Twelfth Night ■ Valentine's Day ■ Mardi Gras ■ Hilda and Mr. John's
rick's Day ■ St. Joseph's Day ■ Easter ■ Straw... ...Jazz
y ■ French Market Tomato Festival ■ Fourth of July ■ Boat Party ■
Race Picnic ■ Annie and Tom's Toasting Party ■ New Iberia Gumbo
■ Omelette Festival ■ Thanksgiving ■ Christmas Tree Trimming ■
tival ■ Sugar Bowl ■ Cigar Dinner ■ Twelfth Night ■ Valentine's Day
Emeril's Tenth Anniversary ■ St. Patrick's Day ■ St. Joseph's Day ■
stival ■ Crab Festival ■ Father's Day ■ French Market Tomato Festival
Sugarcane Festival ■ Pirogue Race Picnic ■ Annie and Tom's Toasting
ristening ■ Pepper Festival ■ Omelette Festival ■ Thanksgiving ■
Day's a Party ■ Oyster Festival ■ Sugar Bowl ■ Cigar Dinner ■ Twelfth
ry ■ Ash Wednesday ■ Emeril's Tenth Anniversary ■ St. Patrick's Day
er's Day ■ Crawfish Festival ■ Crab Festival ■ Father's Day ■ French
al ■ Festivals Acadiens ■ Sugarcane Festival ■ Pirogue Race Picnic ■
ween ■ Alessandro's Christening ■ Pepper Festival ■ Omelette Festival
ear's Eve ■ Every Day's a Party ■ Oyster Festival ■ Sugar Bowl ■ Cigar
John's Anniversary ■ Ash Wednesday ■ Emeril's Tenth Anniversary
l ■ Jazz Fest ■ Mother's Day ■ Crawfish Festival ■ Crab Festival ■
t Party ■ Shrimp Festival ■ Festivals Acadiens ■ Sugarcane Festival
a Gumbo Cook-off ■ Halloween ■ Alessandro's Christening ■ Pepper
■ Christmas Dinner ■ New Year's Eve ■ Every Day's a Party ■ Oyster
y ■ Mardi Gras ■ Hilda and Mr. John's Anniversary ■ Ash Wednesday
ay ■ Easter ■ Strawberry Festival ■ Jazz Fest ■ Mother's Day ■

every day's a
party

also by emeril lagasse

Emeril's New New Orleans Cooking,
with Jessie Tirsch (1993)

Louisiana Real & Rustic,
with Marcelle Bienvenu (1996)

Emeril's Creole Christmas,
with Marcelle Bienvenu (1997)

Emeril's TV Dinners,
with Marcelle Bienvenu
and Felicia Willett (1998)

every day's a
party

Louisiana Recipes for
Celebrating with Family and Friends

**emeril
lagasse**

with Marcelle Bienvenu

and Felicia Willett

photographs by

Philip Gould

William Morrow and

Company, Inc. / New York

It is the policy of William Morrow and Company, Inc., and its imprints and affiliates,
recognizing the importance of preserving what has been written, to print the books we
publish on acid-free paper, and we exert our best efforts to that end.

Library of Congress Cataloging-in-Publishing Data

Lagasse, Emeril
    Every day's a party / Emeril Lagasse, with Marcelle Bienvenu and
Felicia Willett : photographs by Philip Gould. —1st ed.
        p.   cm.
    Including index.
    ISBN 0-688-16430-7 (alk. paper)
    1. Entertaining.   2. Cookery.   I. Bienvenu, Marcelle.
II. Willett, Felicia.   III. Title.
TX731.L324   1999   99–29341
642'.4—dc21   CIP

Printed in the United States of America

First Edition

            5   6   7   8   9   10

BOOK DESIGN BY JILL ARMUS

www.williammorrow.com

IN MEMORIAM

THE VITALITY of Louisiana is embodied in the extraordinary people of the state, who believe that food, fun, and family go hand in hand. Just being together and sharing a meal is a celebration. ■ In this spirit, I dedicate this book in loving memory to a great lady, Rhena B. Bienvenu, Marcelle's mother. ■ She passed away during the writing of the book and I will always remember her fondly as one who possessed grace, love, an incredible sense of life, and a willingness to share her knowledge of the local cuisine. ■ From all of us to her.

contents

JULY

Blow it out at a **Fourth of July** bash with barbecued ribs and peanut butter and chocolate praline ice cream sandwiches!

188

AUGUST

Cool your heels at our **Boat Party** and munch on shrimp at the **Shrimp Festival**.

206

SEPTEMBER

Festivals Acadiens features local music, crafts, heritage, and food at the **Sugarcane Festival**; and eat a picnic lunch at the **Pirogue Festival**.

222

OCTOBER

Party at **Annie and Tom's Toasting Party**, enjoy gumbo at the **New Iberia Gumbo Cook-off**, don a costume for **Halloween**, eat up at **Alessandro's Christening**, and tease your taste buds at the **Pepper Fest**.

242

NOVEMBER

Celebrate the **Omelette Festival** and partake in a **Thanksgiving** feast.

276

DECEMBER

Enjoy the holidays at a **Christmas Tree Trimming** party, **Christmas Dinner**, and a **New Year's Eve** gala event.

294

acknow

FIRST AND foremost, I offer thanks to my family:

Mr. John and Hilda, my parents, with love.

Jessie and Jilly, my daughters, whom I adore.

Mark, my brother, and Dolores Cotter, my sister,

who mean a great deal to me.

THANKS MUCH TO:
✧ Marcelle Bienvenu, a super lady, a dear friend,
and a terrific writer with a vision, for her hard work and support,
and to her husband, Rock-O-Daddy, the king of pig roasts,
a great host, and a true friend.
✧ Felicia Willett, my friend and assistant, who has great creativity and the
drive to always have great food. Thanks for all that you do.
✧ Marti Dalton, for all her hard work, dedication, and understanding.
She always keeps us all on track.
✧ Philip Gould, for his incredibly creative eye, persistence, and talents.
He is responsible for the great photographs.
✧ All the folks at William Morrow:
✧ Michael Murphy, my publisher
✧ Pam Hoenig, my patient editor, and Kate Heddings, editorial assistant
✧ Leah Carlson-Stanisic, cookbook art director, and Jill Armus, a super designer
✧ Rich Aquan, for the great jacket design
✧ Ann Cahn, special projects production editor, and Karen Lumley,
production manager, who performed creative miracles and kept everything on track
✧ Carrie Weinberg, a good friend who keeps us all sane on the road
✧ Mara Warner, who did hours of research.
✧ My dear, dear friends Eric and Gigi Linquest, Tony and Liz Cruz,
and Mauricio and Torre Andrade.

ledgments

✧ The managers and staffs at Emeril's, NOLA, Delmonico Restaurant and
Bar in New Orleans, Emeril's New Orleans Fish House and
Delmonico Steak House in Las Vegas, and Emeril's in Orlando.
Many thanks to all of you who make it happen every day.
✧ Chefs de Cuisine Dave McCelvey, Bernard Carmouche,
Neil Swidler, Sean Roe, and Christian Czerwonka,
and to Pastry Chefs Lou Lynch and Joe Trull.
✧ Julio Hernandez, the sommelier at Emeril's and a great cigar maestro.
✧ At Homebase, Beth Lott, Dana Martinson, Huk Kakish, Carol Ripley, Michele
LeFort, Kathryn Maclean, Maria Eclevia, Anna Hernandez, and Loleta Brooks.
✧ Dr. James Goad, a great guy who is always there to help.
✧ The Food Network and *Emeril Live* teams—you guys are great!
✧ Margo Baumgart, a dear lady and friend, and everyone at *Good Morning America*.

SPECIAL THANKS TO:
Mo and Torre's entire family for the christening.
Saint Rita's Catholic Church.
Tom and Anne Sands and their wedding party.
Henry Lambert and Cary Bond for the roof party.
Marcelle's family at the camp.
The Krewe of Endymion.
Tommy Dantin and his crew on the *Wyoming*.
Nokia Sugar Bowl Classic.
Quint Davis and everyone involved with Jazz Fest.
All the great people at Rock's cracklin' cookoff on Bayou Teche.
Jean Lafitte Oyster Festival.
Festival Acadian.
Louisiana Division, New Orleans Public Library.
The Williams Research Center of the Historic New Orleans Collection.

introd

A COUPLE of years ago, when the hype for the millennium began, I reflected on the fact that it would indeed be a milestone in my life. ■ I remember having what I guess is called an anxiety attack. I wondered if things would change and, if so, could I capture the moment, the time, the experience, and all that has occurred to make me who I am up until this point of my life. ■ It was such a profound feeling, I went for a long walk, down St. Charles Avenue, across Canal Street, and into the *Vieux Carré,* better known as the French Quarter, to sort things out.

In the Quarter, which I think of as the womb of the city, for indeed that is where the city was born, I made a pilgrimage, a walk down memory lane, so to speak. I stopped to get a drink at the Napoleon House, one of my favorite haunts. The narrow streets were busy with visitors who seemed to be enjoying the Old World section of the city and locals who were going about business as usual.

I paid for my drink and walked down Chartres Street to Jackson Square, where local artisans plied their trade and tourists slurped on cocktails carried in the "to-go" cups that are legal here. Noisy pigeons perched on the statue of Andrew Jackson, then flew up to the steeple of St. Louis Cathedral and the rooftops of the adjoining Presbytère and Cabildo, twin structures that flank the historic old church.

From there I ventured to the Moon Walk, which overlooks the mighty Mississippi River, and watched the giant freighters and tankers maneuvering among the busy traffic of the river. The sights, smells, and a gentle breeze calmed my mind.

With a couple of pralines to munch on, I made for the French Market, where local farmers sell their fruits and vegetables. I picked my way down the row of stalls, buying a string of garlic, a spray of bay leaves tied with twine, and a couple of bright red tomatoes for good measure. I was feeling better.

I wound my way to Royal Street and admired the myriad architectural details on the age-old struc-

tures built flush with the *banquettes,* or sidewalks. I have learned from a native to practice looking to both sides of the street, as well as to study the roof lines It's best to wander without a destination or specific purpose, and to be prepared to meet strangers and engage in impromptu conversations. I always marvel at the ornamental ironwork, some wrought iron, some cast iron, that adorns the balconies, and I peer down alleyways to admire the lush inner courtyards and shaded patios.

I pressed my nose to the show windows of the posh antique shops and trendy boutiques and stopped to inspect the gaudy T-shirt and souvenir stores. In the distance, the sound of a lonely moaning saxophone beckoned me to Bourbon Street.

Bourbon Street, named after a duke of Bourbon, a royal family of France, is a mixture of the tawdry and the sublime. A striptease bar may be next door to a fine restaurant or an elegant hotel. Pausing at one corner, I heard traditional Dixieland jazz as well as the chanky-chank of a Cajun band. It is a street that is crowded every day and all night, much like a midway at a carnival. As a friend of mine says, "If you don't make it to Bourbon Street, you haven't been to New Orleans."

The sun was following its path into the western sky when I retraced my steps up Chartres. I waved to the buggy captain of a horse and carriage as he made his spiel to his passengers. Another day in the Crescent City was ending, but the night was young and I knew that the party would continue well into the early morning hours.

During the following months, I made similar expeditions. One early morning, I boarded a streetcar that took me on a thirteen-mile round trip from Canal to South Carrollton and back. The route began in 1835, and the streets through which it passes are lined with trees and gracious homes rising from manicured lawns and gardens.

On a warm, humid night, I went out to the Lakefront and watched sailboats and motor launches ply the waters of Lake Pontchartrain, named by Iberville for the minister of marine in France. The large lake is twenty-five miles wide and forty miles long. Casual restaurants built on stilts over the water are a perfect place to enjoy a meal of boiled or fried seafood.

Another time, I ventured over the Mississippi River Bridge to the West Bank,

which is in Jefferson Parish and contains the communities of Gretna, Harvey, Marrero, and Westwego.

One wondrous weekend in April, when the evenings were still cool and the days warm and breezy, I motored west on Interstate 10 and visited Baton Rouge (French for "red stick"), the state's capital and the home of Louisiana State University and the Fighting Tigers.

My journey took me over both the Bonnet Carré and the Atchafayla spillways, home to alligators, herons, egrets, freshwater fish, frogs, crawfish, and turtles, as well as the majestic bald cypress trees.

My destination was Acadiana, Cajun Country. Acadiana is composed of twenty-two parishes, some of which have unusual names like Point Coupee, Ascension, Calcasieu, Evangeline, Iberia, Avoyelles, and some with saints' names like St. Martin, St. Landry, St. James, St. Charles, St. Mary, and St. John the Baptist. This is the area that was populated by the descendants of the French-Acadians after their exile from what is now known as Nova Scotia. Not only is it rich in history, traditions, and culture, it's wealthy with some of the best food in the world, or so I believe. Bayous meander through the many small, quaint communities and life goes ever so slowly here. It's a place like no other, where I like to kick back, relax, and enjoy the music, the people, and the environs, where the stately live oak trees are draped with Spanish moss and, if you listen, you can hear the sounds of nature floating in the air, broken only by the whine of an outboard as it speeds over the smooth water.

On a cold, clear winter's day, I drove to the northern part of the state, where the piney woods were refreshed by a brisk north wind and the red dirt seemed redder in the brilliant sunshine. In Natchitoches, the oldest town in the Louisiana Purchase, I witnessed the great Christmas Festival of Lights on the sloping banks of the Cane River just as the sun went down. Not only are there a million lights in the displays, but there's a fantastic fireworks show as well, and lots of good food to boot!

Finally, I headed home on a rural road that took me through acres and acres of pecan orchards, and pondered all that I experienced.

That's when the light went on inside my head!

What a state, what a story it tells! I knew then what I wanted to capture about my adopted home state. I had to tell about the people, their history, their foods, and all the cultural events that constitute the true spirit of Louisiana—a place that celebrates its heritage 365 days a year. Here, there is indeed a *joie de vivre* like that of no other place I know.

Young and old, the people love to have fun and that jollity always—and I mean always—includes food and music. Sounds like a party in my book.

After living here for about eighteen years, I've embraced this spirit and feeling. There really is no way of avoiding it—it's contagious. I do admit to being exposed to some of that vitality when I was growing up in Fall River, Massachusetts. Coming from a family with both French-Canadian and Portuguese backgrounds, I shared in a family-oriented lifestyle, with large holiday parties, baseball games, marching bands, and local festivals being a very important part of my childhood.

In many respects, it was easy for me to go with the flow here in Louisiana. I felt quite comfortable being with different groups of people who like to share food. I found that I was as much at home at a crawfish boil as I was at a clambake. The locals showed me a thing or two about cooking, and I, in turn, gave them some new ideas. Hey, that's what it really is all about—sharing. This week the party is at my house or in my town, and it's your turn, buddy, next time. Around here, any occasion or no occasion is reason for a celebration.

Every day's a party—some are just more organized than others. Here there's a festival for just about everything. For instance, we celebrate sugarcane in New Iberia, rice in Crowley, frogs in Rayne, strawberries in Ponchatoula,

blueberries in Mansfield, peaches in Ruston, pecans in Colfax, watermelons in Farmerville, and corn in Bunkie. Nothing is too sacred or too common. We party for the pirate Jean Lafitte at Lake Charles Contraband Days and the world's largest praline at the French Quarter Festival, and listen to some of the hottest performers at the New Orleans Jazz & Heritage Festival. We gather to honor patron saints and feast days, and we amass in great numbers to pray together at religious occasions. Shucks, we even have hurricane parties here! You can't find a day not to party.

We are blessed with great produce—corn, okra, citrus, tomatoes, peppers, eggplant—and other ingredients with which to cook—the best hot sauce, the sweetest crawfish, and incredible fish and shellfish from our waterways and the Gulf of Mexico.

And even when we take a vacation to other parts of the country, we take the party with us. I've seen Louisianians get on planes with ice chests filled with crawfish étouffée, various gumbos,

and even fresh shrimp to take to the beaches, to the slopes, and anywhere else they're destined. If you can't come to their party, they'll take it to you!

Here then, my friends, is my personal invitation to all of you to come to Louisiana, where the fun never stops. I promise you'll "pass a good time" just about anywhere you go in this wonderful state I'm proud to call home!

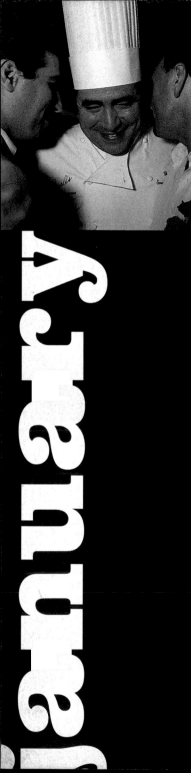

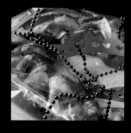

IT'S TRUE what the locals say about the weather down here, in the deepest of the Deep South. ■ "If you don't like the weather, hang around for a couple of hours—it'll change." ■ It's January and the dead of winter, but in Louisiana, you just never know what kind of weather each day will bring. Yesterday, you could have been shivering in thirty-degree

weather in a wet duck blind. Today you might find yourself in shirt sleeves sitting comfortably in a French Quarter courtyard, listening to a murmuring fountain amid subtropical vegetation. Then tomorrow a cold front could blow in from the west, sending the crawfish deep into their mud holes. ■ But that's one of the things that makes New Orleans so captivating, along with the changes in the mood and personality of the city. Take, for instance, the Christmas holidays that are just winding down. Much of the festivities are centered around religious observances and family gatherings. But the week following Christmas is like a lull before a storm. As

December 31 approaches, the excitement spins into a crescendo. ■ Fans of the teams that will be playing in the post-season football classic—the Sugar Bowl, the sweetest of the bowl games—begin flocking to the city. Up and down the streets of the French Quarter they wander, barking football cheers or breaking into impromptu choruses of college fight songs. Pat O'Brien's, the popular watering hole on St. Peter Street, is packed to the rafters with customers swilling Hurricanes, a concoction of rum and fruit juices. The T-shirt and souvenir shops are doing a brisk business, as are the elegant antique emporiums and chic dress shops. ■ Every restaurant, café, and saloon is jammed and the Lucky Dog vendors can barely keep up with their orders. Musicians, artists, and performers at Jackson Square work the throngs that gather in front of St. Louis Cathedral. The horse-

drawn carriages clip-clop along the streets carrying sightseers while their tour guides shout out historical—or is it hysterical?—trivia. ■ In other parts of the city, some of the locals are spending the first day of January making their rounds of

january

visits to family and friends before returning home for a sumptuous family dinner. ■ Once the New Year's festivities draw to a close, there's a brief respite before the season of Carnival begins on Twelfth Night, January 6. Then it's a roller-coaster ride that climaxes on Fat Tuesday, otherwise known as Mardi Gras. ■ Elsewhere in the state, life continues at a more leisurely pace. Down toward the mouth of the Mississippi River, the citrus orchards, if the weather has been cooperating, are at their peak, with branches heavy with fruit. To the west of the Crescent City, in the region known as Acadiana, crawfish farmers are tending their flooded ponds, gearing up for the season that will last until early June, while the pecan season is winding down around Natchitoches, in the central part of the state. Duck hunters are disassembling their duck blinds, picking up their decoys, and closing down their camps until next year. ■ It's January, the first month of the new year, and Louisianians, with their boundless enthusiasm for a good time, are looking forward to another year of fun and excitement in whatever guise it may come.

Oyster Festival

VER WONDER who the first brave soul was who took the initiative to pop an oyster into his mouth? Locals here will tell you it was "Someone who was very hungry." ■ After all, oysters are hardly delectable looking. Rather, they are jelly-like, gray, slimy, and housed in an ugly, spiny shell that is, unless you are skilled in the art, difficult to pry open. ■ Oyster cultivation is as old as the world's oldest profession, dating back to ancient China, Greece, and Rome. Aristotle and Lucullus were supposedly quite fond of the mollusk, and fishermen at Rhodes were wont to throw potsherds into the bays to provide housing for the oysters. ■ Oysters are so productive (thus their reputation for being an aphrodisiac) that one female may lay some five million eggs at one time, but in the wild, only ten to fifteen single eggs are likely to survive. ■ Indians had been eating oysters on Atlantic shores for some ten thousand years when Captain John Smith landed in Virginia and found "savages . . . roasting oysters on the half-shell." ■ It is then not surprising that Louisiana colonists, those brave souls, were

thrilled to find an abundance of oysters in the bays and estuaries along the coast of the Gulf of Mexico. It didn't take these ingenious cooks long to devise ways to vary the routine of eating oysters on the half-shell, and now we have such gastronomic delights as oyster poorboys, oyster panroasts, oysters en brochette, oysters Bienville and Rockefeller, and the list goes on and on. ■

Louisiana is the largest oyster-producing state in America, but oysters are always getting bad press. The state's Wildlife and Fisheries Agency constantly monitors the oyster beds along the state's coast, but it also warns that people with digestive problems should not consume raw oysters. Cooked oysters are usually no threat. ■ It's also interesting to note that oysters may vary in size, looks, and taste because the water, food, climate, and location of the oyster bed all affect their growth. They range from plump and grayish with a bland taste to greenish or coppery with a metallic flavor. Some are as small as a dime, while others can be as big as the palm of your hand. ■ There are several oyster festivals in the southern part of the state and they're all great fun. Philip Gould, our fearless photographer, visited the one held in January in the town of Jean Lafitte, named for the flamboyant pirate and located on Bayou Barataria, south of New Orleans. There he found a treasure hunt in process, an oyster shucking contest, oyster sack races, and, of course, an oyster eating contest. ■ At the peak of the oyster season, in the dead of winter, families often make arrangements with oyster suppliers to provide them with a sack or two for their own oyster festival at home. Some are, of course, eaten on the half-shell, garnished with a ketchup-based cocktail sauce or spiked with nothing more than a squeeze of fresh lemon juice. Others will find their way to the kitchen, where they will be made into a stew, or fried, or served with any number of sauces. ■ Around here, there's an old saying, "Eat Louisiana oysters and love longer." Sounds good to me.

sugar bowl

HELLO OUT there, football fans! Listen up! Did you know that the Sugar Bowl football classic is one of the oldest postseason bowl games in the United States? ■ The idea for the event was first presented in 1927 by James M. Thomson, publisher of the *Orleans Item,* and sports editor Fred Digby, who, by the way, gave it its name. But it wasn't until 1934, when the New Orleans Mid-Winter Sports Association was formally organized, that it became a reality. The first game was played on New Year's Day 1935, pitting Tulane University's Green Wave, unbeaten in the South, against Temple University's Owls, the only unbeaten team in the North. In an exciting contest, Tulane came from behind and won 20–14. The admission prices were $1.50 and $3.50, a far cry from what football tickets cost today. ■ The games were played at Tulane Stadium, which accommodated 24,000. But because of the Bowl's great success, the stadium had to be expanded to 70,000 (later the seating was brought to 81,000) permanent seats just two years later. In June 1939, the first piling was driven, and the double-deck structure was completed in time for the 1940 kickoff. The games were played in Tulane Stadium until 1975, when the Sugar Bowl was moved to the Louisiana Superdome. In 1981, Tulane Stadium was dismantled. The Sugar Bowl has gone through several sponsorships and in 1995 Nokia became the title sponsor of the game. ■ The Sugar Bowl has been a great tourist draw at what was once a slow period for New Orleans hotels, restaurants, and attractions. Parties go on for several days prior to the kickoff and, of course, on the day of the game, just about everyone gathers for "pre-parties," such as brunches and tailgate bashes. ■ How sweet it is!

brunch

BRUNCHES ARE QUITE popular down south and thought to be a very civilized manner in which to work up to another party. Yes, there's nothing like having a party before another party to get everyone in a party mood. ■ Beverages, or eye-openers as they're called here, can run the gamut from Champagne and Bloody Marys to milk punches and the ever-popular Sazerac, perhaps the best known of all New Orleans cocktails. ■ The menu for these affairs usually includes some kind of egg dish but, like everything else here, just about anything goes. All the host must ensure is that whatever is offered is good and that there's plenty of it as you see in this menu that features mushroom tarts, pecan-crusted rabbit tenderloin, and shrimp Creole.

sugar bowl

SAZERAC COCKTAIL

WHEN THE SAZERAC WAS FIRST CREATED, IT CONTAINED AN IMPORTED COGNAC MADE BY A COMPANY CALLED SAZARAC-DEFLORGE ET FILS OF LIMOGES, FRANCE. THE MIXTURE CHANGED IN THE LATE 1870S, WHEN AMERICAN RYE WHISKEY WAS SUBSTITUTED FOR THE BRANDY, SUP-POSEDLY TO PLEASE THE TASTES OF THE LOCALS. ■ MARCELLE HAD AN ASSIGNMENT TO DO A PIECE ON SAZERACS FOR HER WEEKLY FOOD COLUMN FOR THE LOCAL DAILY NEWSPAPER AND DECIDED TO VISIT SEVERAL WATERING HOLES WHERE THE DRINK IS SERVED. HER INVES-TIGATION TOOK HER TO THE SAZERAC BAR AT THE FAIRMONT HOTEL, GALATOIRE'S COMMANDER'S PALACE (WHERE SHE CLAIMS SHE HAD HER FIRST ONE MANY MOONS AGO WITH ELLA BRENNAN), ANTOINE'S, AND MARTI'S (WHICH IS NOW PERISTYLE RESTAURANT). NEEDLESS TO SAY, SHE HAD A GAY OLD TIME. BY THE TIME SHE ARRIVED AT MARTI'S, SHE WAS A LITTLE LIGHTHEADED. SHE WENT TO FRESHEN UP IN THE LADIES' ROOM AND, UPON HER RETURN TO THE BAR, FOUND A GENTLEMAN SIPPING HER DRINK! SHE WAS ABOUT TO HIT HIM OVER THE HEAD WITH HER PURSE, WHEN, TO HER SURPRISE, SHE REALIZED THE FEL-LOW WAS NONE OTHER THAN TENNESSEE WILLIAMS. SHE ORDERED HERSELF ANOTHER SAZ AND TOLD TENNESSEE HIS DRINK WAS ON HER! ■ HERE'S THE RECIPE MARCELLE FAVORS.

Fill a small old-fashioned glass with cracked ice and set aside. In another small old-fashioned glass, put the lump of sugar and just enough water to moisten it. With a spoon, crush the sugar, then add the Pey-chaud's bitters, Angostura bitters, whiskey, and sev-eral ice cubes. Stir. Never use a shaker. Empty the first glass of ice, add the Herbsaint or Pernod, twirl the glass around, and shake the liqueur out. Strain the whiskey mixture into the glass, twist in the lemon peel, and serve immediately.

1 lump sugar
3 drops Peychaud's bitters
1 dash Angostura bitters
1 jigger rye whiskey
1 dash Herbsaint or Pernod
1 strip lemon peel

MAKES 1 DRINK

EXOTIC MUSHROOM TARTS

HERE IN NEW ORLEANS, WE LIKE TO HAVE APPETIZERS WHILE WE ENJOY A COCKTAIL OR TWO, BEFORE WE GET DOWN TO THE MAIN PART OF THE MEAL. THE FILLING FOR THESE TARTS CAN BE MADE A DAY AHEAD AND STORED IN THE REFRIGERATOR. THE MIXTURE SHOULD BE BROUGHT TO ROOM TEMPERATURE, THEN STIRRED BEFORE YOU FILL THE TARTS. TO CHANGE THEM A BIT, SUBSTITUTE CARAMELIZED ONIONS OR ROASTED EGGPLANT FOR THE MUSHROOMS.

2 tablespoons unsalted butter
1 cup thinly sliced yellow onions
1/8 teaspoon plus 1/2 teaspoon salt
1/8 teaspoon plus 1/2 teaspoon freshly ground black pepper
1/2 pound assorted exotic mushrooms, such as shiitakes, oysters, and chanterelles, wiped clean, stems trimmed, and sliced (about 3 cups)
1 teaspoon chopped garlic
1/4 pound goat cheese, crumbled
1/2 cup plus 1 tablespoon freshly grated Parmigiano-Reggiano cheese
1 sheet (15 × 10 inches) frozen puff pastry (found in the frozen food section), defrosted
1 large egg, lightly beaten
1 tablespoon chopped fresh parsley leaves

Preheat the oven to 375° F. Line a baking sheet with parchment paper.

In a medium-size skillet, melt the butter over medium heat. Add the onions, season with 1/8 teaspoon of the salt and 1/8 teaspoon of the black pepper, and cook, stirring occasionally, for 2 minutes. Add the mushrooms and season with the remaining 1/2 teaspoon salt and 1/2 teaspoon black pepper. Cook, stirring, for 2 minutes. Add the garlic and cook, stirring, for another 2 minutes. Remove the skillet from the heat and pour the mushrooms into a medium-size mixing bowl. Add the goat cheese and 1/2 cup of the Parmigiano and stir to blend.

With a 2½-inch cookie cutter, cut 24 rounds out of the puff pastry. Place them on the parchment-lined baking sheet, prick each round randomly with the tines of a fork, and brush with the beaten egg. Spread a tablespoon of the mushroom mixture on each round, leaving a 1/8 -inch border. Bake until lightly browned, about 15 minutes.

Remove from the oven, sprinkle the rounds with the remaining 1 tablespoon Parmigiano and the parsley, and let cool for several minutes before serving.

MAKES 8 SERVINGS (3 TARTS EACH)

PECAN-CRUSTED RABBIT WITH WILTED GREENS AND CREOLE DRESSING

I'M LUCKY. I HAVE A FARMER, DAN CRUTCHFIELD, WHO RAISES THE RABBITS WE USE AT MY RESTAURANTS. BUT YOU CAN USUALLY FIND GOOD-QUALITY DOMESTIC RABBITS AT MOST LARGE SUPERMARKETS OR SPECIALTY FOOD STORES. TALK TO THE BUTCHER TO DETERMINE IF HE'S ABLE TO SUPPLY YOU WITH THE TENDERLOINS. THEY'RE SMALL BUT DELICIOUS. IF YOU CAN'T GET THEM, USE 1 POUND OF BONELESS, SKINLESS CHICKEN BREASTS CUT INTO 8 STRIPS. ■ RABBIT REALLY DOES TASTE LIKE RABBIT, NOT LIKE CHICKEN.

Make the dressing. Put the egg, mustard, garlic, salt, and lemon juice in a food processor or blender and process until smooth, about 15 seconds. With the motor running, pour the oil through the feed tube in a slow, steady stream. Cover and chill for 1 hour in the refrigerator before serving. Best if used within 24 hours.

Make the tenderloins. Preheat the oven to 400°F. Line a baking sheet with parchment paper.

Combine the bread crumbs, pecan pieces, and 1 teaspoon of the Creole seasoning in a food processor or blender and pulse several times to make a fine meal. Transfer the mixture to a shallow bowl and set aside.

Season the tenderloins on both sides with the remaining 4 teaspoons Creole seasoning. Spread the mustard evenly all over the tenderloins, then dredge them in the pecan meal, coating evenly and pressing the meal gently into the tenderloins. Lay the tenderloins about an inch apart on the prepared baking sheet and bake for 15 minutes. Remove from the oven and cut each tenderloin in half diagonally.

FOR THE CREOLE DRESSING

1 large egg (see Note on page 13)
1 tablespoon Creole or whole-grain mustard
1 teaspoon chopped garlic
1/2 teaspoon salt
1 tablespoon fresh lemon juice
1 cup vegetable oil

FOR THE TENDERLOINS

1/2 cup fine dried bread crumbs
1 cup pecan pieces
5 teaspoons Creole Seasoning (recipe follows)
8 rabbit tenderloins (about 2 ounces each)
5 tablespoons Creole or whole-grain mustard

FOR THE WILTED GREENS AND TO FINISH THE DISH

1 tablespoon olive oil

8 cups assorted baby salad
  greens, such as romaine, frisée,
  red oakleaf, and radicchio,
  washed and patted dry
¼ teaspoon salt
¼ teaspoon freshly ground black
  pepper
2 tablespoons chopped fresh
  parsley leaves

Heat the olive oil in a large skillet over medium heat. Add the greens and toss, then quickly remove from the heat.

Spread 2 tablespoons of the Creole dressing in the center of each of eight serving plates. Divide the greens into 8 equal portions and lay them in the center of the dressing. Arrange the tenderloins over the greens, sprinkle with the parsley, and serve.

MAKES 8 SERVINGS

Creole Seasoning

2½ tablespoons sweet paprika
2 tablespoons salt
2 tablespoons garlic powder
1 tablespoon freshly ground
  black pepper
1 tablespoon onion powder
1 tablespoon cayenne
1 tablespoon dried oregano
1 tablespoon dried thyme

Mix all of the ingredients together and store in an airtight container. Can be stored this way for up to 3 months.

NOTE

Salmonella warning: Let's talk about egg safety because I don't want any of you out there to get sick. I personally love homemade fresh mayonnaise and I make it with fresh—and I mean FRESH—raw eggs. I've never had any trouble, but I want you to take some precautions. Always purchase your eggs from a reputable source, a place you can trust with your life. Don't use eggs after the expiration date on the carton. Don't go leaving your eggs in the backseat of your car while you're out and about, and once you get home, keep the eggs in the refrigerator. I use eggs pretty quickly, so I don't have to worry about keeping them too long at home. But I suppose there's a tiny risk some nasty old salmonella could sneak into some eggs, so just be cautious about serving things containing raw eggs to very young kids or the elderly or to people who have health problems. Okay?

MAKES ABOUT ¾ CUP

SHRIMP CREOLE

MARCELLE CLAIMS SHE'S NEVER MET A SHRIMP CREOLE SHE LIKED. THEY'RE TOO THIN OR TOO THICK, OFTEN THEY ARE TASTELESS, AND THE SHRIMP ARE USUALLY OVERCOOKED. BUT WE TRIED THIS ONE TOGETHER AND, BINGO, SHE LIKED IT. ■ IT'S REALLY A SIMPLE DISH COMPOSED OF THE USUAL ONIONS, BELL PEPPERS, AND CELERY, COOKED WITH LOTS OF TOMATOES AND, OF COURSE, SHRIMP. IN NEW ORLEANS, IT'S CLASSICALLY SERVED OVER WHITE RICE, BUT FOR BRUNCH IT SITS ATOP TOASTED FRENCH BREAD AND IS CROWNED WITH PERFECTLY POACHED EGGS AND LEMONY HOLLANDAISE.

In a large saucepan, melt the butter over medium heat. Add the onions, bell peppers, and celery and season with 1 teaspoon of the salt and ½ teaspoon of the cayenne. Cook, stirring, until the vegetables are wilted, about 10 minutes. Stir in the bay leaves, tomatoes, garlic, and ½ teaspoon of the salt. Increase the heat to medium-high and bring to a boil, then reduce the heat to medium-low. Simmer, uncovered, for about 35 minutes, stirring occasionally.

Combine the flour and water in a small bowl and whisk to blend. Add to the tomato mixture and continue to cook for 4 to 6 minutes, stirring occasionally.

Season the shrimp with the remaining 1 teaspoon salt and ¼ teaspoon cayenne. Add to the pan along with the Worcestershire and hot sauce and cook over medium heat until the shrimp turn pink and curl slightly, 4 to 6 minutes. Stir in the green onions and parsley. Keep warm over very low heat.

To poach the eggs, pour cold water into a 10-inch sauté pan to a depth of about 2 inches. Bring to a simmer, then reduce the heat so that the surface of the water barely shimmers. Add the vinegar. Break 4 of the eggs

¼ pound (1 stick) unsalted butter
2 cups chopped yellow onions
1 cup chopped green bell peppers
1 cup chopped celery
2½ teaspoons salt
¾ teaspoon cayenne
2 bay leaves
Two 28-ounce cans crushed tomatoes
1 tablespoon chopped garlic
2 tablespoons bleached all-purpose flour
¼ cup water
2½ pounds medium-size shrimp, peeled and deveined
1 tablespoon Worcestershire sauce
1 teaspoon hot sauce
½ cup chopped green onions or scallions (green part only)
2 tablespoons chopped fresh parsley leaves
1 tablespoon distilled white vinegar

16 large eggs

1 loaf (12 to 14 inches long)
French bread, cut crosswise
into sixteen 1/4-inch-thick
slices and lightly toasted

1 recipe Hollandaise Sauce
(recipe follows)

into individual saucers, then gently slide them one at a time into the water and, with a large spoon, lift the white over the yolk. Repeat the lifting once or twice to enclose each yolk completely in the white. Poach until the whites are set and the yolks feel soft when touched gently, 3 to 4 minutes. Repeat the process until all of the eggs are used. You may have to add more water to keep the depth at 2 inches, but remember, the water must be simmering before adding the eggs. The eggs can be poached ahead of time and kept in a shallow pan of cool water. Reheat the eggs by slipping them into boiling water for about a minute.

To serve, arrange 2 slices of the toasted bread in the center of each serving plate. Remove the bay leaves and spoon equal amounts of the shrimp Creole over the bread. With a slotted spatula, gently lift the eggs out of the water, let them drain for a few seconds, and transfer 2 eggs to top each shrimp Creole serving. Drizzle with the hollandaise sauce and serve immediately.

MAKES 8 SERVINGS

Hollandaise Sauce

4 large egg yolks (see Note on
page 13)

2 teaspoons fresh lemon juice

1/8 teaspoon hot sauce

4 teaspoons water

Salt and freshly ground black
pepper

1/2 pound (2 sticks) unsalted
butter, melted

In a stainless steel bowl set over a pot of simmering water (be careful not to let the bottom of the bowl touch the water), whisk the egg yolks with the lemon juice, hot sauce, and water until pale yellow in color. Season with salt and pepper. Remove the bowl from the pot and, whisking vigorously, add the melted butter 1 tablespoon at a time, whisking until all the butter is incorporated. Keep warm until needed.

MAKES ABOUT 1 1/2 CUPS

ORANGE CREPES

SOUTHEAST OF NEW ORLEANS, IN THE PARISH OF PLAQUEMINES, YOU'LL FIND SOME OF THE BEST CITRUS THAT'S TO BE FOUND ANYWHERE—LOUISIANA SWEET ORANGES, MANDARIN ORANGES, NAVELS, NECTARINES, SATSUMAS, AND LEMONS. AT THEIR PEAK DURING THE WINTER MONTHS, THESE FRUITS ARE IDEAL FOR DESSERTS, SUCH AS THESE ORANGE CREPES. I LOVE THE WAY CITRUS PERKS UP YOUR MOUTH AFTER A RICH MEAL. AT DELMONICO WE PREPARE A SIMILAR CREPE USING LEMONS. ■ FOR THE BEST RESULTS WHEN MAKING CREPES, LIGHTLY OIL THE BOTTOM OF A NONSTICK SKILLET USING EITHER A PASTRY BRUSH OR A PAPER TOWEL DIPPED IN VEGETABLE OIL. WHEN ADDING THE BATTER TO THE PAN, GENTLY AND NEATLY SWIRL IT AROUND TO COMPLETELY COVER THE BOTTOM.

MAKE THE CREPES

Combine the flour, confectioners' sugar, and salt in a large mixing bowl. In a medium-size mixing bowl, combine the melted butter, milk, eggs, and vanilla and whisk until blended. Add the liquid mixture a little at a time to the dry mixture, whisking to dissolve any lumps. Whisk until smooth.

Lightly brush a 6-inch nonstick skillet with vegetable oil and heat over medium heat. When the pan is hot, remove it from the heat and pour in ¼ cup of the batter. Swirl the pan around to spread the batter evenly over the bottom. Return the pan to the heat and cook until lightly golden, 30 to 40 seconds. Turn the crepe over and cook the second side for about 15 seconds. Remove from the pan. Repeat the procedure until all of the batter is used, stacking the crepes between the squares of parchment or waxed paper to prevent them from sticking together. Set the crepes aside.

FOR THE CREPES

2 cups bleached all-purpose flour
6 tablespoons confectioners' sugar
Pinch of salt
2 tablespoons unsalted butter, melted and slightly cooled
2 cups milk
2 large eggs
½ teaspoon pure vanilla extract
Vegetable oil as needed
Sixteen 6-inch squares parchment or waxed paper

FOR THE FILLING

1 pound cream cheese, at room temperature
1/2 cup sour cream
1/2 cup confectioners' sugar
1 tablespoon grated orange zest
1/2 cup fresh orange juice
1/2 teaspoon pure vanilla extract

FOR THE ORANGE SAUCE

1/4 cup (1/2 stick) unsalted butter, at room temperature
3/4 cup granulated sugar
1/2 cup pecan pieces
1 cup fresh orange juice
1 tablespoon grated orange zest
1/2 cup Grand Marnier
2 tablespoons Triple Sec

MAKES 8 SERVINGS

MAKE THE FILLING

Put the cream cheese in a medium-size mixing bowl and beat with an electric mixer until fluffy. Add the sour cream, confectioners' sugar, orange zest, orange juice, and vanilla. Beat to blend well, scraping down the sides of the bowl as needed.

Put 3 tablespoons of the filling in the center of the lower third of each crepe. Fold the bottom of the crepe over the filling and roll up gently but firmly. Place the filled crepes on a large platter or baking sheet, cover lightly, and refrigerate for 1 hour.

MAKE THE ORANGE SAUCE

In a large sauté pan over medium-high heat, melt the butter. Add the granulated sugar and pecan pieces and cook, stirring, for 3 minutes. Add the orange juice and cook, stirring occasionally, for 4 minutes. Add the orange zest and cook for 1 minute. Add the Grand Marnier and Triple Sec and simmer for 2 minutes. Add 8 of the filled crepes to the pan and cook for 1 minute, basting with the orange sauce. Remove the crepes from the pan, set aside, and keep warm. Add the remaining crepes and cook for 1 minute, basting with the orange sauce.

To serve, crisscross 2 crepes on each dessert plate and drizzle with the orange sauce.

tailgate

ON ANY given Saturday during football season, college football fans throughout the state gather at stadiums for pre- and post-game tailgate parties. They come in pickups, motor homes, utility vehicles, or fancy sports cars and hunker down in the parking lots to party hearty. ■ When it comes to having a good time, Louisianians bring all the comforts of home to wherever the party may be. At these tailgate gatherings, you'll see huge tents sheltering tables laden with food, smoking barbecue pits, and an untold number of ice chests chockful of cold beverages. Spontaneous pep rallies and live music work the fans into a frenzy as kickoff time nears. ■ Everyone brings, or prepares on site, a favorite dish, and even strangers are welcome to grab a plate or bowl to fill up with jambalaya, gumbo, fried chicken, chili, or barbecue. Bowls of potato salad, coleslaw, baked beans, and vegetable casseroles are passed around, and huge trays are piled high with poorboys, finger sandwiches, cookies, and other "pick-up" food. ■ Picnic tables are spread with colorful cloths, and blankets and pillows to throw on the ground are readily at hand. If the weather is warm, you might even hear the whir of an electric blender whipping up margaritas, daiquiris, and other icy-cold concoctions. When it's freezing cold, you will probably be offered a strong cup of coffee with a shot of brandy thrown in for good measure. ■

GRILLED CREOLE MUSTARD-MARINATED QUAIL WITH SMOTHERED FIELD PEAS AND ANDOUILLE

YOU MIGHT THINK THIS IS A RATHER COMPLICATED DISH TO SERVE AT A TAILGATE PARTY, BUT THE LOCALS THINK NOTHING OF BRINGING A BUTANE BURNER FITTED WITH A COOKTOP AND PREPARING THE MEAL ON SITE. COOKING IS THE REASON FOR TAILGATE PARTIES. MOST PEOPLE ARRIVE EARLY AND COOK FOR HOURS. BUT YOU CAN COOK THE BEANS IN ADVANCE (THE TASTE WILL ONLY GET BETTER) AT HOME. IN LOUISIANA, WE COOK BEANS UNTIL CREAMY AND SOFT. AND, HEY, THE BEANS CAN BE SERVED WITH A MULTITUDE OF THINGS. ■ BRING ALONG A SMALL GRILL TO COOK THE QUAIL AT THE LAST MINUTE. JUST REMEMBER TO MARINATE THE BIRDS FOR AT LEAST TWELVE HOURS. ■ IF YOU DON'T CARE FOR QUAIL, USE CHICKEN BREASTS, BEEF, OR PORK CHUNKS.

Make the quail: Put the wine, olive oil, cane syrup, mustard, onion, garlic, salt, black pepper, and cayenne in a food processor or blender and process until smooth, about 30 seconds.

Season the quail evenly with the Creole seasoning. Put them in a large 2-gallon plastic storage bag and pour in the marinade. Close the bag securely. Carefully toss to coat the quail evenly and refrigerate for 12 hours.

FOR THE QUAIL

1/2 cup dry white wine
1/2 cup olive oil
1/2 cup Steen's 100% Pure Cane Syrup or other cane syrup
1/4 cup Creole or whole-grain mustard
1/2 cup chopped yellow onion
1 tablespoon chopped garlic
1/2 teaspoon salt
1/4 teaspoon freshly ground black pepper
1/4 teaspoon cayenne
12 quail (about 3 1/2 ounces each), breastbones removed and split down the back
2 tablespoons Creole Seasoning (page 13)

FOR THE BEANS

1 tablespoon olive oil

2 cups chopped yellow onions

1/4 teaspoon freshly ground
black pepper

1/2 pound andouille or fresh pork
sausage, removed from the
casings and crumbled

2 teaspoons chopped garlic

1 pound dried field peas (about
2 cups), picked over and rinsed

1 bay leaf

1 teaspoon fresh thyme leaves

8 cups beef broth

Make the beans. In a large, heavy stockpot or soup pot, heat the oil over medium–high heat. Add the onions and black pepper and cook, stirring, until the onions are soft and lightly golden, about 4 minutes. Add the sausage and cook, stirring, until brown, about 4 minutes. Add the garlic, dried peas, bay leaf, and thyme. Cook, stirring, for 1 minute. Add the broth and bring to a boil, then reduce the heat to medium and cook, uncovered, until creamy and soft, about 1½ hours. Remove the bay leaf. Keep warm.

Prepare the grill.

Remove the quail from the marinade. Grill until cooked through, about 8 minutes total, turning them every 2 minutes.

To serve, mound equal amounts of the beans in the center of each of six serving plates and top each with 2 quail.

MAKES 6 SERVINGS

GARLIC MEATBALL POORBOYS

THESE GARLIC-STUFFED MEATBALLS ARE ONE OF THE FAVORITES OF MARCELLE AND HER HUSBAND, ROCK, AND ARE IDEAL FOR TAILGATE PARTIES. THEY CAN BE MADE AHEAD OF TIME, THEN REHEATED IN A POT ON ONE OF THOSE BUTANE BURNERS THAT ARE SO POPULAR DOWN HERE. OR, YOU CAN HEAT THEM UP AT HOME AND TAKE THEM IN AN INSULATED CONTAINER. ■ PLOPPED ON FRENCH BREAD AND SLATHERED WITH MUSTARD AND MAYONNAISE, THEY'LL CARRY YOU FOR A FEW HOURS. OH, AND JUST SO YOU'LL KNOW, WHEN YOU ORDER A POORBOY IN NEW ORLEANS, YOU'LL BE ASKED IF YOU WANT IT "DRESSED" OR "UNDRESSED." "DRESSED" MEANS THE SANDWICH IS DOLLED UP WITH LETTUCE AND TOMATOES. "UNDRESSED" IS WITH NUT-TIN' ON IT. NEW ORLEANS HAS ITS OWN LANGUAGE SOMETIMES. ■ TO GET THE SEASONING OF THE MEAT JUST RIGHT, I USUALLY FRY A SMALL BALL OF IT, ABOUT THE SIZE OF A PECAN, IN A SKILLET TO TEST IT.

In a large mixing bowl, combine the ground meats, chopped yellow onion, chopped garlic, green onions, egg, bread crumbs, Worcestershire, 1 teaspoon of the salt, and ½ teaspoon of the cayenne. Mix well with your hands and form into 16 meatballs. Insert a garlic clove in the center of each meatball and pinch the meat around it.

Combine the flour and Creole seasoning in a shallow plate. Roll the meatballs evenly in the flour mixture, tapping off any excess. Reserve any remaining flour.

In a large skillet, heat the oil over medium heat. Add the meatballs and brown evenly, using a spoon to turn them. Remove the meatballs from the pan and set aside. With a wooden spoon, scrape the bottom of the pan to loosen any brown bits. Stir in the reserved seasoned

½ pound ground veal
½ pound ground beef chuck
½ pound ground pork
½ cup finely chopped yellow onion
½ teaspoon finely chopped garlic
¼ cup finely chopped green onions or scallions (green part only)
1 large egg
¼ cup fine dried bread crumbs
1 tablespoon Worcestershire sauce
1½ teaspoons salt
¾ teaspoon cayenne
16 small cloves garlic, peeled

¼ cup bleached all-purpose
    flour
1 teaspoon Creole Seasoning
    (page 13)
¼ cup vegetable oil
2 cups thinly sliced yellow onions
One 12-ounce bottle Abita amber
    beer or other amber beer
1 cup water
3 tablespoons chopped fresh
    parsley leaves
1 large (26 to 28 inches long)
    loaf French bread
6 tablespoons Creole or whole-
    grain mustard
6 tablespoons Mayonnaise
    (page 129)
½ pound provolone cheese,
    thinly sliced

flour. Stir constantly for 3 to 4 minutes to make a dark brown roux. Add the sliced onions and season with the remaining ½ teaspoon salt and ¼ teaspoon cayenne. Cook, stirring constantly, until the onions are slightly soft, about 2 minutes. Slowly pour in the beer and water and mix well. Bring to a boil and return the meatballs to the skillet. Reduce the heat to medium-low and simmer, uncovered, for about 1 hour, until the gravy is thick, turning and basting the meatballs with the pan gravy about every 15 minutes.

Remove from the heat and skim off any fat that has risen to the surface. Add the parsley.

Cut the loaf of bread lengthwise in half. Spread one half with the mustard and the other half with the mayonnaise. Arrange the provolone on the bottom half of the bread, overlapping the slices, then arrange the meatballs on top of the cheese. Spoon the gravy over the meatballs. Top with the remaining bread half, cut into 6 equal portions, and serve immediately.

MAKES 6 SERVINGS

cigar
dinner

SINCE ITS opening, Emeril's has been a cigar-friendly restaurant. My staff of managers, sommeliers, and chefs and I believe that having a meal at the restaurant should be an experience, from the first cocktail or glass of wine through the courses of the dinner to the after-dinner coffee or liqueur, ending, if the guest desires, with the enjoyment of a fine cigar. ■ In the summer of 1991, Mauricio Andrade, one of my right-hand men, went on a "Hemingway" trip to Pamplona, Spain, to see the running of the bulls. He savored many fine cigars and brought one back to share with me. Over this cigar, which, by the way, was given to Mauricio by a Spanish gentleman at a bullfight, we discussed the importance of cigars in the lives of friends and ourselves, and their critical place in the dining experience. ■ When we finished our cigars,

I asked Mo to create a cigar program for Emeril's.

"We discovered a whole new clientele of cigar smokers that we might not have otherwise tapped into. We realized that we had to create a niche for these customers even before Marvin Shanken introduced *Cigar Aficionado* and the cigar craze spread," recalls Mo. ■ The first cigar dinner at the restaurant, in 1993, featured Macanudo and Partagas cigars, mostly from the Dominican Republic. It was held on a Friday night to allow the guests to relax without the worry of work the following day. At the first early dinners, no women were allowed and the guests wore black tie. ■ Avo Uvezian, the creator of Avo cigars, was the first cigar celebrity to attend. Another dinner featured George Hamilton and his cigars. In January 1999, the featured guest cigar celebrity was Carlos Fuente, Jr., president of the Dominican Republic–based Tabacalera A. Fuente y Cia., manufacturers of internationally renowned Arturo Fuente handmade cigars. ■ "For this event, we decided to do something more festive. We had a Latin band, we invited women to attend, and we opened the entire restaurant up to accommodate a hundred and thirty guests on a Sunday evening when the restaurant is usually closed. It was an incredible evening," says Mo. "But it takes a lot of work to put on something like this." ■ For months prior to each cigar dinner, Maurico, the entire staff, and I painstakingly work on a menu with complementary wines and, of course, cigars. For instance, the menu for the Fuente dinner highlighted dishes that were Cuban, South American, and Caribbean in inspiration. There were Honduran meat pies, tamales wrapped in banana leaves, seafood seviche, Dominican-style slow-roasted pork, a fabulous banana-rum sorbet, and chocolate-dipped fruits. ■ The following menu, which has a Creole-Caribbean theme, presents several memorable dishes that have been served over the years at cigar dinners. The cigars I've paired with the different courses of this dinner are my personal favorites. Other cigar smokers may

prefer other choices, and that's the fun, finding the cigars that please YOU. ■ You will notice that I don't have a cigar for every single course, simply because I didn't feel that every one needed one—and, too, we took occasional breaks to "smoke out the cigar," in others words, to enjoy an entire cigar without putting it out. ■ During the cocktail hour, I like a Dunhill from the Dominican Republic, with the wrapper being from Connecticut USA and the binder and filler from the Dominican Republic. The cigar is light to mild and has a creamy, silky texture.

After the rich, buttery escargot dish, I would choose an Avo from Davidoff from Geneva, with the wrapper from Connecticut USA, the binder and filler both from the Dominican Republic. The taste is a perfectly balanced marriage of five different types of tobacco that give the Avo line a rich, mild body, and a delicate and toasty taste. ■ Following the snapper course, my choice is a George Hamilton from Hamilton Reserve from Santiago in the Dominican Republic. This cigar features a wrapper from Connecticut USA, a filler and binder from the Dominican Republic. It's ideal, I think, with its full-bodied blend with a sweet brown sugar taste, to follow the firm-fleshed fish. ■ At the end of the meal, after the crème brûlée, I like a full-bodied cigar, with rich flavors of coffee, earthy with toasted vanilla and cream. My choice is the Arturo Fuenta Opus X, A. Fuenta y Cia., Dominican Republic. The wrapper, binder, and filler are all from the Dominican Republic.

SCALLOP SEVICHE

SOMETIMES SPELLED *CEVICHE* OR *CEBICHE*, AND OTHER TIMES SPELLED *SEVICHE*. IT'S ALL THE SAME—A POPULAR APPETIZER IN LATIN AMERICA CONSISTING OF RAW FISH OR SHELLFISH MARINATED IN CITRUS JUICE, USUALLY LIME JUICE. THE ACID OF THE LIME JUICE "COOKS" THE FISH. I LIKE TO MAKE A SEVICHE WITH SCALLOPS. SEA SCALLOPS ARE LARGE AND SLIGHTLY CHEWIER THAN THE SMALL SWEET BAY SCALLOPS. USE WHATEVER YOU CAN FIND THAT'S FRESH, FRESH, FRESH. THEY ARE USUALLY SOLD ALREADY SHUCKED, SO YOU SHOULD SMELL AND PINCH THEM FOR FIRMNESS AND FRESHNESS IF YOU CAN BEFORE YOU TAKE THEM HOME. MOST OF THE SCALLOPS SOLD ON THE MARKET COME FROM ALONG THE ATLANTIC COAST.

Combine all of the ingredients in a medium-size non-reactive mixing bowl and mix well. Cover and refrigerate for 30 minutes. Serve with fried sweet potato chips or tortilla chips or serve on greens for a salad.

1 pound fresh sea scallops, chopped, or 1 pound bay scallops
1/4 cup chopped red bell pepper
1/4 cup chopped yellow bell pepper
1 small fresh jalapeño, seeded and chopped (about 1 tablespoon)
1/2 cup chopped red onion
6 tablespoons fresh lime juice
1 tablespoon extra-virgin olive oil
1/4 cup Coco Lopez coconut cream
1/4 cup chopped fresh cilantro leaves
1 tablespoon chopped garlic
1/2 teaspoon salt
1/8 teaspoon freshly ground black pepper

MAKES 8 APPETIZER SERVINGS

ESCARGOTS IN A PASTRY DOME

IT'S NOT VERY OFTEN YOU SEE ESCARGOTS ON THE MENU, BUT IN THE UNITED STATES, BACK IN THE 1960S AND 1970S, *ESCARGOTS À LA BOUR-GUIGNONNE*, OFFERED AS AN APPETIZER, WERE VERY POPULAR AND CONSIDERED VERY CHI-CHI. SNAILS PREPARED IN THE BURGUNDIAN STYLE, SERVED IN THEIR SHELLS IN BUTTER HEAVILY SEASONED WITH GARLIC AND HERBS, ARE STILL A POPULAR CLASSIC IN FRANCE AND ARE SLOWLY MAKING A REAPPEARANCE IN AMERICA. ■ NOW AND THEN I CAN FIND FRESH SNAILS, AND WHEN I DO, I SERVE THEM AS SPECIALS. I STILL FAVOR THE CLASSIC PREPARATION, BUT FOR ONE OF OUR CIGAR DINNERS, WE SERVED THEM IN RAMEKINS WITH AN HERBED SAUCE TOPPED WITH A PASTRY DOME TO GIVE THE DISH MORE TASTE AND MORE TEXTURE. THEY WERE A HIT! MARTI DALTON LOVES THIS DISH. ■ YOU MAY NOT BE ABLE TO FIND SNAILS FRESH IN YOUR MARKET, BUT THE CANNED ONES ARE QUITE ACCEPTABLE. THE CAN WE FOUND HAD SIX DOZEN SNAILS, BUT YOU MAY BE ABLE TO FIND SMALLER CANS. SINCE OUR MENU IS DESIGNED TO SERVE EIGHT, WE WENT AHEAD AND PUT EIGHT TO NINE SNAILS IN EACH RAMEKIN. YOU CAN PREPARE THE SNAILS IN ADVANCE AND LET THEM STAND IN THE WINE MIXTURE FOR AS LONG AS A WEEK. THE BUTTER MIXTURE CAN ALSO BE MADE IN ADVANCE AND STORED IN THE REFRIGERATOR UNTIL READY TO USE.

Remove the escargots from the can and drain well. Put them in a large bowl, fill with cool water, and drain, then rinse again in cool water. Drain well and return to the bowl. Set aside.

In a medium-size saucepan over medium heat, combine the wine, shallots, 1 tablespoon of the garlic, the thyme, bay leaves, ¼ teaspoon of the salt, and ⅛ teaspoon of the black pepper. Bring to a boil and let boil for 5 minutes. Remove the bay leaves and pour the

1 can (6 dozen count) escargots
1½ cups dry red wine
¼ cup minced shallots
3 tablespoons chopped garlic
1 large sprig fresh thyme
2 bay leaves
¼ teaspoon plus ⅛ teaspoon salt

1/4 teaspoon freshly ground black
  pepper
1/2 pound (2 sticks) unsalted
  butter, at room temperature
1/2 cup chopped fresh parsley
  leaves
1 sheet (11 × 14 inches) frozen
  puff pastry (found in the
  frozen food section), defrosted
1 large egg, beaten with
  1 teaspoon water

mixture over the escargots and let stand at room temperature until completely cool. Drain off 1/2 cup of the wine mixture and reserve. Cover and refrigerate the escargots if not using immediately.

Preheat the oven to 350°F.

With an electric mixer set on low speed, beat the butter until smooth in a small mixing bowl. Add the remaining 2 tablespoons garlic and the parsley and beat to mix. Add the reserved wine mixture and beat until incorporated. Add the remaining 1/8 teaspoon salt and 1/8 teaspoon black pepper and beat to mix.

Put 8 or 9 escargots in each of eight 8-ounce ramekins. Put 2 heaping tablespoons of the butter mixture over the escargots in each ramekin. Cut eight 4-inch rounds out of the puff pastry with a knife and cover the top of each ramekin with a pastry round. With your fingers, press the pastry firmly over the rims and remove any excess. Lightly brush the pastry with the beaten egg.

Place the ramekins on a baking sheet and bake on the middle rack of the oven until the pastry is golden and puffed, 18 to 20 minutes. Remove from the oven and let cool slightly before serving.

MAKES 8 SERVINGS

PISTACHIO-CRUSTED RACK OF LAMB

LOU LYNCH, OUR PASTRY CHEF AT EMERIL'S, LOVES SWEETS, BUT HE ALSO ADORES THIS DISH, SO HERE'S TO YOU, LOU! ■ LET ME EXPLAIN SOMETHING ABOUT WHAT YOU NEED AS FAR AS THE RACK OF LAMB. ONE RACK OF LAMB HAS EIGHT CHOPS. (A "RACK OF LAMB" IS A BIT OF A MISNOMER BECAUSE IT IS STRUCTURALLY HALF THE RACK, THAT IS, EIGHT RIBS OF AMERICAN LAMB.) YOU WILL NEED TWO RACKS, EACH OF WHICH NEEDS TO BE CUT IN HALF SO THAT YOU HAVE FOUR CHOPS PER PIECE. TALK TO YOUR BUTCHER AND HAVE HIM DO THIS FOR YOU AS WELL AS "FRENCHING" THEM, THAT IS, CLEANING THE RIBS SO THAT THE RIB ENDS ARE EXPOSED. ■ IF YOU DON'T CARE FOR PISTACHIOS, YOU CAN SUBSTITUTE PECANS OR WALNUTS.

Preheat the oven to 375°F.

In a medium-size mixing bowl, combine the pistachios, bread crumbs, 2 teaspoons of the Creole seasoning, and ¼ cup of the olive oil. Stir to blend and set aside.

Rub the meat side of the racks with the remaining 1 tablespoon olive oil, then season with the remaining 2 teaspoons Creole seasoning.

Heat a large skillet over medium-high heat, then place the lamb fat side down in the pan and sear for 8 minutes. Using tongs, turn the lamb so that the bones are sticking upward and sear the "eye" of the chops for 2 minutes. Transfer the lamb to a shallow platter and let cool for about 5 minutes. When the lamb is cool enough to handle, brush the meat

1 cup shelled pistachios, finely ground in a food processor
1 cup fine dried bread crumbs
4 teaspoons Creole Seasoning (page 13)
¼ cup plus 1 tablespoon olive oil
2 racks lamb (8 chops each; about 3 pounds total)
¼ cup Creole or whole-grain mustard
1 recipe Goat Cheese Mashed Potatoes (recipe follows)

evenly with the mustard. Spread the bread crumb mixture evenly over the meat, pressing it gently but firmly so it adheres.

Put the racks in a large shallow roasting pan and roast for 22 minutes until medium, then remove from the oven and let rest for about 10 minutes. Cut into individual chops and serve 2 chops per person, with equal portions of the mashed potatoes.

MAKES 8 SERVINGS

Goat Cheese Mashed Potatoes

4 cups peeled and diced white
   potatoes (about 2 pounds)
1 1/2 teaspoons salt
3/4 cup heavy cream
1/4 cup (1/2 stick) unsalted butter
1/2 pound goat cheese, crumbled
1/8 teaspoon freshly ground
   white pepper

Combine the potatoes and 1 teaspoon of the salt in a large saucepan. Cover the potatoes with water, bring to a boil and cook over medium heat until fork-tender, about 20 minutes. Drain.

Return the potatoes to the saucepan and, over low heat, stir them with a fork or wire whisk for about 2 minutes to dry them. And the cream, butter, cheese, the white pepper, and the remaining 1/2 teaspoon salt. Mix well. Serve hot.

MAKES 8 SERVINGS

SALT-AND-HERB-CRUSTED RED SNAPPER

BAKING FISH IN A SALT CRUST IS NOT NEW, BUT YOU DON'T SEE IT DONE TOO OFTEN. THE CRUST SEALS IN THE FISH AND SCENTS IT WITH THE HERBS AND SPICES—THE FLAVOR IS INCREDIBLE. THE CRACKING OPEN OF THE SALT COVERING MAKES FOR A VERY DRAMATIC PRESENTATION. OUR CIGAR GUESTS WERE IMPRESSED WHEN WE BROUGHT THIS OUT.

Preheat the oven to 350°F. Line a baking sheet with parchment paper.

With a sharp knife, make 5 slits, at an angle and about 1½ inches apart, on each side of the fish. Rub 1 table-spoon of the olive oil over each side of the fish, then season each side with 1 teaspoon of the Creole sea-soning.

Place the fish on the prepared baking sheet. Com-bine the kosher salt, herbs, lemon zest and juice, orange zest and juice, and black pepper in a large mixing bowl. Mix well. Mound the mixture evenly on the surface of the fish, leaving the head and tail uncovered. With your fingers, firmly press the mixture into the flesh.

Bake for 1½ hours. Remove from the oven and let cool for 2 minutes. With the back of a heavy spoon or a mal-let, lightly pound the salt crust to crack it open, begin-ning at the tail end. Carefully pull off the salt crust. Then, with a small spatula or wide knife, remove the flesh from the bone from the top side of the fish. Remove the back-bone, then serve the flesh from the bottom side of the fish. Spoon some salsa over each serving.

1 whole redfish or red snapper (about 6½ pounds), cleaned and scaled
2 tablespoons olive oil
2 teaspoons Creole Seasoning (page 13)
One 3-pound box kosher salt
½ cup chopped fresh parsley leaves
¼ cup chopped fresh tarragon leaves
½ cup chopped fresh basil leaves
¼ cup chopped fresh cilantro leaves
¼ cup grated lemon zest
2 tablespoons fresh lemon juice
1 tablespoon grated orange zest
Juice of 2 oranges (½ cup)
1 teaspoon freshly ground black pepper
½ recipe Creole Tomato Salsa (page 184)

MAKES ABOUT 8 SERVINGS

BANANAS FOSTER ICE CREAM PIE

DID YOU KNOW THAT BANANAS FOSTER ORIGINATED IN NEW ORLEANS? BECAUSE NEW ORLEANS IS A BANANA-IMPORTING CITY, THEY WERE A NATURAL FOR A DESSERT ITEM AND THOSE CLEVER RESTAURATEURS THE BRENNANS CAME UP WITH THE IDEA TO COOK THEM IN BUTTER AND BROWN SUGAR, THEN SERVE THEM OVER ICE CREAM. THE DISH WAS NAMED FOR A GENTLEMAN BY THE NAME OF DICK FOSTER, ONE OF BRENNANS' CUSTOMERS BACK IN THE 1950S. ■ HERE IS A NEW TWIST ON THE DESSERT THAT WE DID FOR ONE OF THE CIGAR DINNERS, A PERFECT ENDING TO A PERFECT MEAL.

In a medium-size skillet over medium heat, melt 3 tablespoons of the butter. Add the sugar and stir until it dissolves. Add the bananas and cook, stirring, for 3 minutes. Remove the pan from the stove and carefully add the liqueur and rum. Return the pan to the stove. Using long matches and keeping long hair and hanging sleeves well clear of the pan, carefully ignite the alcohol and stir with a long-handled wooden spoon until the flames die down, about 30 seconds. Remove from the heat and let cool completely. Puree the mixture in a food processor or blender.

In a medium-size nonreactive saucepan over medium heat, heat the milk and cream to the scalding point (when bubbles form around the edges of the pan). Do not let it boil. Remove from the heat.

Beat the egg yolks in a large mixing bowl. Add the cream mixture about ¼ cup at a time to the beaten eggs, whisking well after each addition. Pour the mixture back into the saucepan, and cook, stirring, over medium heat until the mixture becomes thick enough to lightly coat the back of a spoon, 2 to 3 minutes. Do not boil.

¼ pound (1 stick) unsalted
   butter
½ cup firmly packed light brown
   sugar
3 ripe bananas, peeled, sliced
   lengthwise in half, and cut
   crosswise into ¼-inch-thick
   slices
2 tablespoons banana liqueur
2 tablespoons dark rum
2 cups milk
2 cups heavy cream
6 large egg yolks
1¼ cups graham cracker crumbs
1 recipe Caramel Sauce
   (page 85)

Remove from the heat and pour the mixture into a large glass mixing bowl. Add the pureed bananas and stir to mix. Cover the top of the mixture with plastic wrap pressed against the surface (this will keep a skin from forming) and let cool. Place the mixture in the refrigerator and chill completely.

Pour the banana mixture into an ice cream machine and follow the manufacturer's instructions for the churning time. If you leave the ice cream in the freezer for a while before completing the pie, be sure to let it soften up a bit first.

Preheat the oven to 375°F.

Put the graham cracker crumbs in a medium-size mixing bowl. Melt the remaining 5 tablespoons butter and add to the crumbs. Mix well. Press evenly into the sides and bottom of a 9½-inch deep-dish pie pan and bake until browned, about 10 minutes. Let cool completely.

Carefully spread the caramel sauce evenly over the inside of the graham cracker shell. Fill the shell with the ice cream, spreading it evenly with a rubber spatula. Cover with plastic wrap and freeze until the ice cream firms up, about 4 hours.

Cut the pie into wedges to serve.

MAKES ONE 9½-INCH PIE;
8 SERVINGS

twelfth

night

THE TWELFTH Night Revelers is the organization
that officially opens the Carnival season on Epiphany.
The feast of the Epiphany, also called Twelfth Day
because it falls on the twelfth day after Christmas, officially ends the Christmas season and signifies the beginning of the season of Carnival. ■ On January 6, 1870,
the Lord of Misrule, who is essentially the king of
Twelfth Night, first appeared in New Orleans, pre-
senting a pageant depicting a Twelfth Night Revel consisting of eighteen floats and cavalcades. At the tableau
ball, where the court was presented, a great Twelfth
Night cake (also known as King Cake) was cut and slices
distributed with grace and courtesy by the maskers.
Some passed the cake on their spears, and others, in
their enthusiasm, threw slices to the ladies in the boxes.
The young lady who received a slice containing a
golden bean would reign as queen for the evening.

While this method of distribution created much merriment, the bean was lost in the confusion and the Lord of Misrule was without a queen that year. ■ The Twelfth Night Revelers stopped parading in 1877, but they continued to present tableau balls every January, except for the years from 1879 to 1883. The method by which the queen is now chosen was established in 1894 and continues, more or less in the same fashion, to this day. The maskers lead their partners to the King Cake, which the Royal Bakers prepare. Slices in small boxes are obtained by the "maiden ladies" (unmarried debutantes) as they march around. Whoever has the slice of cake in which the golden bean is hidden is declared the queen for the evening. ■ Carnival—the season of merriment that begins annually on January 6 and ends at midnight on Mardi Gras, also known as Fat Tuesday—is either one long raucous celebration or, as it is viewed by everyone who joins in the festivities, the greatest free party on earth.

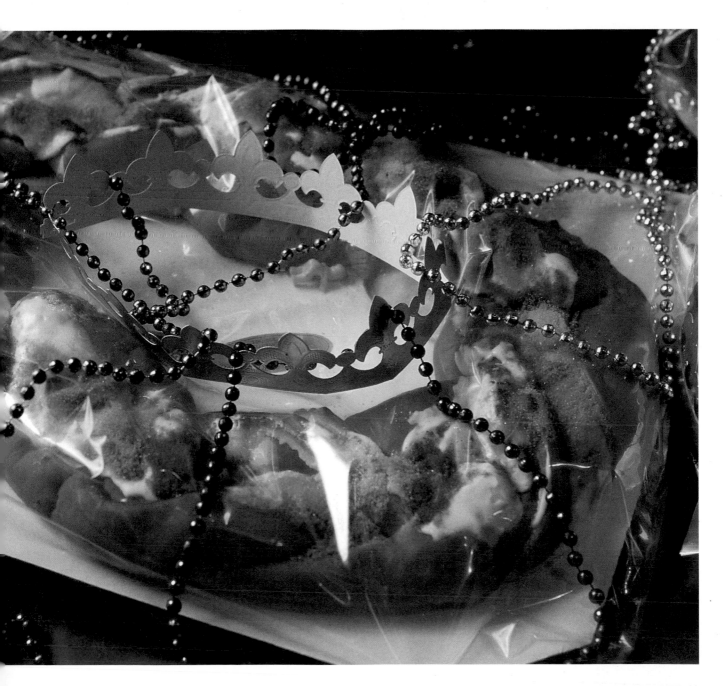

KING CAKE

THE HISTORY OF THE KING CAKE (*GÂTEAU DE ROI*) BEGAN IN TWELFTH-CENTURY FRANCE, WHERE THE CAKE WOULD BE BAKED ON THE EVE OF JANUARY 6, THE FEAST OF THE EPIPHANY. IT WAS MEANT TO CELEBRATE THE VISIT TO THE CHRIST CHILD BY THE THREE KINGS, OR MAGI. A SMALL TOKEN OR COIN WAS HIDDEN IN THE CAKE AS A SURPRISE FOR THE FINDER. ■ IN NEW ORLEANS, THE FIRST KING CAKE OF THE SEASON WAS AND STILL IS SERVED ON JANUARY 6. KING CAKE PARTIES ARE HELD DAILY ALL OVER THE STATE WHERE PEOPLE GATHER TO SHARE THE CAKE. WHOEVER GETS THE SLICE OF CAKE CONTAINING THE PLASTIC OR CERAMIC BABY THAT WAS BAKED INTO IT MUST HOST A KING CAKE PARTY THE FOLLOWING WEEK. YES, WEEKLY KING CAKE PARTIES ARE HELD UNTIL MARDI GRAS. ■ THE CAKE IS CIRCULAR IN SHAPE (TO REPRESENT A CROWN) AND RICHLY DECORATED WITH SUGAR TINTED IN THE CLASSIC CARNIVAL COLORS—GREEN, GOLD, AND PURPLE, SYMBOLIZING FAITH, POWER, AND JUSTICE. THE CAKES ARE USUALLY MADE OF A SIMPLE BUT RICH YEAST DOUGH.

Combine the yeast and granulated sugar in the bowl of a stand mixer fitted with a dough hook. Add the melted butter and warm milk. Beat at low speed for 1 minute. With the mixer running, add the egg yolks, then beat for 1 minute at medium-low speed. Add the flour, salt, nutmeg, and lemon zest and beat until everything is incorporated. Increase the speed to high and beat until the dough pulls away from the sides of the bowl, forms a ball, and starts to climb up the dough hook.

Remove the dough from the bowl. Using your hands, form the dough into a smooth ball. Lightly oil a bowl with the vegetable oil. Place the dough in the bowl and turn it to oil all sides. Cover with plastic wrap and set aside in a warm, draft-free place until doubled in size, about 2 hours.

2 envelopes active dry yeast
1/2 cup granulated sugar
1/4 pound (1 stick) unsalted
    butter, melted
1/2 cup warm milk (about 110°F)
5 large egg yolks, at room
    temperature
41/2 cups bleached all-purpose
    flour
2 teaspoons salt
1 teaspoon freshly grated
    nutmeg
1 teaspoon grated lemon zest
1 teaspoon vegetable oil
1 pound cream cheese, at room
    temperature
4 cups confectioners' sugar

1 plastic king cake baby or a
  pecan half
5 tablespoons milk, at room
  temperature
3 tablespoons fresh lemon juice
Purple-, green-, and gold-tinted
  sugar sprinkles

Meanwhile, make the filling. In a large mixing bowl, combine the cream cheese and 1 cup of the confectioners' sugar. Blend by hand or with an electric mixer on low speed. Set aside.

Line a baking sheet with parchment paper.

Turn the dough out onto a lightly floured work surface. Using your fingers, pat it out into a rectangle about 30 inches long and 6 inches wide.

Spread the filling lengthwise over the bottom half of the dough, then flip the top half of the dough over the filling. Seal the edges, pinching the dough together. Shape the dough into a cylinder and place it on the prepared baking sheet seam side down. Shape the dough into a ring and pinch the ends together so there isn't a seam. Insert the king cake baby or pecan half into the ring from the bottom so that it is completely hidden by the dough.

Cover the ring with plastic wrap or a clean kitchen towel and place in a warm, draft-free place. Let the dough rise until doubled in size, about 45 minutes.

Meanwhile, preheat the oven to 350°F.

Brush the top of the risen cake with 2 tablespoons of the milk. Bake until golden brown, 25 to 30 minutes. Remove from the oven and let cool completely on a wire rack.

Make the icing. Combine the remaining 3 tablespoons milk, the lemon juice, and the remaining 3 cups confectioners' sugar in a medium-size mixing bowl. Stir to blend well. With a rubber spatula, spread the icing evenly over the top of the cake. Sprinkle with the sugar crystals, alternating colors around the cake.

The cake is traditionally cut into 2-inch-thick slices with all the guests in attendance.

MAKES 20 TO 22 SERVINGS

FEBRUARY may be the shortest month of the year, but in Louisiana so much is jam-packed into those few weeks. ■ The weather can be nasty, as winter gives us its last best shot. The landscape is gray and dreary, broken only by the glorious budding of what are locally known as Japanese magnolias. Unlike their cousin the Southern magnolia, which is an evergreen that features grand white blossoms that appear during the heat of the summer, this native Southeast Asian species bursts upon the dismal countryside in varying shades of lavender, purple, and pink as if to announce that although spring has not yet arrived, it's on its way. These tree-like shrubs are quite showy, since they bloom before their bright green leaves fill out. At about the same time, redbud trees, spindly and also leafless, pop out with their tiny delicate purple flowers. ■ But the environmental factors are hardly a concern to revelers whose calendars are filled with balls, parades, and soirees of all sorts, as

february

the celebration of Carnival takes precedence over just about everything. It's just as well, since the winter crops are in and it's too early to plant the summer ones. ■ The City That Care Forgot is packed with revelers in town to attend the many Carnival activities, there's not a hotel or motel room to be found for practically the entire month, and every dining spot, from cafés to fine restaurants, can barely keep up with the customers. It's a madhouse! ■ Elsewhere in the United States, citizens are observing Groundhog Day, Presidents' Day, and Valentine's Day. Here, the predominant Catholic community solemnizes La Chandeleur (Candlemas) on February 2, marking the presentation of the Infant Jesus at the Temple and

the Purification of the Virgin Mother. February 3 is the Feast of Saint Blaise, who once cured a boy who was suffocating because a

fishbone had stuck in his throat, and who is the patron saint of those who suffer from throat ailments. And then, of course, the day after Mardi Gras is Ash Wednesday, which marks the beginning of the Lenten season.

valentine's day

VALENTINE'S DAY is for lovers, and there's nothing better to enjoy with your sweetheart than decadent chocolate desserts. The Aztecs believed chocolate to be an aphrodisiac. They ended their meals with it, and I'm with them. ■ I'm a romantic at heart and I truly believe that the way to a woman's, or man's, heart is through the stomach. After all, food is my business. Nothing gives me more pleasure than watching people enjoy a good meal. At all of my restaurants, the staff and I work very hard to make the meal a wonderful dining experience. We pay a lot of attention to detail, we want our guests to be comfortable and to enjoy good wines, and, of course, the food has to knock their socks off. I want to tantalize all the senses—sight, smell, taste, and feel. ■ Trust me—prepare your sweetheart a meal, pop open a bottle of bubbly, and select appropriate wines for the feast. Be sure to give special care to the dessert. After all, that's the last part of the meal, the part that will (hopefully) put your honey in a loving mood. That's what it's all about!

CHOCOLATE CHESS PIE

CHESS PIE IS A SOUTHERN DESSERT THAT HAS BEEN AROUND FOR A LONG TIME, PROBABLY BECAUSE IT'S VERY EASY TO THROW TOGETHER. MY VERSION IS A LOT LIKE A FUDGE PIE. DESSERTS DON'T NECESSARILY HAVE TO BE ELABORATE, JUST SCRUMPTIOUS, TO TURN YOU ON. YOU'LL NEED SIX 5-INCH TART PANS WITH REMOVABLE BOTTOMS FOR THIS.

Preheat the oven to 325°F.

Roll out the dough to a 12-inch circle ¼ inch thick and cut out six 5-inch rounds. Line each tart pan with a round of dough, pressing it into the bottom and up the sides with your fingers.

In a medium-size mixing bowl, combine the butter and sugar, whisking to blend. Add the melted chocolate and whisk until smooth. Add the eggs, vanilla, and cornmeal and whisk until smooth. Pour about ½ cup of the mixture into each prepared tart pan.

Place the tart pans on a baking sheet and bake until the crusts are lightly browned, about 25 minutes. Remove from the oven and place on a wire rack to cool for 15 minutes. The center of the pies will sink slightly as they cool.

To serve, cool completely before removing the pan bottoms and the pies from the tart pans. Spoon the whipped cream on top of the tarts. Serve at room temperature.

½ recipe Basic Sweet Piecrust (recipe follows)
¼ pound (1 stick) unsalted butter, melted
1 cup sugar
4 ounces semisweet chocolate, chopped and melted
4 large eggs, beaten
1 teaspoon pure vanilla extract
1½ tablespoons yellow cornmeal
1 recipe Sweetened Whipped Cream (recipe follows)

MAKES 6 SERVINGS

Basic Sweet Piecrust

2 cups bleached all-purpose
    flour
1½ teaspoons sugar
½ teaspoon salt
³⁄4 cup vegetable shortening
3 to 4 tablespoons ice water, as
    needed

Combine the flour, sugar, and salt in a medium-size mixing bowl. Add the shortening and work it in with your hands until the mixture resembles coarse crumbs. Add the water 1 tablespoon at a time, working it in with your hands. Add only as much as you need for a smooth ball of dough to form. Wrap the dough in plastic wrap and refrigerate for at least 30 minutes.

Remove the dough from the refrigerator and let it sit for about 10 minutes, then place it on a lightly floured work surface. Cut the dough in half and put the second half back in the refrigerator. For each crust, roll out the dough on the floured surface into a circle about 12 inches in diameter and ⅛ inch thick. Proceed as directed in the recipe.

MAKES TWO 9-INCH PIECRUSTS

Sweetened Whipped Cream

2 cups heavy cream
½ teaspoon pure vanilla extract
2 teaspoons sugar

Combine the cream, vanilla, and sugar in a medium-size mixing bowl and, using an electric mixer, whip until soft peaks form.

MAKES ABOUT 3 CUPS

CHOCOLATE COEUR À LA CRÈME

WITHOUT A DOUBT, THE QUINTESSENTIAL VALENTINE'S DESSERT IS *COEUR À LA CREME*, FRENCH FOR "HEART OF CREAM," AND I CAN UNDERSTAND WHY. A WONDERFULLY RICH MIXTURE OF HEAVY CREAM, CREAM CHEESE, AND CHOCOLATE IS ALLOWED TO SET OVERNIGHT IN HEART-SHAPED MOLDS WITH PERFORATED BOTTOMS SO THE MOISTURE DRAINS OFF. THE DESSERT CAN BE SERVED WITH CHOCOLATE-DIPPED STRAWBERRIES OR SUGAR COOKIES—MAYBE BOTH! ■ YOU CAN USE ONE LARGE HEART-SHAPED MOLD OR INDIVIDUAL ONES, AS WE DID HERE. THEY CAN BE FOUND AT SPECIALTY FOOD STORES OR KITCHEN SHOPS.

Put the cream and vanilla in a medium-size mixing bowl and beat at medium speed until soft peaks form. Add the confectioners' sugar and continue beating until stiff peaks form. Set aside.

In another medium-size mixing bowl, beat the cream cheese at medium speed until fluffy. Add the melted chocolate and beat until smooth, scraping down the sides as needed. Fold in the whipped cream.

Line each mold with a square of the dampened cheesecloth. Divide the chocolate cream mixture evenly among the molds. Fold each overhanging cheesecloth over the top. Place the molds on a wire rack set on a baking sheet. Refrigerate overnight, or at least 8 hours.

FOR THE COEURS
1 cup heavy cream
1/2 teaspoon pure vanilla extract
1/4 cup confectioners' sugar
1/2 pound cream cheese, at room temperature
2 ounces semisweet chocolate, chopped and melted
Six 6-inch squares cheesecloth (or a 12-inch square for a large mold), dampened with water
Six 4-inch coeur à la crème molds (or one 8-inch mold)

**FOR THE CHOCOLATE-
DIPPED STRAWBERRIES**
4 ounces semisweet chocolate,
   chopped
12 fresh strawberries, rinsed and
   dried, at room temperature

TO SERVE
1 recipe Sugar Cookies
   (recipe follows)

Make the chocolate-dipped strawberries. Line a baking sheet with parchment or waxed paper. Stir the
chocolate in the top of a double boiler or in a metal
mixing bowl set over hot (but not simmering) water
until melted and smooth. Remove from the water.
Holding a strawberry by the stem or hull, dip two thirds
of it into the chocolate. Shake gently to remove the
excess. Place the strawberry on the prepared baking
sheet. Repeat with the remaining strawberries. (Set the
chocolate over the hot water to soften if necessary while
working.) Refrigerate the berries until the chocolate is
firm, about 30 minutes.

When ready to serve, carefully remove the hearts from
the molds and gently remove the cheesecloth

Serve the hearts on individual plates with the chocolate-dipped strawberries and the cookies. You can make
this 1 day in advance.

MAKES 6 SERVINGS

Sugar Cookies

Cream the butter and ½ cup of the sugar together with an electric mixer on medium speed until smooth and fluffy, scraping down the sides of the bowl as necessary. Add the egg yolks one at a time, beating after each addition. Scrape down the sides of the bowl. Beat for 1 minute and add the vanilla.

Combine 1¼ cups of the flour and the salt in a small mixing bowl and add to the butter mixture. Mix on low speed until fully incorporated. Increase the speed to medium and mix until the dough is thick and creamy, about 2 minutes.

Generously dust a large sheet of parchment or waxed paper with the remaining 2 tablespoons flour. Spoon the dough down the center of the paper, fold the paper tightly over the dough, and roll into a cylinder about 2 inches in diameter and about 17 inches long. Refrigerate for 4 hours.

Preheat the oven to 350°F. Line a baking sheet with parchment paper.

Remove the dough from the refrigerator and peel away the paper. Using a sharp knife, cut the dough into ½-inch-thick slices. Place them on the baking sheet about 1½ inches apart. Sprinkle with 1 tablespoon of the remaining sugar. Bake until lightly golden, about 15 minutes. Remove the cookies from the oven and let cool completely on the sheet. Remove them from the sheet using a spatula or thin knife. Repeat the process with the remaining dough and sugar.

3/4 cup (1½ sticks) unsalted butter, at room temperature
1/2 cup plus 2 tablespoons sugar
3 large egg yolks
1/2 teaspoon pure vanilla extract
1¼ cups plus 2 tablespoons bleached all-purpose flour
1/4 teaspoon salt

MAKES ABOUT 32 COOKIES

THREE-CHOCOLATE BARK WITH SPICED PECANS AND DRIED CHERRIES

DID YOU KNOW THAT THE LATIN NAME OF THE TREE THAT PRODUCES CACAO BEANS, FROM WHICH WE DERIVE CHOCOLATE, IS *THEOBROMA CACAO* AND THAT *THEOBROMA* MEANS FOOD OF THE GODS IN GREEK? ■ FOR THIS CHOCOLATE TREAT, USE GOOD-QUALITY CHOCOLATE. THIS RECIPE MAKES A LOT, SO YOU MIGHT WANT TO GIVE SOME TO YOUR SWEETHEART AND TAKE THE REST TO FRIENDS TO ENJOY.

Preheat the oven to 400°F. Line two baking sheets with parchment paper.

In a medium-size sauté pan, melt 4 tablespoons of the butter over medium heat. Add the brown sugar and stir until the sugar dissolves and the mixture is bubbly, about 1 minute. Add the pecans, salt, cayenne, nutmeg, and cinnamon and cook, stirring constantly, until the sugar starts to caramelize and coats the pecans evenly, about 3 minutes.

Remove the pan from the heat and spread the pecans over one of the prepared baking sheets. Place the pan in the oven and roast for about 6 minutes. Remove from the oven and, using a fork, place the pecans evenly on the parchment paper. Let cool completely.

Fill three small saucepans halfway with water. Place the pans over medium heat and bring to a simmer, then reduce the heat to medium-low. Put each type of chocolate into a separate stainless steel mixing bowl. Place each bowl over a saucepan and stir until the chocolates are completely melted. Remove from the heat and stir 1 tablespoon of the remaining butter into each bowl until completely melted.

7 tablespoons unsalted butter
1/2 cup firmly packed light brown sugar
2 cups pecan pieces
1/4 teaspoon salt
1/8 teaspoon cayenne
1/8 teaspoon freshly grated nutmeg
1/8 teaspoon ground cinnamon
1 pound semisweet chocolate, chopped
1 pound milk chocolate, chopped
1 pound white chocolate, chopped
2 cups dried cherries

Pour the semisweet chocolate onto the second prepared baking sheet and spread evenly with a rubber spatula. Then pour the milk chocolate over the semisweet layer and spread evenly with a rubber spatula. Repeat with the white chocolate. Sprinkle the pecans and the cherries over the chocolate and press gently but firmly into it. Place the baking sheet in the refrigerator and chill until the bark sets, about 2 hours.

Break the bark into pieces and serve. The bark can be stored between layers of parchment or waxed paper in airtight containers in the refrigerator for up to 2 weeks.

MAKES ABOUT 4 POUNDS

mardi gras

THE FIRST celebration of Mardi Gras in Louisiana dates back to 1699 (so in 1999 New Orleans marked three hundred years of festivities with even more frolicking than usual), when a group of French explorers made camp in a small, swampy bayou near the mouth of the Mississippi. Despite their fatigue and loneliness for their homeland, they noted the date, March 3, and, toasting France's king, named the site Point du Mardi Gras. ■ Mardi Gras (which is French for Fat Tuesday, signifying the last day of feasting before the Lenten fast), always falls forty-six days before Easter. (Some use a formula that says it is the day before Lent, which begins forty days before Easter, excluding Sundays.) The Roman Catholic Church uses a formula to determine the date of Easter. It falls on the first Sunday after the Paschal full moon—the first full moon after the spring equinox. Thus, Mardi Gras is a movable feast, making for the annual lament about Mardi Gras being early or late. ■ In 1970, it was on February 10—that's early. In 1973, it was on March 6, so that's real late. In 1974, it

was on February 26, kinda late. In 1989, it was on February 7, early, early. When is it ever on time? In 1999, it fell on February 16, which is middle of the road, and in the year 2000, it's going to be on March 7, late again.

Without a doubt, New Orleans is best known for its Carnival celebrations. During the French colonial times in New Orleans, the rich celebrated at private masked balls. There were parades of sorts, in which costumed revelers walked the streets. By the mid-eighteenth century, the custom was apparently well established, mainly as an excuse for licentious frolic, but it was not until 1857 that the festivities began to take on their modern-day character, when some socially prominent young blades formed a secret society called the Mistick Krewe of Comus. (The word *krewe* has become the generic term for all Carnival organizations.) This first krewe staged a splendid parade with floats and costumes, and followed it with a *bal masque,* or tableau ball, that included a king, queen, and royal court. ■ Since then, the krewes, the parades, and the balls have proliferated, and Mardi Gras and New Orleans are inseparable. During the week prior to Mardi Gras, the city is in a frenzy. Numerous parades wind through the downtown area as well as the neighboring suburbs, making travel a bit tough, since streets are blocked every which way. ■ The Krewe of Hermes, organized in 1937 and named for the Greek messenger of the gods, takes to the streets on the weekend before Mardi Gras, following a route that takes it from uptown down St. Charles Avenue to Canal Street, ending at the Mississippi River. The popular Endymion rolls on Saturday, Bacchus on Sunday, and, on Monday, Harry Connick, Jr.'s krewe, appropriately named—because of the musical heritage of its founders—for Orpheus, the son of the Greek muse Calliope, a musician and poet who could tame wild animals and set rocks and trees in motion with his singing. ■ Come Fat Tuesday, two major krewes roll. Zulu is one of the season's most anticipated parades, named after the fiercest of the African tribes. The most famous king of Zulu was Louis Armstrong in 1949. The most prized

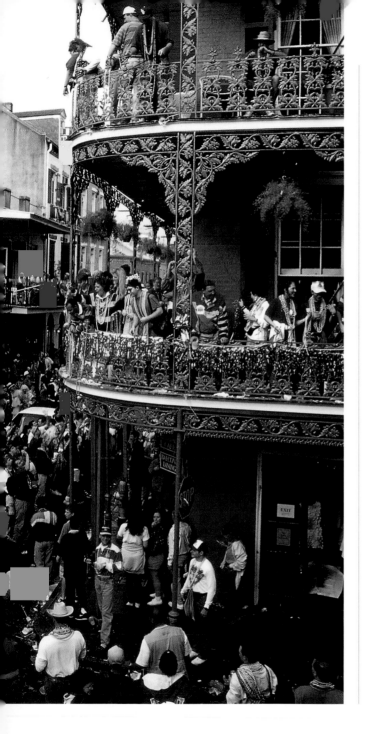

throw (items thrown by the parade riders to the people along the route) in this parade is the treasured Zulu coconut, which is traditionally handed to a lucky few.

The other Tuesday krewe is the Krewe of Rex. The King of Carnival, Rex has been the international symbol of New Orleans's most famous holiday since his first appearance in 1872. This club personifies Mardi Gras, and the throw to catch is the Rex doubloon, introduced in 1960. Rex is never called King Rex—he is the King of Carnival. ■ But there are other celebrations throughout the state. Rollicking street dances, elaborate parades, and costume balls are held in Lake Charles, Shreveport, Thibodaux, Lafayette (where the first recorded observance dates back to 1897), and in just about every small town in between. ■ Perhaps the most unusual style of celebration can be found in the Acadiana towns of Church Point, Mamou, Ville Platte, and Eunice. There the flavor and style is different. Its roots are firmly in the medieval ceremonial begging celebration, which features a performance in anticipation of a donation. The name of the game is *courir du Mardi Gras*, or the running of Mardi Gras. The object of this wild ride through the countryside is to collect ingredients for a gigantic community gumbo—Mardi Gras country-style, you could say. ■ The celebrants contrast sharply with the rhinestoned, sequined, and feathered costumes of the splendid maskers in the larger cities. Underlining it all is the same spirit, the love of a good time shared by the Cajuns and Creoles alike throughout the state. ■ The *courir* usually consists of a group of masked and costumed horseback riders accompanied by a wagon of musicians. They are led by *le capitaine*, who is easily identified by his flowing cape and the flag he carries. The revelers ride from farmhouse to farmhouse, begging for chickens to make the gumbo. The fun ensues when the men have to scramble to catch live chickens. ■ When the riders return to town, they are greeted by a *fais do do*, a Cajun-style dance party. There, the making and eating of the gumbo, together with dancing and frolicking, last well into the night. But

here, as in the Mardi Gras pageants, the high-spirited good times must come to an end at the stroke of midnight, when by law and by custom, Lent begins. ■ I was introduced to all of this some fifteen years ago when I made New Orleans my home, and it was indeed a revelation. I quickly learned why New Orleans is sometimes referred to as the City that Care Forgot. ■ When I was invited to join the krewes of Endymion and Bacchus, I jumped at the opportunity. Endymion, which was founded in 1967, is named for the god of fertility and eternal youth, definitely my kind of group. By 1974, it had grown into a super club. The krewe annually selects celebrity grand marshals and I had the proud honor of being one for the parade in 1999. Seeing young people's eyes watching you and hearing the roar of the voices along the parade route is a rare feeling, one that I can't really put into words. It was an incredible experience to ride through the streets of the city, then end up at the Louisiana Superdome where about fifteen thousand revelers, dressed in evening attire, welcomed the entire parade (about thirty super-floats and probably as many marching bands) and then partied till five A.M. at the Extravaganza. Wow! ■ The Krewe of Bacchus, founded in 1968 to explore new directions for Carnival clubs, honors the Greek god of wine, and it too is right up my alley. It also boasts a parade with huge floats that winds through the city, ending at a supper dance with Las Vegas–type entertainment. Many celebrities, including Raymond Burr, Bob Hope, Dennis Quaid, and Jackie Gleason, have portrayed Bacchus during the festivities. ■ My personal celebration begins four days prior to the big day, starting with a breakfast on Saturday morning at Emeril's. About fifty members of Endymion join me for eye-openers, a huge manly man breakfast, followed by cigars, and then it's on to City Park, where we get costumed and load up the floats.

NOLA BLUE GLACIER MARTINI

THIS IS A SPECIAL DRINK I LIKE TO SERVE AT PARADE PARTIES. SINCE I ADORE VODKA MARTINIS, I HAVE PLAYED AROUND WITH DIFFERENT TYPES OF VODKA AND LIQUEURS AND FINALLY SETTLED ON THIS MIX. IT'S PRETTY AND GOES DOWN REAL EASY. BE CAREFUL!

Chill four martini glasses in the freezer for 1 hour.

In a cocktail shaker, combine the vodka, Curaçao, and ice cubes. With a long-handled bar spoon, stir the mixture 40 times.

Strain the mixture equally into the glasses. Garnish each martini with an orange and lemon twist.

12 ounces high-quality vodka
Several splashes of blue curaçao
1 cup ice cubes
4 orange twists
4 lemon twists

MAKES 4 SERVINGS

ANDOUILLE CORN DOGS

MARDI GRAS FOOD RUNS THE GAMUT FROM HOT DOGS TO CAVIAR, BUT I'M A STREET FOOD JUNKIE AT HEART AND IN MY BOOK, NOTHING IS BETTER THAN CORN DOGS. THIS IS MY VERSION, MADE WITH SMOKY ANDOUILLE AND SLATHERED WITH YELLOW MUSTARD. THEY'RE IDEAL TO SERVE UP AT PRE- OR POST-PARADE PARTIES.

1 large egg

1 cup milk

2 tablespoons baking powder

³/4 cup yellow cornmeal

1¼ cups bleached all-purpose flour

2 tablespoons sugar

1 teaspoon salt

1 teaspoon hot sauce

½ teaspoon Creole Seasoning (page 13), plus some for garnish

8 cups vegetable oil

1½ pounds andouille sausage, cut into eight 3-inch-long pieces

16 bamboo skewers, cut into 6-inch lengths

Yellow mustard for dipping

In a large mixing bowl, whisk the egg and milk together. Add the baking powder, cornmeal, 1 cup of the flour, and the sugar. Whisk until smooth. Season with the salt and hot sauce.

In a small shallow bowl, combine the remaining ¼ cup flour and the Creole seasoning.

Heat the vegetable oil in a large, deep, heavy pot or an electric deep-fryer to 360°F.

Thread a sausage link onto each skewer, leaving 3 inches of the skewer bare at the bottom. Dredge the sausages in the flour mixture, tapping off any excess, then dip in the batter, coating evenly.

Carefully lay 2 to 3 corn dogs at a time (do not crowd them) in the hot oil and fry until golden brown, about 8 minutes, gently rolling them with tongs to brown evenly. Remove from the oil and let drain on paper towels. Sprinkle with Creole seasoning.

Serve the corn dogs with the mustard.

MAKES 8 SERVINGS

CRAWFISH AND SAUSAGE JAMBALAYA

RIGHT AROUND CARNIVAL TIME, CRAWFISH START SHOWING UP AT THE MARKETS AND EVERYONE HAS A HANKERING FOR THEIR FIRST TASTE OF THE SEASON. THIS IS A HEARTY AND FILLING JAMBALAYA THAT IS A MEAL IN ITSELF, JUST WHAT PARTYGOERS NEED TO KEEP THEIR STRENGTH UP! ■ I'VE SEEN MANY AVID PARADE WATCHERS BRING A WHOLE POT OF THIS STUFF TO EAT RIGHT ON THE PARADE ROUTE.

In a large Dutch oven, heat the vegetable oil over medium heat. Add the onions, bell peppers, and celery and season with the salt and cayenne. Cook, stirring, until the vegetables are wilted, about 5 minutes. Add the sausage and cook, stirring, for 2 minutes. Add the bay leaves, tomatoes, garlic, and crawfish and cook, stirring, for 2 minutes. Add the rice and cook, stirring, for 2 minutes, then add the broth and bring to a boil. Reduce the heat to medium-low, cover, and cook until the rice is tender and most of the liquid is absorbed, 25 to 30 minutes.

Stir in the green onions, remove the bay leaves, and serve hot.

2 tablespoons vegetable oil
2 cups chopped yellow onions
1 cup chopped green bell peppers
1/2 cup chopped celery
1 teaspoon salt
1/2 teaspoon cayenne
1 pound smoked sausage, cut lengthwise in half, then cut crosswise into 1/4-inch-thick slices
4 bay leaves
2 cups peeled, seeded, and chopped canned or fresh tomatoes
1 tablespoon chopped garlic
1 pound peeled crawfish tails
2 cups long-grain rice
5 cups chicken broth
1/2 cup chopped green onions or scallions (green part only)

MAKES 6 TO 8 SERVINGS

FRITO PIE

I FIRST SAW THIS WHILE WATCHING ONE OF MY VERY FIRST PARADES AND I COULDN'T GET OVER HOW TWO SIMPLE INGREDIENTS—FRITOS AND CHILI—COULD TASTE SO GOOD. MAYBE BECAUSE IT'S EATEN RIGHT OUT OF THE BAG WITH A PLASTIC FORK ON THE SIDEWALK WITH ALL THE HULLABALOO GOING ON!

2 tablespoons vegetable oil

2 cups chopped yellow onions

2 teaspoons salt

1/2 teaspoon cayenne

2 pounds beef bottom round, trimmed of fat and cut into 1/4-inch cubes

1/2 cup tomato paste

One 28-ounce can whole tomatoes and their liquid

2 cups beef broth

2 tablespoons chopped garlic

1 tablespoon chili powder

2 teaspoons ground cumin

2 teaspoons dried oregano

1/2 teaspoon red pepper flakes

1 cup dried red beans, picked over, rinsed, cooked in salted water to cover until tender, drained, and cooled

Eight 1 1/4-ounce bags Frito corn chips

1 cup grated Monterey Jack cheese

1/2 cup sour cream

1/2 cup pickled jalapeño slices, drained

In a large, heavy pot, heat the vegetable oil over medium-high heat. Add the onions, season with 1 teaspoon of the salt and the cayenne, and cook, stirring, until they are wilted and golden, about 4 minutes.

Season the beef with the remaining 1 teaspoon salt and add to the pot. Cook, stirring, until the beef is browned evenly on all sides, about 4 minutes. Add the tomato paste and cook, stirring, for 2 minutes. Add the tomatoes, beef broth, garlic, chili powder, cumin, oregano, red pepper flakes, and beans. Bring to a boil, then reduce the heat to medium-low and simmer, uncovered, stirring occasionally, until the beef is tender, about 2 hours. Skim off the fat that rises to the surface.

Open each bag of corn chips and remove half of the chips. Spoon 1/2 cup of the chili and 1 tablespoon of the cheese into each bag. Return the remaining chips to each bag and add another 1/2 cup of the chili, another tablespoon of the cheese, 1 tablespoon of the sour cream, and 1 tablespoon of the jalapeños to each one. Eat right out of the bag.

MAKES 8 SERVINGS

FUNNEL CAKES

FUNNEL CAKES ARE FEATURED AT JUST ABOUT EVERY FESTIVAL IN THE STATE, BUT IT'S NOT EVEN A LOUISIANA THING—IT'S A PENNSYLVANIA DUTCH SPECIALTY. THE BATTER IS PUT INTO A FUNNEL, THEN DRIBBLED INTO HOT OIL TO MAKE SPIRALS. WE MAKE SMALL CAKES, BUT YOU CAN MAKE THEM ANY SIZE YOU WANT.

In a small bowl, combine the confectioners' sugar and cinnamon and stir to mix. Set aside.

Into a large mixing bowl, sift the flour, brown sugar, baking powder, and salt. In another large mixing bowl, whisk together the eggs, milk, and vanilla. Fold the dry ingredients into the wet mixture and whisk until smooth.

In a large skillet, heat the vegetable oil to 360°F.

Hold your finger under the opening of an 8-ounce funnel and fill it with about ¾ cup of the batter. Working over the hot oil, carefully remove your finger from the funnel opening and slowly dribble the batter into the oil, making figure 8 designs. Fry until golden brown, about 2 minutes on each side. Remove from the oil, let drain on paper towels, and sprinkle with some of the sugar-cinnamon mixture. Repeat the procedure until all the batter is used. Serve warm.

1 cup confectioners' sugar
1/2 teaspoon ground cinnamon
4 cups bleached all-purpose flour
1 cup firmly packed light brown sugar
1 tablespoon baking powder
1/2 teaspoon salt
3 large eggs
2¼ cups milk
1/2 teaspoon pure vanilla extract
2 cups vegetable oil

MAKES ABOUT 5 DOZEN FUNNEL CAKES

SPLIT PEA SOUP

IN UPTOWN NEW ORLEANS, THE RESIDENTS ALONG THE PARADE ROUTES HOLD GRAND OPENHOUSE PARTIES. WHEN THE WEATHER COOPERATES, EVERYONE GATHERS IN FRONT YARDS, BACKYARDS, OR ON VERANDAHS, SOMETIMES SPILLING OVER ONTO THE SIDEWALKS. THERE ARE TABLES AND TABLES LADEN WITH EVERYTHING IMAGINABLE TO EAT AND DRINK. ■ MARCELLE TELLS ME THAT WHEN SHE LIVED IN THAT PART OF THE CITY MANY MOONS AGO, THERE WERE SEVERAL NEIGHBORS WHO ENJOYED A BIT OF A RIVALRY AS TO WHO COULD PREPARE THE BEST SPLIT PEA SOUP. EVERY FAMILY MADE A POT, PUT IT OUT IN A CAULDRON, AND KEPT IT WARM FOR GUESTS TO HELP THEMSELVES. WHOEVER'S POT WAS EMPTIED FIRST WAS THE WINNER! I'D BE WILLING TO PUT THIS ONE UP IN THE CONTEST.

1 tablespoon olive oil
2 cups chopped yellow onions
1/2 teaspoon salt
1/2 teaspoon freshly ground black pepper
1/4 teaspoon red pepper flakes
1 tablespoon chopped garlic
1 bay leaf
1 pound dried green split peas, picked over and rinsed
8 cups chicken broth
1 cup milk
1/2 teaspoon hot sauce

In a large soup pot over medium-high heat, heat the olive oil. Add the onions, salt, black pepper, and red pepper flakes and cook, stirring, for 2 minutes. Add the garlic, bay leaf, and split peas and cook, stirring, for 1 minute. Add the broth and bring to a boil, then reduce the heat to medium and simmer, stirring occasionally, for 45 minutes, until the peas are tender.

Remove from the heat and let cool slightly. Remove the bay leaf and discard. Add the milk and, using a hand-held immersion blender (or in a regular blender in batches), process until smooth. Add the hot sauce and serve hot.

MAKES ABOUT 8 SERVINGS

ilda and mr. john's anniversary

HILDA AND Mr. John, my mom and dad, celebrate their wedding anniversary on February 11, and it's always a fun occasion for all of us to get together to enjoy a fine meal. As usual, at family affairs such as this, my parents reminisce about when they first met. The story is that they encountered each another when they were in the fifth grade at Longfellow School on Williams Street in Fall River, Massachusetts. They went their separate ways, but they renewed their acquaintance in high school. Their dates were usually to join Mr. John's brother and his girlfriend, Eleanore, to go dancing. As their relationship grew, Mr. John often met Hilda after her work as a seamstress at a curtain shop and walked her home. Finally, after they'd dated seriously for about a year, Mr. John proposed. They were engaged at Christmas and were married in February 1950 at Santo Cristo Church in Fall River. ■ After a three-day honeymoon in Boston, they settled in a little cottage and, as the years rolled on, my sister, Delores, arrived, then me, followed by Mark. ■ Congratulations, Mom and Dad, and thanks for everything!

HILDA'S MAHIMAHI WITH SEASONAL VEGETABLES

HILDA LOVES FISH, AS LONG AS IT'S FRESH. WHEN SHE COMES TO ANY OF MY RESTAURANTS, SHE USUALLY ASKS FOR A FISH DISH, BECAUSE SHE KNOWS WE HAVE GOOD FRESH FISH IN THE HOUSE, ALWAYS. MAHIMAHI IS A FIRM-FLESHED FISH THAT IS FISHED ALONG THE ATLANTIC COAST, MAINLY IN FLORIDA, ALONG THE PACIFIC COAST ALL THE WAY DOWN TO SOUTH AMERICA, AND IN THE HAWAIIAN WATERS. IF YOU CAN'T FIND MAHIMAHI IN YOUR AREA, TALK TO YOUR FISH MAN AND ASK HIM FOR ANY GOOD FIRM WHITE FISH. ■ MAKE THE HERBED VINAIGRETTE A DAY IN ADVANCE IF YOU CAN AND STORE IT IN THE REFRIGERATOR OVERNIGHT TO ALLOW THE FLAVORS TO MINGLE.

Make the vinaigrette. Combine the olive oil, vinegar, honey, garlic, tomatoes, ¼ teaspoon of the salt, ¼ teaspoon of the black pepper, and the herbs in a medium-size mixing bowl and whisk to blend well. Store in an airtight container in the refrigerator for at least 8 hours or as long as 24 hours. Bring to room temperature before using.

Season the fillets with the Creole seasoning. In a large skillet over medium heat, heat 1 tablespoon of the olive oil. Add the fillets and sear until they are lightly golden and flake easily with a fork, 5 to 6 minutes on each side. Transfer to a warm platter.

½ cup extra-virgin olive oil

2 tablespoons balsamic vinegar

1 teaspoon honey

1 teaspoon chopped garlic

¼ cup peeled, seeded, and chopped canned or fresh tomatoes

³/₄ teaspoon salt

½ teaspoon freshly ground black pepper

⅓ cup packed chopped assorted fresh herbs, such as basil, chives, dill, tarragon, and parsley

4 mahimahi fillets (5 to 6 ounces each)

1 tablespoon Creole Seasoning (page 13)

2 tablespoons olive oil

⅛ head white cabbage (about 4 ounces), cored and thinly sliced

¼ small head red cabbage
(about 4 ounces), cored and
thinly sliced

2 cups thinly sliced red onions

4 medium-size carrots (about
8 ounces), julienned or cut on
a mandoline with a shredder
blade

1 medium-size zucchini (about
6 ounces), julienned or cut on
a mandoline with the shredder
blade

1 medium-size yellow squash
(about 6 ounces), julienned or
cut on a mandoline with a
shredder blade

⅓ cup water

MAKES 4 SERVINGS

Heat the remaining 1 tablespoon olive oil in another large skillet over medium-high heat. Add the white cabbage, red cabbage, and the remaining ½ teaspoon salt and ¼ teaspoon black pepper and cook, stirring a few times, for 2 minutes. Add the onions and cook, stirring a few times, for 2 minutes. Add the carrots and cook, stirring a few times, for 2 minutes. Add the zucchini, yellow squash, and water and cook, stirring, for 2 minutes until crisp. Remove from the heat.

To serve, divide the vegetable mixture equally among four plates, place a fillet on each portion, and drizzle about ¼ cup of the vinaigrette over each.

MR. JOHN'S VEAL CHOPS WITH SMOKED GOUDA CHEESE MACARONI

MR. JOHN LOVES VEAL, AND THESE DOUBLE-CUTS REALLY SATISFY HIM. HILDA AND MR. JOHN ARE FANATICS ABOUT CRAWFISH. DURING THE SEASON, THEY HAVE BOILED CRAWFISH EVERY SATURDAY AFTERNOON, SO A CRAWFISH SAUCE IS A NATURAL FOR THIS DISH. AND THE CHEESY MACARONI IS JUST THE RIGHT ACCOMPANIMENT.

Preheat the oven to 375°F.

Season the chops on both sides with the Creole seasoning. Heat the olive oil a large ovenproof skillet over medium-high heat. Add the chops and sear for 5 minutes on each side. Transfer to the oven and roast for 12 minutes. Remove from the oven, transfer the chops to a platter, and keep warm.

In the same skillet, combine the onion, salt, and cayenne over medium-high heat and cook, stirring, for 2 minutes. Add the tomatoes, garlic, and veal reduction and cook, stirring, for 1 minute. Add the crawfish tails and cook, stirring occasionally, for 2 minutes. Add ¼ cup of the green onions and the parsley and return the veal chops and their juices to the skillet. Cook, basting with the sauce, until the veal is cooked the way you like it, about 5 minutes. Remove from the heat.

To serve, divide the macaroni into 4 equal portions and serve with the chops. Garnish with the remaining 1 tablespoon green onions.

4 double-cut veal loin chops (12 to 14 ounces each)
1 tablespoon Creole Seasoning (page 13)
1 tablespoon olive oil
½ cup chopped yellow onion
¼ teaspoon salt
¼ teaspoon cayenne
½ cup chopped, peeled, and seeded canned or fresh tomatoes
½ teaspoon chopped garlic
1 recipe Veal Reduction (recipe follows)
½ pound peeled crawfish tails
¼ cup plus 1 tablespoon chopped green onions or scallions (green part only)
1 tablespoon chopped fresh parsley leaves
1 recipe Smoked Gouda Cheese Macaroni (recipe follows)

MAKES 4 SERVINGS

Veal Reduction

**FOR THE VEAL STOCK
(MAKES 2 QUARTS)**

7 pounds veal marrow bones,
   sawed into 2-inch pieces
   (ask your butcher to do this)
One 6-ounce can tomato paste
2 cups coarsely chopped yellow
   onions
1 cup coarsely chopped celery
1 cup coarsely chopped carrots
2 cups dry red wine
1 teaspoon salt
5 cloves garlic, peeled
1 Bouquet Garni (recipe follows)
6 quarts water

**FOR THE VEAL
REDUCTION
(MAKES 1 CUP)**

1 quart veal stock
1/4 teaspoon salt

Make the veal stock. Preheat the oven to 450°F. Put the bones in a shallow roasting pan and roast for 1 hour.

Remove the pan from the oven and spread the bones evenly with the tomato paste. Combine the onions, celery, and carrots and scatter over the top of the bones. Return to the oven and roast for another 30 minutes. Remove from the oven and drain off any fat.

Place the roasting pan over medium heat on top of the stove and pour the wine over the bones and vegetables. Using a wooden spoon, deglaze the pan, scraping the bottom for browned bits. Put everything into a large stockpot. Add the salt, garlic, bouquet garni, and water and bring to a boil over high heat. Skim off any cloudy scum that rises to the surface, then reduce the heat to medium and simmer, uncovered, for 4 hours.

Strain the stock through a fine-mesh strainer and let cool. Refrigerate for 8 hours, or overnight, then remove any congealed fat from the surface.

The stock will keep in the refrigerator for 3 days or in the freezer, in 1- to 2-cup containers, for up to 1 month.

To make the veal reduction, bring the stock, seasoned with the salt, to a boil in a medium-size saucepan over high heat. Reduce the heat to medium and simmer until reduced by three quarters, about 1 hour. It will keep for 3 days.

continued

Bouquet Garni

Place all the ingredients in the center of a 6-inch square of cheesecloth. Bring the corners together and tie securely with kitchen twine.

5 sprigs fresh thyme
2 bay leaves
10 black peppercorns
3 sprigs fresh parsley

Smoked Gouda Cheese Macaroni

Preheat the oven to 375°F.

Put the water, ½ teaspoon of the salt, and the oil in a large, heavy saucepan over high heat and bring to a boil. Add the macaroni and cook, stirring occasionally, until tender, about 8 minutes. Drain and rinse under cool water. Set aside.

In a small, heavy saucepan, melt 2 tablespoons of the butter over medium heat. Add the flour and cook, stirring constantly, for 2 minutes. Slowly add the milk, whisking constantly. Add the remaining ½ teaspoon salt and the white pepper and continue whisking until the sauce is smooth and thick enough to coat the back of a wooden spoon, about 8 minutes. Remove the white sauce from the heat and stir in the cheese. Continue stirring until the cheese melts.

Lightly grease a 6½ × 10-inch casserole dish with the remaining ½ teaspoon butter. Combine the cheese sauce and macaroni in a large mixing bowl and mix well. Pour into the prepared casserole and bake until lightly golden on top, about 20 minutes. Remove from the oven and serve hot.

6 cups water
1 teaspoon salt
1/8 teaspoon vegetable oil
1 pound ditalini or small elbow macaroni
2 tablespoons plus 1/2 teaspoon unsalted butter
2 tablespoons bleached all-purpose flour
2 1/2 cups milk
1/4 teaspoon freshly ground white pepper
1/4 pound smoked Gouda cheese, grated

MAKES 4 SERVINGS

BLACK FOREST CAKE

SCHWARZWÄLDER KIRSCHTORTE, COMMONLY KNOWN AS BLACK FOREST CAKE, HAILS FROM GERMANY'S BLACK FOREST REGION. IT'S A LUSCIOUS CHOCOLATE CAKE SOAKED WITH KIRSCH, LAYERED WITH CHERRIES LACED WITH KIRSCH, COATED WITH CHOCOLATE ICING, AND GARNISHED WITH WHIPPED CREAM AND CHOCOLATE CURLS OR SHAVINGS.

Preheat the oven to 350°F.

Make the cake. Put the eggs and 1 cup of the granulated sugar in a large mixing bowl and, with an electric mixer fitted with a wire whisk, beat on medium-high speed until the mixture is pale yellow, thick, and tripled in volume, about 8 minutes. Stir in the vanilla.

Sift the flour, cocoa, baking powder, and salt together into a medium-size mixing bowl.

Add the flour mixture ½ cup at a time to the egg mixture mixing at medium speed until all is incorporated. Increase the speed to high and beat for 1 minute.

Grease two 9 × 2-inch round cake pans with the butter. Sprinkle each with 1 tablespoon of the remaining sugar. Pour the cake batter evenly into the pans and bake until the cakes spring back when touched, about 25 minutes.

Remove from the oven and let cool for about 2 minutes. Using a thin knife, loosen the edges of the cakes, then flip them onto a wire rack. Let cool completely.

Make the filling. Combine the granulated sugar and water in a small saucepan over medium heat. Bring to a boil, stirring to dissolve the sugar, and cook for 2 minutes. Remove from the heat and let cool completely, then add 1 cup of the kirsch and stir to mix.

FOR THE CAKE
8 large eggs
1 cup plus 2 tablespoons granulated sugar
1 teaspoon pure vanilla extract
1 cup bleached all-purpose flour
½ cup unsweetened cocoa powder
1 teaspoon baking powder
Pinch of salt
2 teaspoons unsalted butter, at room temperature

FOR THE FILLING
2 cups granulated sugar
1 cup water
1¼ cups kirsch
Two 15-ounce cans dark sweet pitted cherries in heavy syrup
2 tablespoons cornstarch

1 pound confectioners' sugar
1/2 cup unsweetened cocoa
   powder
1/4 pound (1 stick) unsalted
   butter, at room temperature
1 1/2 teaspoons pure vanilla
   extract
1/3 cup boiling water
1 1/2 cups heavy cream
2 teaspoons granulated sugar
3 ounces semisweet chocolate,
   shaved (see Note)

In another saucepan over medium heat, bring the cherries to a boil in their syrup. In a small bowl, dissolve the cornstarch in the remaining 1/4 cup kirsch and add to the cherry mixture. Whisk until it thickens, about 2 minutes. Remove from the heat and let cool completely.

Assemble the cake. Using a serrated knife, carefully cut each cake horizontally in half to make four layers. Brush the tops of all the layers with equal amounts of the sugar syrup. Allow the liquid to soak into the layers for about 30 minutes.

Place the bottom layer on a large cake plate. Spread 1 cup of the filling evenly over this layer, then top with a second layer of cake. Spread 1 cup of the filling evenly over it. Repeat the same process with the third layer and another cup of filling. Top with the fourth layer.

To finish the cake, sift together the confectioners' sugar and cocoa powder into a medium-size bowl. Add the butter and mix with an electric mixer until incorporated. Add 1 teaspoon of the vanilla and the boiling water and mix until smooth. Let cool.

Combine the cream, the remaining 1/2 teaspoon vanilla, and the granulated sugar in a medium-size mixing bowl and, using an electric mixer, whip until soft peaks form.

Ice the side and top of the cake evenly with the chocolate frosting. Spoon the whipped cream over the top of the cake and sprinkle with the chocolate shavings. Slice to serve.

NOTE

To make shaved chocolate, chill the block and, using a vegetable peeler, shave the side of the block.

MAKES ONE 4-LAYER
9-INCH CAKE; 10 SERVINGS

ash wednesday

ASH WEDNESDAY, the day after Mardi Gras, begins the forty-day season of Lent, which ends on Easter Sunday. ■ Ash Wednesday is so called from the ceremony of placing ashes on one's forehead as a sign of penitence. In the Roman Catholic Church, a priest places blessed ashes on the foreheads of the congregation while saying, "Remember that you are dust, and unto dust you shall return." ■ Ash Wednesday is a day of fasting and abstinence, to help make Christians aware that Lent is beginning and to help them turn away from sin. ■ Marcelle turned me on to a novel set in New Orleans, written by a friend of hers, Sheila Bosworth, called *Almost Innocent*. In the book, two characters, Rand and Airey, meet every Ash Wednesday at St. Louis Cathedral to get ashes, then walk to Antoine's, where they have their ". . . annual White Lunch: vichyssoise, accompanied by vodka martinis, followed by filet de truite au vin blanc, pommes de terre soufflées, a bottle of Pouilly-Fuissé, and, for dessert, Baked Alaska. No green salad, or coffee, or cigars, in keeping with the Tout Blanc dictum." ■ I so liked this tale that I devised my own menu for a white lunch.

CRABMEAT WITH CELERY ROOT MAYONNAISE

CELERY ROOT, ALSO KNOWN AS CELERIAC, IS A KNOBBY, BROWN TUBEROUS ROOT. IT TASTES, SOME SAY, LIKE A CROSS BETWEEN A STRONG CELERY AND PARSLEY, AND IT CAN BE EATEN RAW OR COOKED. I DECIDED TO TRY IT IN A MAYONNAISE TO DRESS FRESH LUMP CRABMEAT FOR AN APPETIZER. THE FLAVORS ARE SMOOTH AND PLEASANT FOR THIS FIRST MEAL AFTER THE DEBAUCHERY OF CARNIVAL.

Put the celery root, onion, mustard, lemon juice, parsley, egg, ¼ teaspoon of the salt, and the cayenne in a food processor or blender and blend for 30 seconds. With the motor running, slowly drizzle in the vegetable oil. The mixture will thicken slightly.

Put the crabmeat in a medium-size mixing bowl and season with the remaining ¼ teaspoon salt and the black pepper. Add 1 cup of the dressing and toss lightly to mix. Cover and chill for 30 minutes.

Remove several leaves from the inside of each lettuce wedge and thinly slice. Toss with the remaining ¼ teaspoon salt and ½ cup of the remaining dressing in a bowl. Divide this mixture into 4 equal portions and arrange in the center of four salad plates. Place a lettuce wedge on top of each portion. Spoon a tablespoon of the remaining dressing over each wedge, then put ½ cup of the crab mixture in the center of each wedge of lettuce. Serve with the croutons.

2 ounces celery root, peeled and finely chopped (about 1 cup)
¼ cup chopped yellow onion
2 teaspoons Dijon mustard
2 tablespoons fresh lemon juice
2 teaspoons chopped fresh parsley leaves
1 large egg (see note on page 13)
³/₄ teaspoon salt
¹/₈ teaspoon cayenne
1 cup vegetable oil
1 pound lump crabmeat, picked over for shells and cartilage
¹/₈ teaspoon freshly ground black pepper
1 medium-size head iceberg lettuce, cored, rinsed, and cut into 4 wedges
1 recipe Toasted Croutons (recipe follows)

MAKES 4 SERVINGS

Toasted Croutons

1 loaf French bread (about
   8 inches in diameter and
   15 inches long), ends trimmed
   and cut crosswise into
   1/4-inch-thick slices
5 tablespoons olive oil
1/4 teaspoon salt
1/4 teaspoon freshly ground
   black pepper

Preheat the oven to 400°F. Line a baking sheet with parchment paper.

Arrange the bread slices on the baking sheet and brush them with half of the olive oil, then sprinkle them with 1/8 teaspoon of the salt and 1/8 teaspoon of the black pepper. Turn the slices over, brush with the remaining oil, and sprinkle with the remaining 1/8 teaspoon each salt and pepper.

Bake for about 6 minutes, then turn the baking sheet around in the oven to ensure even browning. Bake until the croutons are lightly browned, about 6 minutes. Remove from the oven and let cool completely before serving.

MAKES ABOUT 32 CROUTONS

POACHED TROUT WITH LEMON BUTTER SAUCE AND PARSLEY POTATOES

FOR THE MAIN COURSE OF THIS WHITE LUNCH, I'VE CHOSEN TO POACH FRESH WHITE-FLESHED TROUT IN A COURT-BOUILLON, A BROTH FLAVORED WITH WHITE WINE, CARROTS, AND HERBS. THIS PREPARATION IS AN OLD FRENCH CLASSIC. THE SAUCE IS A TRADITIONAL LEMON BUTTER SAUCE THAT IS POPULAR HERE IN LOUISIANA TO SERVE NOT ONLY WITH FISH BUT WITH OTHER SEAFOOD AS WELL.

Make the court-bouillon. In a shallow pan or a fish poacher, combine the water, wine, carrots, onions, thyme, and bay leaves. Squeeze the juice from the lemon into the pan and add the lemon shells. Add the salt and the black pepper and bring to a boil over medium-high heat. Reduce the heat to medium-low and simmer for 30 minutes. Remove and discard the lemon shells. Simmer for 12 minutes more.

Meanwhile, make the potatoes. Put the water and ½ teaspoon of the salt in a large saucepan and bring to a boil over high heat. Add the potatoes and reduce the heat to medium. Cook until fork-tender, about 25 minutes. Drain.

Season the fillets with the salt. Add the fillets to the court-bouillon, cover, and cook until the fish flakes easily with a fork, about 10 minutes.

FOR THE COURT-BOUILLON
3 cups water
1 cup dry white wine
¼ cup sliced carrot
1 cup sliced yellow onions
1 large sprig fresh thyme
2 bay leaves
1 medium-size lemon, cut in half
½ teaspoon salt
1 teaspoon freshly ground black pepper

FOR THE POTATOES
8 cups water
¾ teaspoon salt
12 new potatoes (about 1½ pounds), peeled
1 tablespoon unsalted butter
1 tablespoon chopped fresh parsley leaves
¼ teaspoon freshly ground black pepper
4 trout fillets (5 to 6 ounces each)
½ teaspoon salt

FOR THE LEMON BUTTER SAUCE

1/4 cup chopped shallots

6 medium-size lemons, skin and pith removed and quartered

1 cup dry white wine

1/8 teaspoon salt

1/8 teaspoon cayenne

1/4 cup heavy cream

3/4 cup (1 1/2 sticks) unsalted cold butter, cut into pieces

1/8 teaspoon hot sauce

1/4 teaspoon Worcestershire sauce

Meanwhile, make the lemon butter sauce. In a small nonreactive saucepan, combine the shallots, lemons, wine, salt, and cayenne over medium heat, bring to a gentle boil, and cook until as thick as syrup. Add the cream and cook, stirring a few times for 2 minutes, then remove from the heat. Add the butter 1 tablespoon at a time, whisking after each addition, until all is incorporated. Add the hot sauce and Worcestershire and whisk to blend. Strain through a fine-mesh sieve and keep hot.

Finish the potatoes. In a medium-size skillet over medium heat, melt the butter. Add the potatoes, parsley, the remaining 1/4 teaspoon salt, and the white pepper and cook until heated through, 2 to 3 minutes.

To serve, put a fillet on each serving plate, spoon 1/4 cup of the sauce over each, and serve with equal portions of the potatoes.

MAKES 4 SERVINGS

FLOATING ISLANDS

FLOATING ISLANDS, ALSO CALLED *OEUFS À LA NEIGE* (SNOW EGGS), HAVE BEEN POPULAR IN NEW ORLEANS FOR YEARS. THIS IS A SIMPLE DESSERT, CONSISTING OF A COLD LIGHT EGG CUSTARD IN WHICH SCOOPS OF MERINGUE FLOAT.

In a large nonreactive saucepan, combine 2½ cups of the milk, ½ cup of the sugar, and the vanilla over medium heat and whisk to dissolve the sugar. Bring to a gentle boil.

In a large mixing bowl, beat the egg whites with an electric mixer on medium speed until soft peaks form. Add the remaining 1 tablespoon sugar and continue beating until stiff peaks form.

With a wooden spoon, scoop 2 balls of the meringue into the simmering milk mixture. Poach the balls for 2 to 3 minutes, rolling them over with the spoon and basting them with the milk. When all sides are cooked (they are slightly firm to the touch), lift them out with a slotted spoon and set aside on a platter. Scoop 2 more balls from the remaining meringue and repeat the process. The meringues can be stored for about 1 hour, loosely covered with plastic wrap, in the refrigerator until ready to use.

In a small mixing bowl, combine the remaining ½ cup milk, the egg yolks, and cornstarch and whisk together. Slowly whisk ½ cup of the warm milk mixture into the egg mixture, then pour into the warm milk mixture in the saucepan. Whisking constantly, bring the mixture to a gentle boil and cook until it thickens enough to coat the back of a wooden spoon, about 2 minutes.

3 cups milk
½ cup plus 1 tablespoon sugar
1 teaspoon pure vanilla extract
4 large eggs, separated
2 teaspoons cornstarch
1 recipe Caramel Sauce
    (recipe follows)

Remove from the heat, pour into a glass bowl, and let cool to room temperature. Cover with plastic wrap, pressing the wrap down against the surface of the custard to keep a skin from forming. Refrigerate for at least 4 hours or up to 8 hours.

To serve, gently stir the custard and spoon equal amounts into four dessert bowls. Set a meringue ball on top of each and drizzle with the caramel sauce.

MAKES 4 SERVINGS

Caramel Sauce

1 cup sugar
1/2 cup water
1 cup heavy cream

In a small, heavy saucepan, combine the sugar and water and bring to a boil, stirring often. Cook, stirring occasionally, until the mixture is a deep caramel color and has the consistency of a thick syrup, 10 to 15 minutes. Remove from the heat. Stir in the cream, return the saucepan to high heat, and boil the sauce until it regains the consistency of a thick syrup, about 2 minutes. Let cool.

The sauce can be refrigerated until ready to use. Allow it to reach room temperature before using it.

MAKES ABOUT 3/4 CUP

march

HEN the month of March rolls in, everyone is champing at the bit to get outdoors. There's a hint of spring in the air and whispers of green leaves peek out of the dense, dreary landscape along country roads. The bald cypress, willows, and live oaks are slowly sprouting as the warmer weather prods their growth. ■ Wildflowers—bright yellow milkweed and tiny lavender violets—dance in the warm southerly winds. Fathers and their children head for the levees that contain the mighty Mississippi River and the Atchafalaya to try their hand at getting multicolored kites aloft. Fishing and pleasure boats, retrieved from their winter storage, skim along the chocolate-colored bayous and streams, their exhilarated occupants gulping the fresh air after being indoors for the past few months. ■ With the weather being so pleasant, city folk take to the streets of the French Quarter. It's a good time to relax at an outdoor table at the Café du Monde and enjoy the sugary square doughnuts and café au lait, or to spend a day in a park. ■ The huge 1500-acre New Orleans City Park is a public recreation mecca, with four eighteen-hole golf courses, a large tennis center, horseback riding, fishing lagoons, gardens, and the New Orleans Museum of Art. Audubon Park, located in the uptown section of the city, is named for John James Audubon, the naturalist, and he would be mighty proud of this tree shaded area. The 340-acre park also has an eighteen-hole golf course that was the site of the World's Industrial and Cotton Centennial Exposition in 1884–85. Also in the park is the outstanding Audubon Park Zoo. ■ Those who want to get out of the city might choose to spend the day traveling along the Great River Road, which winds along the Mississippi River. There

were plantations along the river even before the steamboat appeared in 1812, and quite a few of the antebellum mansions, many lovingly restored, are still standing. These magnificent homes face the river, which, for the inhabitants, was their main street. ■ Oak Alley Plantation, constructed in 1832, is so named for the grand "alley" of twenty-eight live oaks that

march

form an archway from the river to the main house. San Francisco Plantation, begun in 1849 and completed in 1854, looks much like a grand ornate steamboat. The beautiful Houmas House is probably the most photographed plantation house (it was the set for the movie *Hush, Hush, Sweet Charlotte*). Visiting this area is like taking a step back in time, to a time that was perhaps more gracious and definitely more romantic. ■ In the country, farmers are readying their fields for spring planting and home gardeners are

busy preparing the soil for vegetable gardens. Soft-shell crabs are beginning to come in and the crawfish season is drawing near its peak. ■ The Irishmen are ready to party and parade on St. Patrick's Day, the Italians are busy preparing food for the annual St. Joseph's Day altars, and the whole state is gearing up for spring festivals. ■ Springtime is upon us!

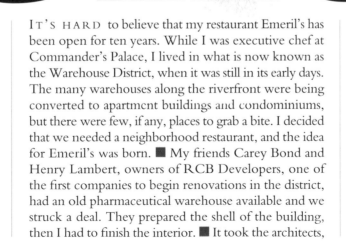

emeril's tenth

anniversary

I T ' S H A R D to believe that my restaurant Emeril's has been open for ten years. While I was executive chef at Commander's Palace, I lived in what is now known as the Warehouse District, when it was still in its early days. The many warehouses along the riverfront were being converted to apartment buildings and condominiums, but there were few, if any, places to grab a bite. I decided that we needed a neighborhood restaurant, and the idea for Emeril's was born. ■ My friends Carey Bond and Henry Lambert, owners of RCB Developers, one of the first companies to begin renovations in the district, had an old pharmaceutical warehouse available and we struck a deal. They prepared the shell of the building, then I had to finish the interior. ■ It took the architects,

designers, and my small crew about six months to complete the project. Used kitchen equipment that I found in Mississippi arrived contained in one truck. Eric Linquest and his wife, Gigi, I, and anybody else who could wield a paint brush helped with custom paint finishes. We worked long hours with no pay for some time, but we all agreed we were investing in the dream. ■ My initial staff was composed of myself as executive chef and proprietor, Eric as general manager, Andre Begnaud as the only sous-chef, and Harold Geravis and Mauricio Andrade as waiters. When we finally opened our doors in March 1990, we were astonished at the response! People lined up in the street, the telephones rang off the wall, and it was all we could do to keep up with the orders. But somehow, with the help of a great, loyal, tireless staff, we made it. In 1991, Emeril's was named Restaurant of the Year by *Esquire* magazine and we were ecstatic. ■ In March 2000, we'll celebrate our tenth anniversary, and I thank all of you out there for making it a great decade! ■ Looking back over the years, I realize how much things have changed, and have not. When I first opened, I promised myself and my customers that I would always feature on the menu the freshest local ingredients I could find. In the beginning, we changed the menu about three times a year to roughly coincide with the seasons. (Fall and winter were joined together, because the seasons are not that distinct.) Later we added specials and the dégustation (tasting) menu to better please our customers and to use local products that are in season for a short time. Doing this allows me to showcase the products and to be creative with them. The following recipes are some of my very favorites that have appeared on the menu over the years.

OYSTERS ON THE HALF-SHELL WITH MIGNONETTE SAUCE AND CAVIAR

AS YOU CAN IMAGINE, LOUISIANIANS EAT A LOT OF OYSTERS, RAW OR OTHERWISE PREPARED. AND THEIR FRENCH COUSINS WHO RESIDE IN FRANCE ALSO LOVE OYSTERS. WHEN THE COOL WEATHER SETS IN AROUND OCTOBER, CRATES OF OYSTERS BEGIN APPEARING ON THE SIDEWALK IN FRONT OF FRENCH CAFÉS AND RESTAURANTS. IN FRANCE, RAW OYSTERS ARE SERVED WITH A SMALL SAUCEBOAT OF SAUCE MIGNONETTE, WHICH IS VERY DIFFERENT FROM THE KETCHUP-BASED COCKTAIL SAUCE SERVED WITH OYSTERS HERE IN LOUISIANA. ■ THE WORD *MIGNONETTE* IS USED IN THE KITCHEN TO MEAN CRUSHED PEPPER. SINCE MOST PEOPLE USE ONLY ABOUT A TEASPOON PER OYSTER, A LITTLE GOES A LONG WAY. ■ IN THE COOLER MONTHS OF THE FALL AND WINTER, WHEN OYSTERS ARE IN SEASON, THIS IS A DELIGHTFUL APPETIZER COURSE. IT'S SIMPLE, CLASSIC, AND LIGHT, AND I LIKE THE IDEA OF SPOONING JUST A TAD OF CAVIAR ON THE OYSTERS RIGHT BEFORE SERVING TO GIVE THEM AN ELEGANT TOUCH.

2 teaspoons finely crushed white pepper
1/8 teaspoon salt
1/4 cup dry red wine
2 tablespoons olive oil
2 tablespoons finely chopped shallots
8 cups finely crushed ice
1/2 cup kosher salt
2 dozen freshly shucked oysters on the half-shell
1 ounce beluga, osetra, or sevruga caviar

MAKES 8 SERVINGS

Combine the white pepper, salt, wine, olive oil, and shallots in a small bowl and whisk to blend. Set aside.

Put 1 cup of the ice in each of eight small shallow rimmed soup bowls and press down gently to make a level bed. Sprinkle 1 tablespoon of the kosher salt over each bowl of ice. Place 3 oysters in their shells on each bed and spoon an equal amount of the sauce over each. Dot with the caviar and serve cold.

PAN-SEARED ESCOLAR WITH CRABMEAT AND CHANTERELLES

ESCOLAR, CAUGHT IN THE GULF OF MEXICO, IS ONE OF MY FAVORITE FISH. IT'S FIRM AND WHITE AND HOLDS UP WELL IN MANY PREPARATIONS. EMERIL'S WAS THE FIRST RESTAURANT IN THE CITY TO SERVE THIS FABULOUS FISH. BECAUSE IT WASN'T ALWAYS AVAILABLE, I OFFERED IT AS A SPECIAL WHENEVER I COULD FIND IT. SERVED WITH FRESH CRABMEAT AND CHANTERELLES FROM A LOCAL FORAGER, IT'S POSSIBLY ONE OF THE BEST DISHES THAT YOU CAN ORDER. ■ THIS IS ONE OF FELICIA'S FAVORITES AND WE USE CHANTERELLES, THE GOLDEN ONES, WHICH ARE FORAGED IN SOME HARDWOOD FORESTS IN MISSISSIPPI, NOT FAR FROM NEW ORLEANS. ONCE I SPIED THEM SPROUTING OUT OF MATTED LEAVES AFTER A GENTLE RAIN AND IT WAS GLORIOUS—THEY LOOKED LIKE BRIGHT YELLOW FLOWERS! IF YOU CAN'T FIND CHANTERELLES, USE ANY KIND OF SMALL MUSHROOMS, LIKE REGULAR BUTTONS OR WHOLE SHIITAKES (DO NOT USE THE STEMS). IF YOU USE LARGER MUSHROOMS, SIMPLY SLICE THEM.

In a medium-size skillet, heat 1 tablespoon of the olive oil over medium heat. Add the onion, bell pepper, ½ teaspoon of the salt, and ¼ teaspoon of the white pepper. Cook, stirring, for 1 minute. Add the mushrooms and cook, stirring, for 1 minute until the mushrooms are slightly soft. Add the crabmeat and garlic and cook, stirring, for 1 minute. Add 1 tablespoon of the chives and remove from the heat. Keep warm.

Season the fish with the remaining 1 teaspoon salt and 1 teaspoon white pepper. In a large skillet, heat the remaining 2 tablespoons olive oil over medium heat. Add the fish and cook for 3 minutes on each side. Remove from the heat.

3 tablespoons olive oil

1/2 cup thinly sliced yellow onion

1/4 cup thinly sliced red bell pepper

1 1/2 teaspoons salt

1 1/4 teaspoons freshly ground white pepper

2 cups chanterelles, cleaned and trimmed

1 pound lump crabmeat, picked over for shells and cartilage

1/2 teaspoon chopped garlic

2 tablespoons snipped fresh chives

1 pound escolar fillet, cut into eight 2-ounce pieces

1 recipe Muscat Sabayon
  (recipe follows)
8 teaspoons 25-year-old
  balsamic vinegar, balsamic
  syrup, or balsamic extraction
  (found in gourmet stores)

To serve, pool about 2 tablespoons of the sabayon in the center of each of eight serving plates. Divide the mushroom mixture into 8 equal portions and arrange over the sabayon. Top each serving with a fillet of fish and drizzle each with 2 teaspoons of the balsamic vinegar. Garnish with the remaining 1 tablespoon chives.

MAKES 8 SERVINGS

Muscat Sabayon

4 large eggs
2 teaspoons minced shallots
1/4 teaspoon pure vanilla extract
1/2 cup muscat wine
1/4 teaspoon salt
1/8 teaspoon freshly ground
  white pepper
1 teaspoon snipped fresh chives

Combine all of the ingredients in a small stainless steel bowl. Set the bowl over a pot of simmering water and whisk until the mixture begins to thicken, about 2 minutes. Remove from the heat and use immediately.

MAKES ABOUT 1 CUP

PETITS FILETS WITH BLUE CHEESE GLAÇAGE

ERIC LINQUEST, MY GOOD FRIEND, SAYS THIS IS ONE OF HIS FAVORITE DISHES. HE'S A SMART GUY. A *GLAÇAGE* IS SIMPLY A GLAZE. THE DISH CAME ABOUT WHEN I DISCOVERED THAT WONDERFUL BLUE CHEESE FROM THE MAYTAG PEOPLE. IT WAS FIRST SERVED AS A SPECIAL, BUT IT BECAME SO POPULAR I HAD TO PUT IT ON MY REGULAR MENU TO SATISFY MY REPEAT CUSTOMERS—A GRAND DISH!

Preheat the oven to 400°F.

Put the cheese, buttermilk, ⅛ teaspoon of the black pepper, the Worcestershire, and hot sauce in a food processor or blender and process until smooth. Set aside.

In a medium-size skillet, fry the bacon until crispy, about 10 minutes. Drain on paper towels and set aside. Drain off most of the bacon grease, leaving 2 tablespoons in the skillet. Add the onions, season with the remaining ¼ teaspoon black pepper, and cook, stirring, until slightly softened, 2 to 3 minutes. Add the haricots verts and toss to mix. Remove from the heat and keep warm.

Season the filets with the Creole seasoning. Heat the vegetable oil in a large ovenproof skillet over medium-high heat. Add the filets and sear for about 4 minutes on each side. Spread 1 tablespoon of the blue cheese mixture on top of each filet and put in the oven. Roast for 8 minutes for medium-rare (130° to 140°F), 10 minutes for medium (145° to 150°F), or 12 minutes for well-done (155° to 160°F).

To serve, divide the haricots verts into 8 equal portions and arrange in the center of eight serving plates. Place the filets on top of the beans, spoon the pan juices over, and garnish with the parsley.

¼ pound blue cheese, crumbled, preferably Maytag Blue
¼ cup buttermilk
⅛ teaspoon plus ¼ teaspoon freshly ground black pepper
1 teaspoon Worcestershire sauce
1 teaspoon hot sauce
½ pound sliced bacon, chopped
2 cups thinly sliced yellow onions
¾ pound haricots verts (thin green beans), blanched in boiling salted water for 4 minutes, drained, and rinsed in cool water
8 filet mignons (about 6 ounces each)
2 tablespoons Creole Seasoning (page 13)
2 tablespoons vegetable oil
1 tablespoon chopped fresh parsley leaves

MAKES 8 SERVINGS

SEARED DUCK WITH CARAMELIZED ONION BREAD PUDDING

EVERYONE SAYS TO USE DAY-OLD BREAD FOR BREAD PUDDING, BUT I LIKE IT SO MUCH I USE WHATEVER BREAD I HAVE HANDY. IN LOUISIANA, WE MAKE LOTS OF SWEET BREAD PUDDINGS, BUT I'VE BORROWED THE TECHNIQUE AND MAKE SAVORY ONES ALL THE TIME. THIS CARAMELIZED ONION BREAD PUDDING WAS THE FIRST SAVORY PUDDING I OFFERED AT EMERIL'S. I'VE ALWAYS HAD DUCK ON THE MENU, AND THIS DISH IS A SURE WINNER. ■ YOU CAN USE THIS BASIC BREAD PUDDING RECIPE AND ADD ALL SORTS OF THINGS, LIKE ASSORTED MUSHROOMS OR CHOPPED ZUCCHINI AND SQUASH. ■ TONY CRUZ, MY FRIEND AND BUSINESS MAN-AGER, LIKES THIS DISH VERY MUCH. WHENEVER WE GO OUT TO DINNER AT JUST ABOUT ANY RESTAURANT, HE GOES FOR THE DUCK DISH.

Make the bread pudding. Preheat the oven to 350°F.

In a large skillet over medium-high heat, melt 2 table-spoons of the butter. Add the onions, ½ teaspoon of the salt, and ¼ teaspoon of the black pepper, and cook, stirring, until the onions are caramelized, about 12 min-utes. Add the garlic and cook for 2 minutes. Remove from the heat and let cool.

In a large mixing bowl, whisk the eggs, cane syrup, the remaining 1 teaspoon salt and ½ teaspoon black pepper, the Worcestershire, and hot sauce together to blend. Add the cream and whisk to blend. Add the bread and mix well, pushing the bread down into the cream mixture.

Grease a 12 × 8½-inch baking dish with the remain-ing 1 teaspoon butter. Fold the onions into the bread pudding mixture and pour into the prepared baking dish.

FOR THE BREAD PUDDING

2 tablespoons plus 1 teaspoon unsalted butter

4 cups sliced yellow onions

1½ teaspoons salt

³/4 teaspoon freshly ground black pepper

2 teaspoons chopped garlic

5 large eggs

¼ cup Steen's 100% Pure Cane Syrup or other cane syrup

1 teaspoon Worcestershire sauce

1 teaspoon hot sauce

2 cups heavy cream

4 cups cubed French bread

1 cup freshly grated Parmigiano-Reggiano cheese

FOR THE DUCK AND FOIE GRAS

4 boneless duck breasts (about 6 ounces each)

1 tablespoon Creole Seasoning (page 13)

½ pound foie gras, cut into eight 1-ounce pieces and each scored with 2 cuts

½ teaspoon salt

½ teaspoon freshly ground black pepper

2 cups Veal Reduction (page 73)

1 tablespoon chopped green onion or scallion (green part only)

Top with the cheese. Bake until golden brown, about 40 minutes. Remove from the oven and let cool slightly before serving.

Make the duck. Preheat the oven to 400°F.

Score the duck breasts on the skin side, making 3 cuts about ¼ inch apart in each. Season the breasts on both sides with the Creole seasoning. Heat a large ovenproof skillet over medium heat. Place the breasts skin side down in the pan and cook for 10 minutes. Turn the breasts over, transfer the skillet to the oven, and roast for 5 minutes for medium-rare, 7 minutes for medium, or 10 minutes for medium-well. Remove from the oven and let rest for 5 minutes, then cut diagonally into eight ¼-inch-thick slices.

Season the foie gras with the salt and black pepper. Heat a medium-size skillet over high heat, add the foie gras, and sear for 1 minute. Turn and sear for 30 seconds on the second side. Remove and drain on paper towels. In the same skillet, over medium heat, slowly whisk in the veal reduction and cook for 2 minutes. Remove from the heat.

Put ½ cup of the bread pudding in the center of each of eight serving plates. Fan 4 slices of duck breast on the side of each pudding. Place a piece of foie gras on top of the bread pudding and pour ¼ cup of the veal reduction over the pudding, duck, and foie gras. Garnish with the green onion and serve.

MAKES 8 SERVINGS

CRÈME BRÛLÉE

CRÈME BRÛLÉE, OR LITERALLY, BURNT CREAM, HAS BEEN A POPULAR DESSERT IN NEW ORLEANS FOR YEARS, PROBABLY BECAUSE IT'S IDEAL TO SERVE AFTER A LARGE, RICH MEAL, AS WE SO OFTEN HAVE HERE IN THIS GASTRONOMIC CITY. ■ IT'S ONE OF THOSE CLASSIC DESSERTS THAT I LIKE TO SERVE PERIODICALLY BECAUSE IT'S SO APPEALING TO SO MANY PEOPLE. WE MAKE SOME FLAVORED ONES, BUT I LIKE THIS ONE THE BEST.

In a medium-size nonreactive saucepan, combine the cream, ½ cup of the granulated sugar, and the vanilla bean and pulp over medium heat. Bring to a gentle boil, whisking to dissolve the sugar.

In a small mixing bowl, whisk the egg yolks and the remaining ½ cup of granulated sugar together. Whisk 1 cup of the hot cream mixture into the egg yolk mixture until smooth. Slowly pour this mixture into the hot cream mixture, whisk for 2 minutes, and remove from the heat. Strain the mixture through a fine-mesh sieve. Let cool completely.

Preheat the oven to 300°F.

Fill eight 6-ounce custard cups with equal portions of the cream mixture. Place the cups in a deep baking dish large enough to accommodate them comfortably without touching. Fill the baking dish with enough water to come halfway up the sides of the cups.

Bake in the lower third of the oven until lightly golden brown and just set, about 45 minutes. Remove from the oven and let cool. Cover and refrigerate for at least 4 hours or up to 12 hours.

1 quart heavy cream
1 cup granulated sugar plus 8 teaspoons raw sugar
1 vanilla bean, split and scraped (see Note)
8 large egg yolks

About 2 hours before serving, sprinkle 1 teaspoon of the raw sugar on the top of each custard. One at a time, using a kitchen blowtorch, approach the sugar with the torch at a low angle until the inner blue flame is ¼ inch above the surface and move the flame in a continuous motion over the surface until the sugar has caramelized. Or, preheat the broiler, sprinkle the sugar over the custards, and slide the dishes under the broiler. Broil until the sugar caramelizes, 2 to 3 minutes. Remove and allow the custards to cool again. Refrigerate and serve chilled.

NOTE

Vanilla beans are long and thin. To get the essence of the bean, it must be split lengthwise, then scraped to remove the resinous, pasty insides. Lay the bean on a flat surface with its seam as the center and split to one end. Place the point back at the center and split it to the other end. Use the blade of the knife to scrape the pasty seeds out.

MAKES 8 SERVINGS

EMERIL'S MARTINI WITH CHOCOLATE GRAPES

I'VE SAID IT BEFORE, BUT I'LL SAY IT AGAIN—I ADORE MARTINIS AND I'VE DABBLED WITH LOTS OF RECIPES. NEW ORLEANIANS HAVE ALWAYS BEEN FOND OF THEIR MARTINIS AND WE HAVE OFFERED THEM AT EMERIL'S FROM THE DAY WE OPENED TO PLEASE THEM. THIS IS ONE I CREATED THAT'S ON THE SWEET SIDE AND I LIKE TO GIVE IT TO CUSTOMERS ON SPECIAL OCCASIONS. IT MAY NOT APPEAL TO THE PURISTS OUT THERE, BUT I THINK IT'S REFRESHING AND FUN TO SERVE AFTER DINNER.

Line a baking sheet with parchment paper. Dip each cluster of grapes into the chocolate, allowing the chocolate to cover half of the grapes. Place the grapes on the baking sheet and refrigerate until the chocolate sets, about 30 minutes.

Mound 1 cup of the shaved ice in the center of each martini glass. Pour 2 ounces of the vodka over each mound of ice. Add a splash of Chambord to each. Garnish each with a cluster of the chocolate grapes. Serve the cookies on the side.

4 small clusters white grapes, washed and patted dry
4 ounces semisweet chocolate, melted and kept warm
4 cups shaved ice
8 ounces Absolut currant vodka
8 splashes Chambord
1 recipe Sugar Cookies (page 52)

MAKES 4 SERVINGS

st. patrick's day

THE CITY of New Orleans was appealing to the Irish, if for no other reason than that there was a strong anti-British sentiment among the French and Spanish who had colonized the lower Mississippi Valley. Forever enterprising, the Irish also recognized the opportunity for mercantile prospects in this port city and immigrated in the late 1700s and early 1800s to take advantage of the growing area. ■ During the horrendous potato famine, beginning in 1845, thousands and thousands of Irish fled their native country; many settled in Boston, but a large number entered at New Orleans. ■ Some time after the Civil War, an area of the city between Constance Street and the river, extending from St. Joseph Street to Louisiana Avenue, was named the Irish Channel. There is no history as to why it was so designated, but some believe that it may have been called such for Irish sailors who came into port and would head for a light kept burning all night in an Irish saloon much as they would a channel marker. ■ Because of their strong Catholic beliefs and because they couldn't understand the French sermons at St. Louis Cathedral, the Irish set about building their own church, named for the patron saint of Ireland, St. Patrick. In 1833, the church parish was established. In 1840, a small church was built. Because the Irish population grew rapidly, a larger structure was completed in 1851. The structure remains today as the oldest original church structure in New Orleans. ■ The Irish also gave the city of New Orleans, and the gastronomical world, that great restaurant dynasty, the Brennans, who are responsible for so many fine restaurants, like Brennans' in the French Quarter, Commander's Palace, the Palace Café, Mr. B's, and Bacco, to name just a few. ■ The Irish are a party people and they have been observing St. Patrick's Day in New Orleans since way back in 1809. The tradition continues to this day with a day-long celebration that begins with a solemn mass, then continues with parades, general feasting, and, of course, toasting at neighborhood pubs. In fact, all over the state, where there may be as few as two Irishmen who gather to toast their native country and St. Paddy, March 17 is considered a celebration. And as we all know, everyone, even those with no Irish blood coursing through their veins, wants to be Irish on St. Patrick's Day. ■ So, no matter what your ancestry or name is, you'll enjoy this Irish dinner.

IRISH SODA BREAD

IRISH SODA BREAD IS A MUST TO SERVE ON ST. PATRICK'S DAY. AT LEAST, THAT'S WHAT MY IRISH FRIENDS TELL ME. THEY ALSO TELL ME THAT ANCIENT LORE DICTATES THAT A CROSS CUT INTO THE TOP OF THE UNBAKED SODA BREAD IS NECESSARY TO LET THE FAIRIES OR DEMONS OUT. WHATEVER!

Preheat the oven to 450°F.

Combine the flour, baking soda, salt, and black pepper in a large mixing bowl and stir to mix. Add the buttermilk and mix gently with a fork. Transfer the dough to a lightly floured work surface. Gently fold the edges into each other four times, turn once, then pat the dough out into a circle about 9 inches in diameter and about 1 inch thick. With a sharp knife, make two large slashes in the shape of a cross on the top.

Lightly grease a 2 × 10-inch round cake pan with the vegetable oil. Place the dough in it and sprinkle the top with the bacon. Bake for 15 minutes. Reduce the oven temperature to 400°F and bake until the bread is brown and sounds hollow when thumped with your fingers, about another 25 minutes.

Remove from the oven, then remove the bread from the pan and let cool on a wire rack before slicing to serve.

4 cups bleached all-purpose flour
1 teaspoon baking soda
1 teaspoon salt
1 teaspoon freshly ground black pepper
2 cups buttermilk
1 teaspoon vegetable oil
4 slices bacon, chopped

MAKES 8 SERVINGS

POTATO SOUP

GIVE AN IRISHMAN A POTATO AND HE'LL COME UP WITH A LONG LIST
OF WAYS TO PREPARE IT AS A SOUP, MASHED, FRIED, IN SALADS, IN
OMELETTES, AND GOD ONLY KNOWS WHAT ELSE. THIS SOUP IS DEFI-
NITELY A WINNER IN MY BOOK. IT'S CREAMY AND COMFORTING, ALL
THAT A SOUP SHOULD BE.

¼ cup (½ stick) unsalted butter
2 cups chopped yellow onions
1 cup chopped celery
½ teaspoon salt
¼ teaspoon cayenne
1 bay leaf
2 tablespoons chopped garlic
8 cups chicken broth
2 large baking potatoes (about
   2 pounds), peeled and diced
¼ cup heavy cream

Melt the butter in a large, heavy pot or Dutch oven
over medium-high heat. Add the onions, celery, salt,
and cayenne and cook, stirring, until the onions are soft
and lightly golden, about 5 minutes. Add the bay leaf
and garlic and cook, stirring, for 2 minutes. Add the
broth and potatoes and bring to a boil. Reduce the heat
to medium-low and simmer, uncovered, until the potatoes are soft, about 30 minutes.

Remove the soup from the heat. Discard the bay leaf.
With a hand-held immersion blender, or in a food
processor or regular blender in batches, process until
smooth. Slowly add the cream and stir to blend.

To serve, ladle into soup bowls and serve hot.

MAKES 8 SERVINGS

BRAISED CABBAGE WITH CORN BEEF HASH

CORNED BEEF AND CABBAGE IS A TRADITIONAL COMBINATION FOR THE IRISH AND AT ONE TIME WAS THE MEAL SERVED ON EASTER SUNDAY. THIS HASH MAKES ONE GREAT MEAL ON ANY SUNDAY.

Melt the butter in a large, heavy saucepan or Dutch oven over medium heat. Add 2 cups of the onions, ¾ teaspoon of the salt, and ¾ teaspoon of the black pepper. Cook, stirring, until the onions are soft, about 4 minutes. Add the cabbage and sugar and stir until the cabbage is slightly wilted, about 3 minutes. Add the mustard and garlic and stir to mix. Add the water, stir, cover, and cook for 20 minutes, stirring occasionally. Add the cream, stir to mix, and cook, covered, for 10 minutes. Remove from the heat and keep warm.

In a large nonstick skillet over medium-high heat, heat the olive oil. Add the remaining 1½ cups onions, the remaining 1 teaspoon salt, and the remaining 1 teaspoon black pepper. Cook, stirring, for 2 minutes. Add the potatoes and spread evenly over the onions. Cook, flipping the potatoes about every minute and gently mashing them, until golden brown, about 8 minutes.

Add the corned beef and cook, stirring and pressing it into the hash browns, for 2 minutes. One by one, crack the eggs over the mixture, placing them about ¼ inch apart, reduce the heat to low, cover, and cook until the eggs are set, 7 to 8 minutes.

To serve, spread about ½ cup of the cabbage in the center of each serving plate and top with a wedge of corned beef hash with an egg. Sprinkle with the parsley and serve.

2 tablespoons unsalted butter
3½ cups thinly sliced yellow onions
1³/₄ teaspoons salt
1³/₄ teaspoons freshly ground black pepper
½ head white cabbage (about 1½ pounds), cored and thinly sliced
1 teaspoon sugar
3 tablespoons Creole or whole-grain mustard
2 teaspoons chopped garlic
1 cup water
½ cup heavy cream
¼ cup olive oil
2 large baking potatoes (about 2 pounds), peeled and grated (squeeze the grated potatoes with your hands to remove excess water)
1 pound thinly sliced corned beef, shredded
8 large eggs
1 tablespoon chopped fresh parsley leaves

MAKES 8 SERVINGS

LAMB STEW

I NEVER SEEM TO GET A STRAIGHT ANSWER AS TO WHAT GOES INTO AN AUTHENTIC IRISH STEW. SOME SAY IT CAN BE MADE WITH EITHER PORK OR LAMB. THE PURISTS TELL ME THAT CARROTS MIGHT NOT HAVE BEEN IN THE ORIGINAL IRISH STEW. WELL, I LISTENED TO ALL MY IRISH FRIENDS AND LET THEM EACH HAVE THEIR SAY, THEN CAME UP WITH THIS VERSION, WHICH I THINK IS ABSOLUTELY OUTSTANDING, EVEN IF I DO SAY SO MYSELF. I WISH YOU COULD HAVE SEEN MARCELLE AND FELICIA CLEAN OUT THE POT WHEN WE HAD IT FOR SUPPER AFTER THE ST. PATRICK'S DAY PARADE!

2 pounds lamb shanks
1 teaspoon salt
3/4 teaspoon freshly ground black pepper
3 tablespoons bleached all-purpose flour
2 tablespoons olive oil
2 medium-size yellow onions, quartered
3 ribs celery, cut into 1/2-inch-thick slices
3 carrots, cut into 1/2-inch-thick slices
2 sprigs fresh thyme
4 bay leaves
2 tablespoons tomato paste
10 cups beef broth
10 small red potatoes (about 1 pound), peeled and halved
1 large turnip (about 8 ounces), peeled and cubed
2 parsnips (about 4 ounces total), peeled and cubed
1/4 cup water

Season the lamb with 1/2 teaspoon of the salt and 1/4 teaspoon of the black pepper and dust with 1 tablespoon of the flour. Heat the olive oil in a large, heavy deep pot or Dutch oven over medium-high heat. Add the shanks and cook, turning to brown evenly, about 10 minutes.

Add the onions, celery, carrots, the remaining 1/2 teaspoon salt, and the remaining 1/2 teaspoon black pepper and cook for 2 minutes. Add the thyme, bay leaves, and tomato paste, stirring to mix. Cook for 2 minutes, then add the beef broth and stir to mix. Bring to a boil, reduce the heat to medium, cover, and cook until the meat is very tender, about 1 1/2 hours.

Add the potatoes, turnip, and parsnips and cook, uncovered, until the vegetables are fork-tender, about 30 minutes. Dissolve the remaining 2 tablespoons flour in the water and add to the stew, stirring to blend. Simmer for 30 minutes. Remove from the heat. Using a fork, remove the meat from the bones and discard the bones. Remove the bay leaves.

Serve the stew in deep bowls and accompany with Irish Soda Bread (page 108).

MAKES 8 SERVINGS

APPLE CUSTARD PIE

MY IRISH FRIENDS TELL ME THAT APPLE DESSERTS, LIKE DUMPLINGS, FRITTERS, AND CRUMBLES, ARE MUCH FAVORED. I THINK THEY WOULD LIKE THIS CUSTARD PIE AS WELL IN THEIR NATIVE COUNTRY.

In a medium-size mixing bowl, combine the flour, salt, and 2 tablespoons of the granulated sugar. Add the shortening and work it in with your hands until the mixture resembles coarse crumbs. Add the water 1 tablespoon at a time, working it in with your hands. Form the dough into a smooth ball, wrap in plastic wrap, and refrigerate for at least 30 minutes.

Preheat the oven to 350°F.

In a large skillet over medium heat, melt the butter. Stir in the brown sugar and cook, stirring, for 1 minute. Add ½ teaspoon of the cinnamon and the apples. Cook, stirring to coat the apples with the sugar syrup, for 3 minutes. Remove from the heat and turn into a 9-inch deep-dish pie pan.

Remove the dough from the refrigerator and let stand for about 5 minutes.

Lightly flour a work surface and roll out the dough into a circle 12 inches in diameter and ⅛ inch thick. Gently fold the dough in half, and then in half again. Place it over the apples in the pie pan and unfold it. Crimp the edges around the rim of the pan. Brush the

1 cup bleached all-purpose flour
Pinch of salt
2 tablespoons plus ¼ cup granulated sugar
⅓ cup vegetable shortening
2 tablespoons ice water
2 tablespoons unsalted butter
1 cup firmly packed light brown sugar
½ teaspoon plus ⅛ teaspoon ground cinnamon
2 pounds Granny Smith apples, peeled, cored, and cut into ¼-inch-thick slices
1 large egg, lightly beaten
1 cup heavy cream
1 large egg yolk
½ teaspoon pure vanilla extract
1 tablespoon confectioners' sugar
1 recipe Sweetened Whipped Cream (page 49)

dough with the beaten egg. With a sharp knife, make a 1-inch circle in the center of the pie. Bake for 15 minutes. Remove from the oven.

In a mixing bowl, whisk together the remaining ¼ cup granulated sugar, the cream, egg yolk, vanilla, and the remaining ⅛ teaspoon cinnamon. Pour the custard through the hole in the piecrust. Return to the oven and bake until the custard sets, about 30 minutes. Remove from the oven and let cool completely.

Sprinkle the top of the pie with the confectioners' sugar, spoon onto serving plates, and garnish with the whipped cream to serve.

MAKES ONE 9-INCH PIE; 8 SERVINGS

st. joseph's day

THE ITALIANS who came to New Orleans believed it to be a sort of paradise, similar in climate to the balmy Mediterranean lands of southern Italy and Sicily. The Italians also felt comfortable in the Creole culture, since the French and the Spanish were neighbors in Europe. ■ Perhaps the first Italian to set foot in Louisiana was one Enrico Tonti, who accompanied LaSalle in his exploration of the New World. Tonti is honored by having a street in the city named for him. By the mid-1800s, Italians were arriving in increasing numbers and even more so after the Civil War, during Reconstruction. After World War II, the Italian population in New Orleans, as well as in other parts of the state, drew a new wave of immigrants and added yet another flavor to the melting pot of Louisiana. ■ To Italians, St. Joseph is the patron saint of carpenters, widows, unwed mothers, and orphans, and they gather each year on March 19 to honor him with a St. Joseph's Day altar. To the people who make devotions to him, the day means a break from the Lenten rigors (the Creoles called the feast day *la mi-carême,* the middle of Lent) and is a day for feasting and, of course, prayers and attendance at mass. ■ The tradition of staging the St. Joseph altar was brought by the Sicilian immigrants and is specific to Sicily, not found anywhere else in Italy. Here in New Orleans, as well as in other towns and cities across Louisiana, their descendants continue the custom. ■ How the food-filled altars came to honor St. Joseph is subject to doubt. Some say the altar had its origin in a famine in Sicily. With so many people starving, all that the people could do was to turn to their faith. They offered prayers and asked for St. Joseph's help to intercede for them so that they would have successful crops. Another version is that a group of Italians, in the days of political persecution, was put on a ship and cast adrift without food. Day and night they prayed to St. Joseph, the protector of the Holy Family, to save them. When they reached landfall in Sicily, they prepared a feast for the hungry in the saint's honor. ■ It doesn't matter which story you believe, it only matters that the loyal Italians continue to have their altars which are offered in thanksgiving for some favor or request that was granted. During wartime, the altar was offered for the safe return of a loved one. At other times it was offered for the healing of the sick. ■ Much of the preparation of the food is done by family members or helpful volunteers for weeks or days in advance of St. Joseph's Day. ■ The St. Joseph's altar is layered with food, and the food is layered with significance. The altar itself is constructed in three levels, connoting the Catholic belief in the Trinity. There are breads baked in the form of crosses, palm fronds, rosaries, and the crown of thorns, or in the shape of St. Joseph's beard or of his staff, and these breads have great importance.

Every visitor is given a piece of the bread to take home and keep all year to protect the family from starvation. ■ The fava bean is called the lucky bean by Sicilians and dried fava beans are also distributed to those who visit the altar. It is said that if you carry a fava bean in your pocket or purse, you'll never go broke. ■ Throughout the night before the feast, families prepare stuffed artichokes or fried cauliflower since no meat can be on the altar because the season of Lent is in progress. There are many cakes, some made with figs, and cookies featuring dates, raisins, honey, almonds, sesame, lemon, and anise. ■ The altar is blessed by a priest, then three people representing the Holy Family—sometimes a young boy, an old man, and a virgin of sixteen, sometimes three young children—sit down to eat the meal. ■ Custom and tradition holds that all visitors to an altar, a private or public one, must be fed, and any food left over is distributed to the needy.

BAKED MACARONI WITH CALAMARI TOMATO SAUCE

THE PASTA DISH USUALLY FEATURED ON THE ALTAR IS MILANESE—THAT IS, IT'S SPRINKLED NOT WITH CHEESE BUT WITH BREAD CRUMBS TO REPRESENT THE SAWDUST OF ST. JOSEPH, THE CARPENTER. THIS VERSION IS MADE WITH CALAMARI, SINCE NO MEAT IS ALLOWED AT THE MEAL.

In a medium-size saucepan, heat the olive oil over medium-high heat. Add the onions, bay leaves, ½ teaspoon of the salt, the cayenne, and pepper flakes. Cook, stirring, for 3 minutes. Add the tomatoes, tomato paste, garlic, wine, 1 cup of the water, the basil, parsley, and sugar. Stir to mix. Bring to a boil, reduce the heat to medium, and simmer until thick, for 45 minutes. Add the calamari and simmer for 12 minutes.

Preheat the oven to 350°F.

In a large saucepan over high heat, combine the remaining 6 cups water, ½ teaspoon of the salt, and the vegetable oil. Bring to a boil, then add the macaroni and cook, stirring occasionally, until tender, about 8 minutes. Drain and rinse under cool water. Pour into a 2-quart baking dish. Pour the calamari sauce over the macaroni and stir to mix. Arrange the olives over the top of the macaroni.

In a small mixing bowl, combine the bread crumbs with the remaining ½ teaspoon salt, the black pepper, and extra-virgin olive oil. Mix well and sprinkle over the olives.

Bake until the bread crumbs are golden brown, about 30 minutes. Serve hot.

2 tablespoons olive oil
1 cup chopped yellow onions
2 bay leaves, crushed
1½ teaspoons salt
⅛ teaspoon cayenne
1 teaspoon red pepper flakes
3 cups chopped, peeled, and seeded canned or fresh tomatoes
2 tablespoons tomato paste
1 teaspoon chopped garlic
1 cup dry white wine
7 cups water
¼ cup chopped fresh basil leaves
1 tablespoon chopped fresh parsley leaves
½ teaspoon sugar
¾ pound cleaned calamari, tentacles and bodies, cut into rings
⅛ teaspoon vegetable oil
1 pound ditalini or small elbow macaroni
½ cup Kalamata olives, pitted and halved
1 cup fine dried bread crumbs
¼ teaspoon freshly ground black pepper
2 tablespoons extra-virgin olive oil

MAKES 8 SERVINGS

BRAIDED BREAD WITH ARTICHOKES

NOT ONLY DOES A PIECE OF ST. JOSEPH'S BREAD IN THE HOUSE KEEP THE FAMILY FROM STARVATION, IT IS ALSO BELIEVED CAPABLE OF DIVERTING STORMS. THE CUSTOM IS TO TAKE A PIECE OF THE BREAD, THROW IT OUTSIDE, AND SAY "ST. JOSEPH, MAKE THE STORM GO AWAY." ■ IT'S PREFERABLE TO BAKE THE BREADS ON TWO PANS, BUT YOU CAN ALSO PUT THEM ON ONE LARGE BAKING SHEET. IF NOT, BAKE THE BREADS SEPARATELY. IT WON'T MATTER THAT ONE BREAD RISES A LITTLE MORE THAN THE OTHER.

In a food processor, combine the artichoke hearts, garlic, ¼ teaspoon of the salt, the pepper, and olive oil and pulse several times to finely chop; do not puree. Remove from the processor and set aside.

Combine the yeast, sugar, and water in the bowl of stand mixer fitted with a dough hook. Beat on low speed for 1 minute. Add the artichoke mixture, the remaining 1 teaspoon salt, and the flour. Beat until all of the flour is incorporated, about 1 minute. Then beat on medium speed until the dough forms a ball, leaves the sides of the bowl, and starts to climb up the dough hook.

Remove the dough from the bowl. Using your hands, form the dough into a smooth ball. Lightly oil a bowl with the vegetable oil. Place the dough in the bowl and turn it to oil all sides. Cover with plastic wrap and set aside in a warm, draft-free place until doubled in size, about 1 hour.

Line two baking sheets with parchment paper.

Remove the dough from the bowl and invert it onto a lightly floured work surface. With your fingers, pat the dough into a rectangle about ¾ inch thick. Divide

One 14-ounce can quartered artichoke hearts packed in water, drained
1 teaspoon chopped garlic
1¼ teaspoons salt
¼ teaspoon freshly ground black pepper
2 tablespoons olive oil
1 envelope active dry yeast
1 tablespoon sugar
1 cup warm water (about 110°F)
3½ cups bleached all-purpose flour
1 teaspoon vegetable oil
1 large egg, beaten

the dough into 4 equal portions and form into flattened balls. Using your hands, roll two of the balls of dough into two thick ropes, each about 1 inch in diameter and about 22 inches long. Join the ropes together at one end and pinch together. Braid the ropes together, lapping each one over the other as you go, then pinch the other ends together. Tuck the pinched ends underneath the braided bread. Place the bread on one of the prepared baking sheets and form it into the shape of a staff (like a candy cane).

Divide the remaining 2 balls of dough in half. You now have four pieces. Using your hands, roll each piece into a thick rope, each about 1 inch in diameter and about 16 inches long. Pinch 2 of the ropes together at one end and braid them together, lapping one over the other as you go. Pinch the other ends together. Repeat the process with the remaining 2 ropes. Tuck the pinched ends together and tuck them underneath each loaf.

Arrange the 2 braids in the form of a cross on the second baking sheet, gently pulling the lengthwise braid to make it about 2 inches longer and gently compressing the cross braid to make it fit across the narrow part of the pan.

Cover both breads with plastic wrap and set aside in a warm, draft-free place until doubled in size, about 1 hour.

Preheat the oven to 350°F.

With a pastry brush, brush the beaten egg evenly over the breads. Bake until they are lightly brown and sound hollow when tapped, about 30 minutes. Let cool on a wire rack.

MAKES 2 BRAIDED BREADS; EACH SERVES 8

WHILE MARCH can be wet and windy, with just a hint of spring, April breezes in with brilliant splashes of color—bright pink and magenta azaleas, stark white bridal wreaths, radiant yellow and regal purple wild irises, and creamy wild dogwood—much like a Monet canvas. ■ The Garden District of New Orleans, the area bounded by Jackson Avenue to Louisiana Avenue, about thirteen blocks, and St. Charles Avenue to Magazine Street toward the river, a distance of five blocks, is at its loveliest. This section, with its palatial mansions on beautifully landscaped grounds, was settled by rich Americans who had been snubbed by the French Quarter Creole society. The Americans showed the Creoles that they too could construct grand homes, and the residential streets are shaded by live oaks, magnolias, and palm trees and the yards protected by ornamental cast-iron fences and gates. During Spring Fiesta, which begins the first Friday after Easter and continues for about nineteen days, many of the private homes in the Garden District, as well as in the Quarter, are open to the public. ■ In the rural southern area of the state, strong southerly currents turn the murky brown bayous into languid, limpid waterways where, along the lush banks, giant wild elephant ears rise in full glory. Graceful and towering live oaks suddenly burst forth with new growth. Even the unwanted water hyacinths (they can deprive fish of the phytoplankton necessary for them to thrive) are an extravagant sight, like a river of lavender orchids. ■ The cypress-

filled swamps are dotted with colorful wild hibiscus and water lilies. Delicate water lettuce and pea-green duckweed appear overnight on the surface of stillwater ponds and lakes. ■ Shrimp boats head out to the open waters of the Gulf of Mexico in

search of a good harvest. Sport fishermen ply the waters of the adjacent bays in hopes of reeling in redfish, speckled trout, and flounder. ■ Out of the rich soil of truck farms and home gardens spring young tender plants that will bring forth okra, tomatoes, bell peppers, beans, and eggplant.

april

■ To the north, the piney upland is fresh and green, like the forest primeval. ■ It's a time of reawakening, both physically and spiritually, as the season of Lent ends with the celebration of Easter, one of the most important of all religious holidays. ■ Now that spring, and the longer days associated with it, has indeed arrived, the locals are ready to enjoy the balmy weather and all that goes with it—crawfish boils, fish fries, and a host of festivals. One of these is the annual Jazz and Heritage Festival, which  spans two weeks in late April and early May, when countless music- and food-hungry party lovers flock to the New Orleans Fairgrounds Racetrack for this incredible open-air event. Another celebration, also featuring food and music, but on a smaller scale, is the Festival International de Louisiane held in Lafayette in the heart of Acadiana in the southern part of the state.

Festival International de Louisiane

ESTIVAL INTERNATIONAL de Louisiane in Lafayette is always held the last full weekend of April. It was first staged in 1987 and has grown in size ever since. ■ Over the years, it has become an artistic, cultural crossroad of the world music scene. With several stages set in the downtown area of the city, you might hear a calypso beat, a Canadian folk song, Cajun waltzes, reggae, Caribbean chants, zydeco, soukous from Zaire, a Haitian rara, or a ballad from Senegal, as well as New Orleans rhythm and blues. ■ International performers, crafters, and cuisine make it a festival that's not only fun but educational. Local chefs host cooking demonstrations, but there's a taste of the exotic as well, with samples of French, Jamaican, Philippine, and Greek foods at the food court. ■ *Allons à Lafayette!*

easter

AS THE Lenten season draws to a close, Cajun and Creole families observe Holy Week, which begins on Palm Sunday, the commemoration of the triumphant arrival of Jesus Christ in Jerusalem, where the crowds put down their cloaks and waved palm branches to hail him as King. On Holy Thursday, the cooking and eating of *gumbo z'herbes*, a dish of nine greens, is observed to ensure having something to eat the whole year. Legend has it that for every green put in the pot, a new friend would be made in the year. Thus cooks gathered as many greens as possible. On Good Friday, churches are filled to capacity for services, and no meat is eaten on that day. ■ On Easter Sunday, families decked out in new Easter outfits and bonnets gather to attend glorious church services, then retire to their homes or camps to enjoy a fun-filled day that will include a lavish feast and egg hunts or a game called *pacquer*, or *pacque-pacque*, derived from the French word for Easter, *Pacques*. Participants select hard-boiled eggs, pair off, and tap the eggs together. The player whose egg does not crack is the winner. ■ Marcelle's family has a tradition of getting their camp ready for the opening of the season on the Easter weekend. All the brothers and sisters, their spouses, children, cousins, and old aunts and uncles spend several days before Easter cleaning, mowing, painting, planting, and spiffing everything up for the long three-day weekend, during which they enjoy crawfish boils, fish fries, barbecues, homemade ice cream, and, of course, a grand egg hunt in the woods and meadows on the property. ■ No matter on what date Easter falls, it marks the beginning of the warm-weather season that will last until Labor Day, a time for fun in the sun!

HAM AND CHEESE BITES

HAM HAS BEEN THE SYMBOL OF SPRING AND THE CENTERPIECE OF EASTER TABLES FOR CENTURIES. ■ I PREFER LAMB FOR MY MAIN COURSE, BUT I DARE NOT FORGET TO HAVE SOMETHING MADE WITH HAM TO OFFER MY GUESTS. THESE LITTLE HAM BITES HAVE BECOME A FAVORITE AT OUR FAMILY GATHERINGS.

1/4 pound boiled ham, cut into small dice
2 ounces Swiss cheese, grated
2 ounces sharp cheddar cheese, grated
1/8 teaspoon freshly ground black pepper
1/2 teaspoon Worcestershire sauce
1/4 teaspoon hot sauce
3 tablespoons minced shallots
1/4 cup Mayonnaise (recipe follows)
1 sheet (14 × 10 inches) frozen puff pastry (found in frozen food section), defrosted and cut into 2-inch squares
1 large egg, beaten with 1 teaspoon water

Preheat the oven to 375°F. Line a baking sheet with parchment paper and set aside.

In a medium-size mixing bowl, combine the ham, cheeses, black pepper, Worcestershire, hot sauce, shallots, and mayonnaise. Mix well.

Brush 24 of the pastry squares with the beaten egg wash, then put a heaping teaspoon of the ham mixture in the center of each square. Top with the remaining 24 pastry squares and, using your fingers, gently seal the edges together. Put the squares on the prepared baking sheet and brush the tops with the egg wash. Bake until lightly golden brown, about 15 minutes. Serve warm.

MAKES 24 HORS D'OEUVRES

Mayonnaise

1 large egg (see Note on page 13)
1 tablespoon Creole or whole-grain mustard
1/2 teaspoon salt
1 tablespoon fresh lemon juice
1 cup vegetable oil

Combine the egg, mustard, salt, and lemon juice in a food processor or blender and process until smooth, about 15 seconds. With the motor running, pour the vegetable oil through the feed tube in a slow, steady stream. Cover and chill for 1 hour in the refrigerator before serving. Best if used within 24 hours.

MAKES ABOUT 1 CUP

ROASTED LEG OF LAMB WITH A BOUQUET OF SPRING VEGETABLES

IN *THE PICAYUNE'S CREOLE COOK BOOK,* FIRST PUBLISHED AT THE TURN OF THE CENTURY, A TYPICAL EASTER DINNER FEATURED ROAST LAMB, MINT SAUCE, GREEN PEAS, CAULIFLOWER, AND ASPARAGUS. THE LAMB WAS SYMBOLIC OF THE SACRIFICIAL LAMB'S BLOOD ASSOCIATED WITH THE BIBLE.

Put the mint, parsley, onions, chopped garlic, lemon juice, ½ teaspoon of the salt, and ¼ teaspoon of the black pepper in a food processor or blender, and pulse several times to blend. With the motor running, slowly pour in the olive oil through the feed tube. The mixture should thicken.

In the top of the leg of lamb, where the meat is exposed, make 15 holes using a knife. Insert the garlic cloves into the holes. Season the leg evenly with 2 teaspoons of the salt and 1 teaspoon of the black pepper.

Put the lamb in a large shallow dish. Add the reserved lemon shells and pour in the marinade, spreading it evenly all over the lamb and rubbing it into the meat with your hands. Cover the dish and refrigerate for 8 to 12 hours.

Preheat the oven to 400°F.

Remove the lamb from the marinade. Put the lamb in a large roasting pan and roast on the bottom rack of the oven for 1 hour. Reduce the oven temperature to 300°F and roast until the internal temperature of the lamb reaches 160°F on a meat thermometer for a delicate pink center, about another hour. If you prefer the lamb to be medium-rare, roast just until the internal temperature reaches 140°F to 145°F, about another 45 minutes.

½ cup fresh mint leaves
½ cup fresh parsley leaves
1 cup chopped yellow onions
1 tablespoon chopped garlic
6 tablespoons fresh lemon juice (reserve the lemon shells)
1 tablespoon plus ½ teaspoon salt
1½ teaspoons freshly ground black pepper
1 cup olive oil
1 leg of lamb (about 9½ pounds), trimmed of excess fat
15 cloves garlic, peeled
2 cups beef broth
¼ cup (½ stick) unsalted butter
¼ cup minced shallots
2 teaspoons chopped garlic
3 pounds assorted vegetables, such as asparagus, baby carrots, green beans, cauliflower florets, and broccoli florets, each blanched in boiling salted water until tender and refreshed under cold running water
1 tablespoon chopped fresh parsley leaves

Remove from the oven and let the lamb rest for 15 to 20 minutes to settle the juices before carving.

Pour off the excess fat from the pan, place the pan on top of the stove over medium heat, and whisk in the beef broth. Continue whisking to loosen any browned bits from the bottom of the pan. Bring to a boil, then remove the pan from the heat.

To prepare the vegetables, melt the butter over medium heat in a large skillet. Add the shallots and chopped garlic and cook, stirring, for 2 minutes. Add the vegetables and season with the remaining 1 teaspoon salt and ¼ teaspoon black pepper. Toss to coat with the butter. Remove from the heat and garnish with the parsley.

To serve, carve the meat and serve with the vegetables and roasted potatoes (recipe follows).

MAKES ABOUT 12 SERVINGS

ROASTED POTATOES

TINY NEW RED POTATOES ARE CALLED CREAMERS IN LOUISIANA.

24 new or small red potatoes (about 2½ pounds), washed and halved
2 tablespoons olive oil
2 tablespoons bleached all-purpose flour
1 teaspoon salt
1 teaspoon freshly ground black pepper

Preheat the oven to 400°F. Line a baking sheet with parchment paper.

In a large mixing bowl, toss the potatoes with the olive oil. In a small bowl, combine the flour, salt, and black pepper and stir to mix. Sprinkle the potatoes with the mixture and toss to coat evenly. Arrange the potatoes on the prepared pan and roast for 1 hour.

MAKES ABOUT 12 SERVINGS

SWEET DOUGH COCONUT PIE

FOR YEARS, MARCELLE'S FAMILY SPENT THE LATTER PART OF HOLY WEEK AT THEIR CAMP IN CATAHOULA, A VILLAGE ON THE ATCHAFALAYA BASIN LEVEE. ON GOOD FRIDAY, AFTER ATTENDING THE AFTERNOON SERVICES, THEY WOULD RETURN FOR BOILED CRAWFISH. BY THE TIME THEY WERE SUCKING THE LAST OF THE HEADS AND PEELING THE TAILS, AN ENTOURAGE OF LADIES WOULD ARRIVE BEARING SWEET DOUGH PIES. GOOD FRIDAY WAS LONG KNOWN AS "PIE DAY" IN THE VILLAGE, AND IT WAS CUSTOMARY FOR THE LADIES TO LABOR FOR SEVERAL DAYS MAKING THE PIES TO CONSUME ON THE HOLY DAY. ■ YOU SEE, THE CATHOLIC CHURCH DEEMS THAT ON THAT DAY EVERYONE MUST FAST AND HAVE ONLY ONE MEAL. THE LADIES MADE SURE THEIR ONE MEAL WAS A LONG AND GOOD ONE. THEY WOULD BEGIN IT EARLY IN THE MORNING, AND IT WOULD STRETCH ON INTO THE AFTERNOON. ■ THOSE LADIES WERE NOT ONLY CLEVER, THEY WERE FINE BAKERS. YOU WILL NEED TWELVE 4-INCH ROUND TART PANS.

FOR THE CRUST

1/2 cup sugar
6 tablespoons vegetable
   shortening
1/2 cup milk
1 large egg
1/2 teaspoon pure vanilla extract
2 cups bleached all-purpose flour
2 teaspoons baking powder

Make the crust. In a medium-size mixing bowl, cream together the sugar and shortening. In a small mixing bowl, combine the milk, egg, and vanilla and mix well. Add the milk mixture to the shortening mixture and blend well. Combine the flour and baking powder in a medium-size mixing bowl. Then add the shortening mixture, about 1/4 cup at a time, to the dry mixture, blending well between each addition. The dough should come away from the sides of the bowl. Form the dough into a smooth ball, wrap it in plastic wrap, and chill for 30 minutes.

Preheat the oven to 350°F.

Lightly dust a work surface with flour. Divide the dough in half. Gently pat one half of the dough out into a disk. Roll it out into a 12-inch round about 1/4 inch thick. Cut out six 5-inch rounds and line each of

FOR THE FILLING

3 cups milk

1 cup sugar

4 large egg yolks

¼ cup cornstarch

1 teaspoon pure vanilla extract

2 tablespoons unsalted butter, cut into pieces

12 ounces frozen unsweetened flaked coconut, defrosted

TO FINISH

³/₄ cup frozen unsweetened flaked coconut, defrosted

six 4-inch round tart pans with a round of dough, pressing it into the bottom and up the side with your fingers. Repeat the process with the remaining ball of dough. With the tines of a fork, randomly prick the dough all over. Put the tart shells on a baking sheet and bake until lightly golden, 12 to 14 minutes. Remove from the oven, then transfer to a wire rack to let cool completely.

Make the filling. In a medium-size nonreactive saucepan over medium heat, combine 2½ cups of the milk and the sugar. Bring to a gentle boil, stirring to dissolve the sugar. Meanwhile, in a medium size mixing bowl, combine the egg yolks, cornstarch, and the remaining ½ cup milk. Whisk until smooth.

Add 1 cup of the hot milk mixture to the egg mixture, whisking to blend. Pour the mixture into the saucepan and cook, stirring constantly, until it thickens, about 4 minutes.

Remove from the heat and pour into a large mixing bowl. Add the vanilla, butter, and coconut. Mix well. Press a piece of plastic wrap down against the surface to prevent a skin from forming. Let cool completely.

Spoon an equal amount of the filling into each tart shell, cover loosely with plastic wrap, and refrigerate for at least 2 hours before serving.

Preheat the oven to 400°F.

Spread the coconut on a baking sheet and bake until just golden, 4 to 6 minutes. Remove from the oven and let cool slightly.

Sprinkle the toasted coconut on the tarts. Serve immediately.

MAKE 12 TARTS

strawberry april festival

THE FIRST Pontchatoula Strawberry Festival was held in 1972, cosponsored by the Chamber of Commerce and the Jaycees. Today it draws in excess of 225,000 visitors and features 54 booths highlighting music, food, and crafts. ■ Since the 1930s, the area north of Lake Pontchartrain has been a stronghold of Louisiana's berry crop, which, by the way, came about rather curiously. There simply wasn't much else that could be grown in that part of the state. The climate and soil couldn't support a major crop like sugarcane, but the railroad went right through the region and the freight trains needed something to carry back north. It was at this time that Italian immigrants first settled in those parishes north of New Orleans, and they began cultivating strawberries. It wasn't long until the locals realized what a treasure they had and began demanding more for their own use. Now the strawberry crop stays home. ■ When the season is in full swing, customers from Louisiana and neighboring states find their way to Tangipahoa and Livingston parishes to pick and buy the fruit, which can be popped into the mouth fresh from the plant, or baked in a pie or made into jams or toppings.

APRIL ✧ **STRAWBERRY FESTIVAL**

CHOCOLATE STRAWBERRY SHORTCAKE

SHORTCAKE IS LIKE A SWEET RICH BISCUIT. THE CLASSIC AMERICAN VERSION IS MOST OFTEN SPLIT IN HALF, THEN FILLED WITH FRESH STRAWBERRIES, AND *VOILÀ*—STRAWBERRY SHORTCAKE! THIS VERSION IS DIFFERENT; IT IS FILLED WITH ICE CREAM AND TOPPED WITH BERRIES. ■ AT THE PONTCHATOULA STRAWBERRY FESTIVAL, YOU'LL SEE A GREAT VARIETY OF STRAWBERRY TREATS, BUT STRAWBERRY SHORTCAKE IS A STANDARD OFFERING. SINCE I'M SUCH A CHOCOLATE LOVER, I ADDED COCOA TO THE SHORTCAKE MIX TO GIVE IT A NEW TWIST. ■ YOU CAN USE CHOCOLATE MILK INSTEAD OF THE COCOA AND HALF-AND-HALF AND YOU'LL HAVE A SIMILAR RESULT.

Combine the strawberries, kirsch, and ½ cup of the granulated sugar in a medium-size mixing bowl. Toss to mix. Cover and chill for 2 hours.

Preheat the oven to 350°F. Line a baking sheet with parchment paper.

Sift the flour, cocoa powder, baking powder, and salt into a large mixing bowl. Add the remaining 3 tablespoons granulated sugar and mix well. Add the butter and, using your hands, work it into the dry ingredients until the mixture resembles coarse crumbs. Add the half-and-half and gently mix to incorporate. The dough will be sticky.

Dust your work surface with 1 tablespoon of the flour. Turn the dough onto the floured surface. Gently fold each edge toward the center. Pick up the dough and dust the work surface with the remaining 1 tablespoon flour. Return the dough to the work surface and fold each edge toward the center again. Turn the dough over and lightly press it out to a ¾-inch thickness. Cut out 8 shortcakes using a 2½-inch round cookie cutter.

2 pints fresh strawberries, rinsed, hulled, and sliced
¼ cup kirsch
2 cups plus 2 tablespoons bleached all-purpose flour
2 tablespoons unsweetened cocoa powder
2 teaspoons baking powder
Pinch of salt
3 tablespoons plus ½ cup granulated sugar
¼ pound (1 stick) unsalted butter
¾ cup half-and-half
8 scoops Vanilla-Praline Ice Cream (page 204)
Confectioners' sugar for dusting

Place them on the prepared baking sheet and bake for 25 minutes. Remove from the oven and let cool on a wire rack.

To serve, cut the shortcakes horizontally in half. Put a scoop of ice cream on each bottom half, then cover with the top half. Spoon the strawberries in equal amounts over the tops and sprinkle with confectioners' sugar. Serve immediately.

MAKES 8 SERVINGS

STRAWBERRY SABAYON CAKE

SPONGE CAKE, CREAM, AND STRAWBERRIES ALL COME TOGETHER TO MAKE THIS ONE HECK OF A FESTIVE CAKE. I SUGGEST YOU MAKE IT A DAY AHEAD TO LET IT CHILL THOROUGHLY. COOL AND LUSCIOUS— SERVE IT AT YOUR FIRST SPRING PARTY.

Preheat the oven to 350°F.

Make the sponge cake. In a small saucepan, warm the milk and 2 teaspoons of the butter together over medium-low heat.

With an electric mixer fitted with a wire whip, beat the eggs and 1 cup of the sugar on medium-high speed in a large mixing bowl until the mixture is pale yellow, thick, and tripled in volume, about 8 minutes. With the mixer on low speed, beat in the warm milk mixture.

Sift the flour, baking powder, and salt into a small mixing bowl. Add half the flour mixture to the egg mixture and blend thoroughly until smooth. Repeat with the other half. Add the vanilla and mix gently.

Grease a 17 × 12-inch baking pan or jelly-roll pan with the remaining 2 tablespoons butter. Sprinkle evenly with the remaining 2 tablespoons sugar. Pour the cake batter into the pan, spreading it evenly. Bake until the cake springs back when touched, about 15 minutes. Cool for about 2 minutes, then gently flip it out onto a large wire rack or a large sheet of parchment paper. Let cool completely.

Make the filling. In a medium-size mixing bowl, combine the sliced strawberries, Grand Marnier, and 1 cup of the sugar. Stir gently to mix. Cover and let stand for 1 hour.

FOR THE SPONGE CAKE
1/4 cup milk
2 teaspoons plus 2 tablespoons
  unsalted butter
8 large eggs
1 cup plus 2 tablespoons sugar
1 cup bleached all-purpose flour
1 teaspoon baking powder
1/8 teaspoon salt
1 teaspoon pure vanilla extract

**FOR THE FILLING AND
   TO FINISH**

3 pints fresh strawberries, rinsed,
   hulled, and thinly sliced
1 cup Grand Marnier
2 cups sugar
1 pound mascarpone cheese
4 large egg yolks
1/2 cup dry white wine
1/4 cup (1/2 stick) unsalted butter,
   melted
2 cups heavy cream, whipped to
   stiff peaks
1 pint fresh strawberries, rinsed
   and hulled

Combine the mascarpone cheese with 1/2 cup of the sugar in a medium-size mixing bowl and mix well. Set aside.

Combine the egg yolks, the remaining 1/2 cup sugar, and the wine in a medium-size stainless steel mixing bowl and whisk until frothy. Set the bowl over a pot of simmering water and whisk until the mixture thickens, about 5 minutes. Add the melted butter in a steady stream, whisking constantly until it is well blended. Remove from the heat and continue whisking to cool slightly. Set aside and let cool for 10 minutes.

Whisk the mascarpone mixture, a little at a time, into the sabayon. Whisk in half the whipped cream.

Cut the cake vertically in half. Spread the strawberry mixture evenly over both halves.

To assemble, spread 1 cup of the sabayon evenly over the bottom of a deep glass dish (about 10 × 13 inches). Carefully place one piece of the cake on top of the sabayon and gently press down to remove any air pockets.

Spoon half of the remaining sabayon over the cake and spread evenly. Top with the remaining piece of cake and spread the remaining sabayon over the top. Cover and refrigerate for at least 12 hours.

When ready to serve, spread the top with the remaining whipped cream, then arrange the whole strawberries on the whipped cream. Spoon into dessert dishes.

MAKES 10 TO 12 SERVINGS

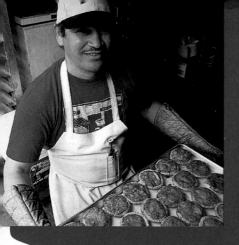

may

H, THE MERRY month of May! It is perhaps the most glorious of all the months! Along the sloping levees and the meandering country roads, lush clover and delicate pink and lavender buttercups dance in the warm southerly breezes that waltz in from the Gulf of Mexico. ■ Wild honeysuckle, wisteria, and Confederate jasmine twist and climb along fences and over arbors, scenting the night air with their sweet-smelling blossoms. Along the bayous and streams, turtles sun on driftwood and white egrets float overhead. Graceful blue herons swoop quietly to their nests in the lush foliage of the willow trees. ■ Young Catholic children gather at church to honor the Blessed Mother with May crownings, using fragrant gardenias to fashion her a headpiece. ■ Farmers and home gardeners are tending their summer crops—cucumbers and tomatoes are the first to appear—while shrimpers and fishermen are bringing in their hauls from the seas. Boat launches are crowded with sport fishermen trying their luck in the freshwater streams and saltwater bays. Tenacious crawfishermen make their final rounds in their ponds, netting the last of the crawfish for the season. ■ Families head out to their local parks for picnics and barbecues, volleyball games, and water sports. ■ With the weather being close to ideal, the weekends are jammed with festival activities. Hordes flock to the second weekend of the Jazz Fest, and the small town of Breaux Bridge is packed with visitors for the annual crawfish festival. In Lake Charles, in the southwestern part of the state, the townspeople are honoring the pirate Jean Lafitte, while in Gonzalez, near Baton Rouge, jambalaya is being paid tribute. In Shreveport, in the northwest corner of the state, everyone's heading to the First Bloom Festival. They're

cooking pigs at the Cochon de Lait Festival in Mansura, and in New Orleans, it's the Zoo-To-Do, a gigantic fundraising gala held at the zoo  that features many booths where local chefs sell small samples of their most popular dishes. ■ It's time to let the good times roll, enjoy some music, eat some good food, and ply the waters in whatever vessel you can get your hands on!

jazz fest

ONCE A small local event, which began in 1970 with 300 musicians performing for a crowd of 150 or so, the Jazz Fest has become an international attraction for more than 300,000 people. ■ It all started in the fall of 1969, when a New York–based jazz pianist and impresario named George Wein met with several New Orleans civic leaders who wanted to establish an annual jazz festival. The idea had been tried before, but it had proven too gigantic a task. Wein, then forty-four, had launched the Newport Jazz Festival, a world-class stage of talent that attracted large crowds and was more than successful. If a New Orleans festival could be organized, Wein would be the man to do it. The first festival was well received, and it has grown to be much larger than anyone dreamed. ■ To get the ball rolling, however, took some doing. Wein needed, and found, some local organizers who did incredible groundwork. (One was Quint Davis, then a part-time Tulane ethnomusicology student, and, coincidentally, the son of Arthur Davis,

the architect who worked with me on the development of Emeril's Restaurant.) Davis and Dick Allen, curator of the William Ransom Hogan Jazz Archive at Tulane University, and Allison Miner, a full-time staff member at the archive, knew enough musicians, local and otherwise, and had enough contacts to get it all rolling. ■ And the rest is history. ■ The highlights are two long weekends at the New Orleans Fair Grounds with several concerts at local clubs, theaters, and performing arts centers. The festival features traditional and contemporary jazz, as well as groups representing every facet of Louisiana's rich musical heritage: Afro-Caribbean, blues, Cajun, zydeco, country, ragtime, rockabilly, bluegrass, folk, gospel, Latin, Mardi Gras Indian, pop, rock, and rhythm and blues. There is also talent that includes the best regional styles as well as a number of those who have broken into the mainstream: Bois Sec Ardoin & Canray Fontenot, Beausoleil, Clarence "Gatemouth" Brown, C. J. Chenier & the Red Hot Louisiana Band, the Dixie Cups, Rockin' Doopsie & the Zydeco, Dr. John, Irma Thomas, the Neville Brothers, and on and on. ■ Over the years, the food has become almost as important as the music, with more than sixty booths featuring everything from jambalaya, poorboys, boudin, Jamaican chicken, and crawfish beignets to strawberry shortcake, mango freeze, pecan pralines, sno-balls, and a long list of cool drinks. ■ And if that's not enough to entertain you, be assured it's one of the best people-watching festivals in the state. It's amazing to see thousands of people jamming together, and although it's called the Jazz Fest, it should be hailed as the Feast of Music. ■ All of Emeril's New Orleans restaurants are packed with not only visitors, but musicians, like Paul Simon, Bonnie Raitt, and a host of others, who sneak in to get a bite to eat and enjoy the mayhem. The staffs of the restaurants are so constantly busy, they can't wait for the last Sunday, when they themselves can go to celebrate at the Gospel Tent at the Fest. Alleluia and amen!

CRAWFISH BREAD

CRAWFISH BREAD IS A VERY POPULAR JAZZ FEST FOOD. IT'S ONE OF THOSE "WALK AND EAT" KINDS OF EDIBLE THAT'S A MUST AT FESTIVALS. IT IS WITHOUT QUESTION FELICIA'S FAVORITE JAZZ FEST FOOD ITEM, AND SHE CANNOT OR WILL NOT GO TO THE FEST WITHOUT HAVING ONE, TWO, OR THREE CRAWFISH BREADS. AT JAZZ FEST, THEY'RE MADE IN INDIVIDUAL SIZES AND ARE WRAPPED IN ALUMINUM FOIL, PERFECT FOR CHOMPING ON WHILE LISTENING TO THE NEVILLES, JIMMY BUFFET, OR IRMA THOMAS. THE TRUE TEST THAT THE BREAD IS MADE JUST RIGHT IS THAT THE CHEESE DRIPS DOWN YOUR CHIN. I MEAN IT!

Combine the yeast, sugar, and 2 tablespoons of the vegetable oil in the bowl of a stand mixer fitted with a dough hook. Add the warm water. With the mixer on low speed, beat the mixture for about 1 minute to dissolve the yeast. If the yeast mixture doesn't begin to foam after a few minutes, it means it's not active and you will have to start over with fresher yeast.

In a large mixing bowl, combine the flour and 1 teaspoon of the salt. Add it ¼ cup at a time to the yeast mixture, mixing on low speed until the dough lightly comes together. Increase the speed to medium and beat until the dough pulls away from the sides of the bowl, forms a ball, and starts to climb up the dough hook.

Coat a large bowl with the remaining 1 teaspoon vegetable oil. Put the dough in the bowl and turn it to oil all sides. Cover the bowl with plastic wrap, set aside in a warm, draft-free place, and let rise until doubled in size, about 1 hour.

Meanwhile, in a large skillet, melt the butter over medium heat. Add the onion, bell pepper, the remaining 1½ teaspoons salt, and the cayenne. Cook, stirring,

1 envelope active dry yeast
1 tablespoon sugar
2 tablespoons plus 1 teaspoon vegetable oil
1¼ cups warm water (about 110°F)
3½ cups bleached all-purpose flour
2½ teaspoons salt
1 tablespoon unsalted butter
½ cup chopped yellow onion
1 tablespoon finely chopped red bell pepper
1 tablespoon finely chopped yellow bell pepper
½ teaspoon cayenne
1½ pounds peeled crawfish tails
½ pound sharp cheddar cheese, grated
½ pound Monterey Jack cheese with jalapeños, grated
1 large egg, beaten
1 teaspoon kosher salt
¼ teaspoon freshly ground black pepper

for 4 minutes. Add the crawfish and cook, stirring, for 5 minutes until they are soft. Remove from the heat, drain off any excess liquid from the pan, and set aside to cool.

Remove the dough from the bowl and turn it onto a lightly floured work surface. Push it down, then, using your hands, pat it out to flatten it. Pick it up, dust the work surface with flour, and return the dough to the work surface. Roll it out to a 20 × 15-inch rectangle, about ⅛ inch thick.

Combine the cheeses in a medium-size mixing bowl. Sprinkle half of the cheese over the upper half of the rectangle of dough, leaving a ½-inch border. Spoon the crawfish mixture evenly over the cheese. Top with the remaining cheese. Fold the other half of the dough up over the filling, forming a half-moon shape, and pinch the edges tightly to seal completely. Fold the edges over, seal securely, and then crimp. Carefully transfer the dough to a baking sheet lined with parchment paper. With a sharp, pointed knife, make three slits on top, about 6 inches apart. Brush the surface of the dough with the beaten egg and sprinkle with the kosher salt and black pepper. Cover with plastic wrap and set aside in a warm, draft-free place until doubled in size, about 1 hour.

Preheat the oven to 400°F.

Remove the plastic wrap and bake the bread until golden brown, 30 to 35 minutes. Let cool slightly. Cut crosswise into 12 equal portions and serve warm.

MAKES 1 LARGE LOAF, 12 SERVINGS

FIFIELD'S BLACKBERRY COBBLER

JIM FIFIELD, WHO USED TO BE IN THE MUSIC BUSINESS, HAS BECOME A GREAT FRIEND OF MINE. HE ALWAYS ATTENDED THE JAZZ FEST WITH SOME OF HIS TALENTS, LIKE THE LATE CHARLES BROWN, STEVEN CURTIS CHAPMAN, AND RUTH BROWN. THE SECOND WEEKEND DURING JAZZ FEST IS ALWAYS NEAR HIS BIRTHDAY. WE'VE HAD SOME BLOW-OUT DINNERS, BUT IT SEEMS HIS ALL-TIME FAVORITE DESSERT IS THIS RATHER MODEST COBBLER. ■ DURING LATE SPRING AND EARLY SUMMER, BIG, JUICY BLACKBERRIES GROW WILD IN DITCHES AND ALONG FENCE LINES ON RURAL ROADS ACROSS THE STATE. WHAT BETTER WAY TO USE THEM THAN IN THIS DESSERT?

Preheat the oven to 350°F.

In a large mixing bowl, combine the blackberries, Grand Marnier, granulated sugar, and 2 tablespoons of the flour. Toss to mix and let sit for 15 minutes.

Grease four 8-ounce ramekins with 1 teaspoon of the butter. Divide the berry mixture equally among the ramekins.

In a small mixing bowl, cream the remaining stick of butter with the brown sugar until smooth. Add the cinnamon, the remaining ½ cup flour, and the oats. Mix well.

Spread the oat mixture evenly over the berries. Put the ramekins on a baking sheet and bake until lightly golden, about 30 minutes. Remove from the oven and let cool slightly.

Top each cobbler with a scoop of ice cream, if you wish, to serve.

4 pints fresh blackberries, rinsed and picked over
¼ cup Grand Marnier
¼ cup granulated sugar
2 tablespoons plus ½ cup bleached all-purpose flour
1 teaspoon plus ¼ pound (1 stick) unsalted butter, at room temperature
1 cup firmly packed light brown sugar
½ teaspoon ground cinnamon
½ cup rolled oats
4 scoops Vanilla-Praline Ice Cream (page 204; optional)

MAKES 4 SERVINGS

JAMBALAYA GRITS

TRADITIONAL JAMBALAYA IS MADE WITH RICE, BUT GRITS WORK EQUALLY WELL, FOR A DIFFERENT TWIST ON THIS LOUISIANA STAPLE. THIS IS ONE HEARTY DISH AND NOT FOR THE WEAK OF HEART. SOMETIMES I LIKE TO ACCOMPANY IT WITH A LINK OF WARM BOUDIN, THE FANTASTIC LOCAL SAUSAGE MADE WITH BITS OF PORK, RICE, AND, OF COURSE, THE PERFECT BLEND OF SEASONINGS.

1 tablespoon olive oil
1 cup chopped yellow onions
1/2 cup chopped green bell pepper
1/2 cup chopped celery
1 1/2 teaspoons salt
1/8 teaspoon freshly ground black pepper
1/2 teaspoon cayenne
1/4 pound andouille or other smoked sausage, cut crosswise into 1/4-inch-thick slices
1/4 pound boiled ham, cut into small dice
1 tablespoon chopped garlic
1/2 cup peeled, seeded, and chopped vine-ripened tomato
6 cups milk
2 cups quick-cooking white grits
1/2 pound medium-size shrimp, peeled and deveined
1/4 cup chopped green onions or scallions (green part only)
1/4 pound sharp white cheddar cheese, grated

In a large, heavy pot, heat the olive oil over medium high heat. Add the onions, bell pepper, celery, salt, black pepper, and cayenne. Cook, stirring, until the vegetables are soft and lightly golden, about 4 minutes. Add the sausage and ham and continue to cook, stirring occasionally, for 2 minutes. Add the garlic and tomato and cook for 2 minutes. Add the milk and bring to a boil. Reduce the heat to medium and stir in the grits. Stir for 2 minutes, then add the shrimp. Cook, stirring, until the grits are tender and creamy, 7 to 8 minutes. Stir in the green onions, then add the cheese and stir until it is completely melted, about 30 seconds.

Serve hot right from the pot.

MAKES 8 APPETIZER SERVINGS OR 4 MAIN-COURSE SERVINGS

LOUISIANA OYSTER AND SAUSAGE BAKE

AS I'VE SAID BEFORE, YOU'LL FIND OYSTERS PREPARED IN ANY NUMBER OF WAYS AROUND HERE, AND THIS IS ONE OF MY FAVORITES. OYSTER BAKES USUALLY COMBINE THE MOLLUSKS WITH LOTS OF GARLIC, SOMETIMES HAM OR BACON, AND BREAD CRUMBS. SINCE I'M SUCH A SAUSAGE FAN, I'VE ADDED IT TO THIS RECIPE. IT'S A DISH THAT GOES WELL WITH AN ICE COLD BEER. BRING ON THE MUSIC!

Preheat the oven to 400°F.

In a large skillet over medium-high heat, heat 1 tablespoon of the olive oil. Add the sausage and cook, stirring, until the meat is browned and all the pink has disappeared, about 4 minutes. Add the onions and cook, stirring, for 2 minutes. Stir in the garlic, salt, and black pepper. Remove from the heat and pour into a medium-size mixing bowl. Let cool to room temperature.

In another medium-size mixing bowl, combine 2 tablespoons of the olive oil, the bread crumbs, parsley, cheese, and Creole seasoning. Mix well. Add the sausage mixture and mix well. Combine the oyster liquor and enough water to make a total of 1¼ cups of liquid. Add this to the bread crumb–and–sausage mixture and mix well.

Grease the bottom of a 10-inch pie pan with the remaining 1 tablespoon olive oil. Arrange the oysters in one layer in the bottom of the pan. Cover the oysters evenly with the sausage mixture, packing it firmly down onto them.

Bake on the center rack of the oven until the top is golden brown, 18 to 20 minutes. Remove from the oven and serve hot.

¼ cup olive oil
½ pound finely ground andouille or fresh pork sausage removed from the casing and crumbled
1 cup chopped yellow onions
1 tablespoon chopped garlic
¼ teaspoon salt
⅛ teaspoon freshly ground black pepper
1½ cups fine dried bread crumbs
1 tablespoon finely chopped fresh parsley leaves
½ cup freshly grated Parmigiano-Reggiano cheese
1 tablespoon Creole Seasoning (page 13)
2 dozen freshly shucked large (or 4 dozen medium-size) oysters, drained well; reserve the oyster liquor
Up to ¾ cup water

MAKES 8 APPETIZER SERVINGS

ROASTED PORK AND FRENCH FRY POORBOY

LET ME TELL YOU ABOUT THE FOOD SERVED AT THE BOOTHS AT JAZZ FEST. VENDORS CAN'T JUST SHOW UP AND START SELLING THEIR FARE. THEY MUST APPLY TO THE NEW ORLEANS JAZZ & HERITAGE FESTIVAL. ALL APPLICATIONS ARE CAREFULLY SCRUTINIZED AND A SPECIAL COMMITTEE DECIDES WHO MAKES THE CUT. THE TRICK IS TO GET THE RIGHT MIX OF FOODS SO THAT THERE'S SOMETHING FOR EVERYBODY. ■ THIS POORBOY WAS ONE OF MY FAVORITES AND I DON'T KNOW IF IT'S STILL AROUND, BUT IT SHOULD BE.

Preheat the oven to 400°F.

Rub the pork with the olive oil, then season it with 1 teaspoon of the salt, ½ teaspoon of the black pepper, and the cayenne. Place it fat side up in a roasting pan and roast for 1 hour. Reduce the oven temperature to 325°F and bake for another 3 hours. Remove from the oven and transfer the pork to a shallow bowl. Let cool slightly, then shred the meat into small pieces.

In a heavy, deep pot or an electric deep-fryer, heat the vegetable oil to 360°F.

Fry the potatoes in batches until golden brown, 7 to 8 minutes, stirring constantly to brown them evenly. Remove from the oil with a slotted spoon and drain on paper towels. Season with the remaining ¼ teaspoon salt and ⅛ teaspoon black pepper.

Slice the loaf of bread lengthwise in half. Spread the mayonnaise on one half and the mustard on the other. Arrange a layer of the pork on the bottom half of the bread. Arrange the fried potatoes on top of the meat. Replace the top of the bread. Slice the poorboy into 4 equal portions and serve.

1 Boston butt pork roast
   (3½ to 4 pounds)
1 tablespoon olive oil
1¼ teaspoons salt
½ teaspoon plus ⅛ teaspoon
   freshly ground black pepper
¼ teaspoon cayenne
4 cups vegetable oil
2 large Idaho potatoes (about
   1½ pounds), peeled and cut
   into thin french fries
1 crusty loaf French bread
   (22 to 24 inches long)
¼ cup Mayonnaise (page 129)
¼ cup Creole or whole-grain
   mustard

MAKES 4 SERVINGS

STUFFED ARTICHOKES

THERE ARE ALL SORTS OF STUFFED ARTICHOKES SERVED IN AND AROUND NEW ORLEANS, SOME STUFFED WITH A BREAD CRUMB MIXTURE, OTHERS WITH SHRIMP. JUST ABOUT EVERY COOK HAS HIS OWN RECIPE. HERE'S ONE THAT I LIKE.

4 large artichokes, rinsed in cool water
1 tablespoon salt
1 teaspoon freshly ground black pepper
2 bay leaves
1 tablespoon liquid Zatarain's Concentrated Crab & Shrimp Boil (optional)
1 medium-size lemon, halved
1 cup fine dried bread crumbs
2 teaspoons Creole Seasoning (page 13)
¼ cup olive oil
¼ cup chopped fresh parsley leaves
1 tablespoon chopped garlic
¼ cup freshly grated Parmigiano-Reggiano cheese
3 tablespoons fresh lemon juice
½ pound lump crabmeat, picked over for shells and cartilage

Trim off the stems of the artichokes and the thorny tips of each leaf until the artichokes can stand up on their own. Put them in a deep pot and add enough water to cover. Add the salt, black pepper, bay leaves, and crab boil. Squeeze the lemon halves over the pot and add the lemon shells. Bring to a boil, then reduce the heat to medium and simmer, covered, until the artichokes are tender when pierced with the tip of a knife, 20 to 30 minutes. Drain. Return the artichokes to the pot, cover with ice water, and let cool completely.

Remove the artichokes from the water and pat dry with paper towels. To remove the chokes, grasp the central core of leaves of each artichoke and, with a quick twist, lift it out. Carefully scoop out the choke with a teaspoon or melon baller and discard it.

Preheat the oven to 400°F.

In a medium-size mixing bowl, combine the bread crumbs, Creole seasoning, olive oil, parsley, garlic, cheese, and lemon juice. Gently fold in the crabmeat. Stuff the center of each artichoke with about ¼ cup of the crabmeat mixture, pressing it in firmly. Stuff the remaining mixture between the outer leaves of the artichokes.

Put the artichokes in a large shallow baking dish or on a baking sheet. Bake for 12 minutes until warmed through. Remove from the oven and let cool slightly before serving.

may

mother's day

LIKE EVERYWHERE else in America, Louisiana honors its mothers in a big way. The usual custom of giving Mom a day off from the kitchen and taking her out for a fancy feast is observed here, making Mother's Day the busiest restaurant day of the year. (Thank goodness Emeril's is closed, so I can either cook for my mother or take her out.) ■ Marcelle and Felicia recall that when they were children, it was their custom to go with their siblings and their father to pick out the corsage that was to be presented to Mama on her day. It was indeed a thrill to be able to pick out not only the flowers but also the ribbon, the brighter and gaudier the better, or so they thought! And poor Mama had to wear the thing with her best outfit, topped off with a flower-bedecked hat as well! ■ In our family, Hilda rules all year, not just on Mother's Day. She especially likes crab cakes, and, for that matter, anything made with lump crabmeat. She is also fond of fish, but it had better be the freshest you can find! And believe me, she can tell! ■ So here's to you, Mom, and thanks for all that you did and continue to do for me!

COLD CUCUMBER SOUP

THERE ARE MULTIPLE METHODS OF SERVING THIS WONDERFUL COOL SOUP. IN THE COOLER MONTHS, HILDA LIKES SERVING IT POURED OVER FRESHLY SHUCKED LOUISIANA OYSTERS, DABBED WITH OSETRA CAVIAR. WHEN I HAVE FRESH CHERVIL AND HEIRLOOM OR THE SMALL TEARDROP TOMATOES, I MAKE A LITTLE RELISH TO GARNISH THE SOUP. MAKE UP YOUR OWN GARNISHES, USING WHATEVER IS FRESH LOCALLY. I SUGGEST MAKING YOUR GARNISH A DAY AHEAD OR AT LEAST A FEW HOURS AHEAD TO ALLOW THE FLAVORS TO MELD.

In a large, heavy pot, heat the olive oil over medium heat. Add the onions, garlic, 1 teaspoon of the salt, and the white pepper. Cook, stirring, for 4 minutes. Add the chopped cucumbers. Cook, stirring, for 2 minutes. Add the chicken broth and bring to a boil. Reduce the heat to medium-low and simmer for 30 minutes.

Remove from the heat and stir in the parsley leaves. Let cool completely.

Process the soup, in batches, in a food processor or blender until smooth. Strain through a fine-mesh sieve. Cover and chill for 2 hours.

Meanwhile, in a small bowl, combine the tomatoes, red onions, diced cucumbers, chervil, the remaining ¼ teaspoon salt, the black pepper, and extra-virgin olive oil. Stir to mix. Cover and chill until ready to use.

When ready to serve, add the yogurt to the soup and stir to mix. Ladle the soup into soup bowls and garnish with the tomato relish.

1 tablespoon olive oil
1 cup chopped yellow onions
1 tablespoon chopped garlic
1¼ teaspoons salt
½ teaspoon freshly ground white pepper
6 large cucumbers (about 2 pounds), peeled, seeded, and chopped
8 cups chicken broth
1 cup loosely packed fresh parsley leaves
¼ pound yellow teardrop tomatoes, sliced lengthwise in half
¼ pound red teardrop tomatoes, sliced lengthwise in half
¼ cup small-diced red onions
½ cup small-diced peeled and seeded cucumbers
½ cup fresh chervil leaves
⅛ teaspoon freshly ground black pepper
2 tablespoons extra-virgin olive oil
One 1-pound container plain yogurt

MAKES 8 SERVINGS

GOAT CHEESE–STUFFED SOFT-SHELL CRABS WITH A PECAN-PESTO BUTTER SAUCE

SOFT-SHELL CRABS, BLUE CRABS THAT HAVE JUST SHED THEIR HARD SHELLS, ARE A REAL DELICACY. WHEN THE OLD SHELL SPLITS, THE CRAB CREEPS OUT WITH ITS NEW PAPER-THIN SHELL AND IS ALMOST ENTIRELY EDIBLE. AROUND THIS TIME OF THE YEAR IS WHEN THEY'RE PLENTIFUL AND PERFECT, I THINK, FOR A SPECIAL OCCASION LIKE MOTHER'S DAY. ■ NOW REMEMBER, YOU HAVE TO CLEAN SOFT-SHELL CRABS BEFORE YOU COOK 'EM. USE KITCHEN SHEARS TO CUT THE FACE, REMOVING THE EYE SOCKETS AND THE LOWER MOUTH. TURN THEM OVER, CAREFULLY LIFT UP THE APRON, AND REMOVE THE GILLS. CUT OFF THE TAIL-LIKE PART OF THE APRON AND YOU'RE READY TO GO.

Combine the basil, garlic, pecans, cheese, salt, and black pepper in a food processor or blender and process until smooth. With the machine running, add the olive oil in a steady stream and process to make a paste.

Transfer the pesto to a medium-size saucepan over low heat. Whisk in the butter, a cube at a time, until all of it is incorporated. Set aside and keep warm.

In a large, heavy, deep pot or an electric deep-fryer, heat the vegetable oil to 360°F.

Season the soft-shells with 1 tablespoon of the Creole seasoning. Put the flour in a large bowl and season it with 2 teaspoons of the Creole seasoning. Put the eggs and milk in another bowl and season it with 1 teaspoon of the Creole seasoning. Put the bread crumbs in another bowl and season the bread crumbs with 1 tablespoon of the Creole seasoning.

Carefully lift the "shoulders" of each crab and stuff the cavity with 2 tablespoons of the goat cheese. Press the cheese firmly into the cavity. Dredge the crabs in the sea-

1 cup fresh basil leaves
6 cloves garlic, peeled
1/3 cup pecan pieces, toasted (see Note)
1/2 cup freshly grated Parmigiano-Reggiano cheese
1/2 teaspoon salt
1/8 teaspoon freshly ground black pepper
1/4 cup extra-virgin olive oil
1/2 pound (2 sticks) cold unsalted butter, cubed
6 cups vegetable oil
8 large soft-shell crabs, cleaned (see above)

1/4 cup Creole Seasoning
   (page 13)
1 cup bleached all-purpose flour
2 large eggs, beaten
1 tablespoon milk
2 cups fine dried bread crumbs
1 cup crumbled goat cheese
1 recipe Mashed Potatoes
   (recipe follows)

soned flour, tapping off any excess, then dip them in the egg wash, letting the excess drip off. Dredge them in the bread crumbs, making sure to coat the legs completely.

One at a time, holding the body of each crab, carefully drag the legs in the hot oil for about 30 seconds, then carefully drop the crab into the oil. Fry until golden brown, flipping the crabs with tongs two to three times to brown evenly, 3 to 4 minutes. Remove from the oil with tongs and drain on paper towels. Season each crab as it comes out of the oil with some of the remaining 1 tablespoon Creole seasoning. Repeat the procedure until all of the crabs are cooked.

To serve, spoon the pesto sauce into the center of each plate. Mound the mashed potatoes in the center of the sauce. Place a soft-shell on top of each mound of potatoes.

NOTE

Combine 2 tablespoons unsalted butter and the pecans in a nonstick skillet over high heat. Cook, stirring, until they are toasted and brown, about 3 minutes.

MAKES 8 SERVINGS

MASHED POTATOES

4 large Idaho potatoes, peeled
   and cubed
1/2 teaspoon salt
1/4 cup (1/2 stick) unsalted
   butter, cut into pieces
1 cup milk
1/8 teaspoon freshly ground
   white pepper

Put the potatoes in a large saucepan and cover with water. Add 1/4 teaspoon of the salt and bring to a boil. Reduce the heat to medium and cook, covered, until tender, 15 to 20 minutes. Drain, then return the potatoes to the pot. Add the butter and stir and mash until it melts completely. Add the milk, the remaining salt, and the white pepper and stir to mix. Serve hot.

MAKES 8 SERVINGS

MINT JULEP ICE CREAM

DOWN SOUTH, THERE ARE MANY KINDS OF MINT JULEP, ONE FOR JUST ABOUT EVERY SOUTHERN STATE. BUT THERE'S EVEN SOMETHING BETTER—MINT JULEP ICE CREAM. NOW, THAT'S REJUVENATING! HILDA CLAIMS THIS ICE CREAM IS SO GOOD IT SHOULD BE SERVED REGULARLY DURING THE WARM WEATHER.

Combine the sugar, water, and the 8 mint sprigs in a small saucepan over medium heat and bring to a boil, stirring to dissolve the sugar. Cook for 2 minutes. Remove from the heat and let cool completely. Strain through a fine-mesh strainer, then add the bourbon.

Combine the milk and cream in a large nonreactive saucepan and bring to a gentle boil. In a small mixing bowl, whisk the egg yolks together. Whisk 1 cup of the hot cream mixture into the egg mixture. In a slow, steady stream, add the egg mixture to the hot cream mixture. Continue to cook for 4 minutes, stirring occasionally, until the mixture thickens enough to coat the back of a spoon. Remove from the heat and let cool completely.

Whisk the bourbon mixture into the cream mixture. Cover with plastic wrap, pressing the wrap down against the surface of the mixture to keep a skin from forming, and chill in the refrigerator for at least 2 hours.

Remove from the refrigerator and pour the mixture into an ice cream machine. Churn according to the manufacturer's directions.

To serve, put a large scoop of the ice cream in the center of each serving dish and garnish with the remaining mint sprigs. Pass a tray of Pecan Florentines (recipe follows), if you wish.

1 cup sugar
1/2 cup water
1/2 cup bourbon
2 cups milk
2 cups heavy cream
6 large egg yolks
8 large sprigs fresh mint, plus several small sprigs for garnish

MAKES ABOUT 8 SERVINGS

PECAN FLORENTINES

MICHELLE, WHO WORKS AT EMERIL'S HOMEBASE (OUR HEADQUARTERS IN NEW ORLEANS), HAD A GRANDMOTHER NAMED PRISCILLA WHO DIED AT THE RIPE OLD AGE OF EIGHTY-FIVE WHILE COOKING IN HER KITCHEN. I HOPE THAT I CAN GO THAT WAY! ACCORDING TO MICHELLE, ONE OF PRISCILLA'S SPECIALTIES WAS THESE PECAN FLORENTINES, SOMETIMES CALLED PECAN LACE COOKIES, SINCE, ONCE THEY'RE BAKED, THEY ARE AS DELICATE AS OLD LACE. MICHELLE SHARED HER GRANDMOTHER'S RECIPE WITH US AND THEY'RE A LITTLE DIFFERENT FROM MOST, AS THEY ARE MADE WITH OATMEAL AS WELL AS PECANS. SERVE WITH MINT JULEP ICE CREAM OR WITH ANY ICE CREAM. STORE THEM IN AN AIRTIGHT CONTAINER FOR A WEEK.

¼ pound (1 stick) unsalted butter, at room temperature
1 cup sugar
1 large egg
1 teaspoon pure vanilla extract
¼ teaspoon baking soda
Pinch of salt
1 cup quick-cooking oats
1 cup pecan pieces

Preheat the oven to 350°F. Line a baking sheet with parchment paper.

Cream the butter and sugar together with an electric mixer or hand-held mixer on medium speed until smooth. Add the egg and beat until incorporated. Add the vanilla, baking soda, and salt and beat until smooth.

In a food processor or blender, combine the oats and pecan pieces and pulse several times to grind. Add this to the dough and beat until incorporated. The dough will be stiff but sticky.

Drop the dough by the teaspoonful, about 3 inches apart, onto the prepared sheet pan. Flatten the dough slightly with your fingertips. Bake for 6 minutes until lightly golden. Remove from the oven, carefully remove from the sheet, and let cool completely on wire racks. Repeat the process until all the dough is used, relining the sheet each time with new parchment.

MAKES ABOUT 5 DOZEN COOKIES

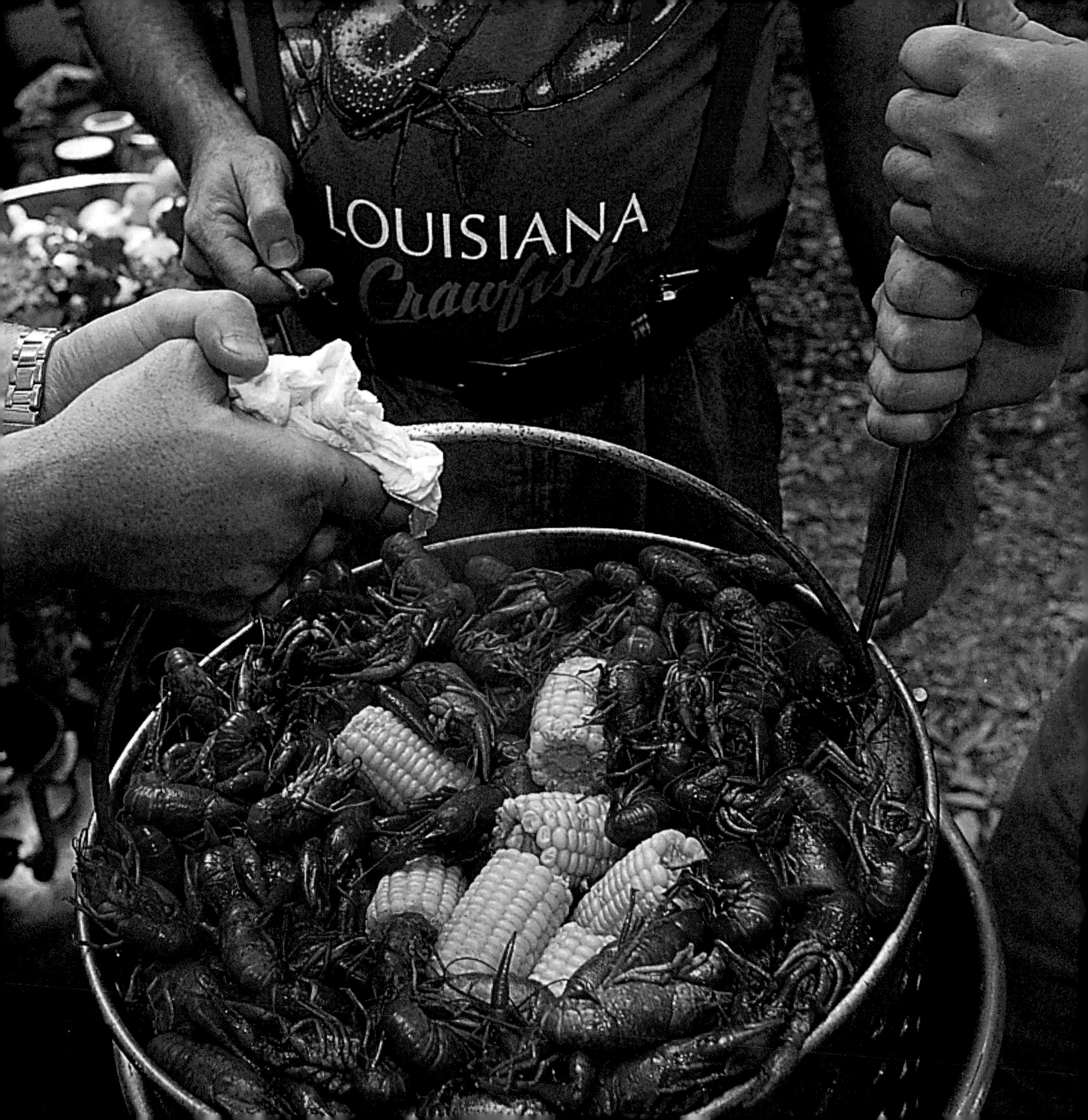
LOUISIANA
Crawfish

may

crawfish

festival

IN 1959, through the efforts of the late Robert Angelle, who was then the Speaker of the House for the Louisiana Legislature, a resolution was passed proclaiming Breaux Bridge *La Capitale Mondiale de l'Écrevisse*, the Crawfish Capital of the World. ■ The following year, the Breaux Bridge Crawfish Festival began as a spin-off of the Breaux Bridge Centennial Celebration. It has since developed into a celebration of Cajun heritage. People from around the world come to the small community the first full weekend of May each year to enjoy Cajun and zydeco bands, a crawfish-eating contest, crawfish races, a crawfish étouffée cook-off, and other events. ■ It's hard to believe that up until the 1960s, crawfish wasn't popular, at least outside southwest Louisiana. Local fishermen brought up crawfish from the swampy waters primarily for consumption by their own families. If they had more than they needed, the fishermen would peddle the crawfish to friends and neighbors. It was practically unheard of

to get crawfish, boiled or prepared otherwise, in a restaurant or café. Sucking the heads and pinching the tails was done only in the privacy of one's home. ■ But once Monsieur Écrevisse was discovered for his sweet tasty meat, the world clamored for more. To meet the demand, crawfish farming has developed into a science. The crawfish industry has been a boon to south Louisiana. Besides the farmers, there are businesses that peel and boil crawfish for fresh or frozen tails that are shipped all over the country. ■ Locally, during the crawfish season, which runs roughly from January to June, thousands of pounds of crawfish find their way into boiling pots, étouffées, pies, and stews. ■ Each year, Marcelle's family, numbering about thirty-five, gather at the camp, spending the better part of the day boiling over two hundred pounds for their consumption. ■ It is therefore only right that these freshwater crustaceans are honored with their very own celebration. ■ *Vive le festival de l'écrevisse!*

CRAWFISH PIES, MY WAY

THERE'S A PLACE ON LAKE PONTCHARTRAIN JUST ACROSS THE NEW ORLEANS CITY LIMITS, IN METAIRIE, CALLED R & O PIZZA PLACE. THE PIZZAS ARE GREAT, BUT THEY ALSO SERVE ALL KINDS OF SEAFOOD, LIKE SOFT-SHELL CRABS, SHRIMP, OYSTERS, AND, IN SEASON, BOILED CRAWFISH. ■ ON SUNDAYS DURING THE SPRINGTIME, I LIKE NOTHING BETTER THAN TO SPEND THE BETTER PART OF THE AFTERNOON EATING MY WAY THROUGH THEIR MENU. THAT'S HOW I DISCOVERED THEIR SMALL CRAWFISH PIES. BOY, ARE THEY TASTY. OF COURSE, THEY WOULDN'T GIVE ME THE RECIPE, BUT I BROUGHT SEVERAL HOME AND DISSECTED THEM. THIS IS ABOUT AS CLOSE AS I COULD GET. ■ YOU SHOULD KNOW THAT ALL OVER LOUISIANA YOU'LL FIND ALL KINDS OF FRIED PIES, SOME STUFFED WITH A MEAT MIXTURE LIKE THE NATCHITOCHES MEAT PIES, OTHERS STUFFED WITH CRAWFISH LIKE THESE.

Make the filling. Heat the olive oil over medium heat in a large skillet. Add the onions, bell pepper, salt, and cayenne and cook for 2 minutes, stirring a few times. Add the crawfish tails and cook, stirring, for 2 minutes. Add the green onions, garlic, and parsley and cook, stirring, for 1 minute.

Pour the mixture into a medium-size mixing bowl and let cool for about 3 minutes. Add the egg and bread crumbs and mix well. Set aside.

Make the pastry. Sift the flour, salt, and baking powder into a large mixing bowl. With a pastry cutter or two knives, cut in the shortening until the mixture resembles coarse meal. In a small mixing bowl, beat the egg with the milk. Gradually add the egg mixture to the flour mixture, working it to make a thick dough.

FOR THE FILLING
3 tablespoons olive oil
3/4 cup chopped yellow onions
1/4 cup chopped green bell
 pepper
1 tablespoon salt
3/4 teaspoon cayenne
1 1/2 pounds peeled crawfish tails
1/2 cup chopped green onions or
 scallions (green part only)
1 tablespoon chopped garlic
3 tablespoons chopped fresh
 parsley leaves
1 large egg
3/4 cup fine dried bread crumbs

FOR THE PASTRY

3 cups bleached all-purpose flour

1 1/2 teaspoons salt

3/4 teaspoon baking powder

6 tablespoons vegetable
shortening

1 large egg

3/4 cup milk

TO FRY THE PIES

4 cups vegetable shortening

1/2 teaspoon Creole Seasoning
(page 13)

Divide the dough into 12 equal portions. On a lightly floured work surface, roll out each dough piece into a thin round about 5 inches in diameter.

Put about 1/4 cup of the crawfish mixture in the center of each round, fold the dough over, and crimp the edges together with a fork.

Heat the shortening in a heavy, deep pot or an electric deep-fryer to 360°F. Fry the pies, two to three at a time, until golden brown. Drain on paper towels, sprinkle with the creole seasoning, and serve hot.

MAKES 12 HAND PIES

CRAWFISH VOL-AU-VENT

A *VOL-AU-VENT* IS A PUFF PASTRY SHELL THAT RESEMBLES A SMALL POT.

Preheat the oven to 400°F. Line a baking sheet with parchment or waxed paper.

Thaw the pastry at room temperature for 20 to 30 minutes before gently unfolding. With a sharp knife, divide the pastry in half, wrap the remaining piece in plastic wrap, and return to the freezer for another use.

Cut the pastry into 4 equal triangles. With the tip of a sharp knife, make a ¼-inch score on all edges of the triangles, being careful not to cut all the way through. Put them on the prepared baking sheet and brush the tops lightly with the beaten egg. Bake until golden brown, 8 to 10 minutes. Remove from the oven and let cool.

With the tip of a sharp knife, carefully remove the top of each pastry and set it aside.

In a skillet over medium heat, combine the butter and flour and cook, stirring slowly and constantly for 2 to 3 minutes, to make a blond-colored roux. Add the onion and garlic and cook, stirring, for 2 minutes. Slowly whisk in the broth and cook, whisking occasionally, until it thickens slightly, about 25 minutes.

Season the crawfish with the Creole seasoning and add to the sauce. Cook, stirring, for 2 to 3 minutes. Add the cream, Worcestershire, and hot sauce. Cook, stirring, for 1 minute, then stir in the green onions.

Spoon equal amounts of the crawfish and sauce into the center of the pastries and top with the pastry tops. Serve warm.

1 sheet (about 10 inches square) frozen puff pastry (found in the frozen foods section)
1 large egg, lightly beaten
2 tablespoons unsalted butter
2 tablespoons bleached all-purpose flour
¼ cup minced yellow onion
1 teaspoon minced garlic
2 cups chicken broth
1 pound peeled crawfish tails
½ teaspoon Creole Seasoning (page 13)
¼ cup heavy cream
1 tablespoon Worcestershire sauce
1 tablespoon hot sauce
¼ cup chopped green onions or scallions (green part only)

MAKES 4 SERVINGS

TROUT STUFFED WITH CRAWFISH DRESSING

THIS IS ANOTHER DISH THAT IS ON THE MENU AT DELMONICO WHENEVER WE CAN GET GOOD, FRESH CRAWFISH. IT'S REALLY SIMPLE, BUT WHEN YOU HAVE GOOD FRESH INGREDIENTS, THAT'S ALL YOU NEED. ■ BERNARD CARMOUCHE, ONE OF MY CHEFS, CAN'T GET ENOUGH OF THIS DISH.

2 tablespoons unsalted butter
1/2 cup chopped yellow onion
1/4 cup chopped green bell
  pepper
2 1/4 teaspoons salt
1/2 teaspoon cayenne
1 pound peeled crawfish tails
1/4 cup chopped green onions or
  scallions (green part only)
1 tablespoon chopped garlic
2 tablespoons plus 2 teaspoons
  chopped fresh parsley leaves
1 large egg
1/2 cup fine dried bread crumbs
4 whole trout (6 to 8 ounces
  each), dressed
1/4 teaspoon freshly ground black
  pepper
1 teaspoon olive oil
1 recipe Lemon Butter Sauce
  (page 83)

Preheat the oven to 400°F.

Melt the butter over medium heat in a medium-size skillet. Add the onion, bell pepper, 2 teaspoons of the salt, and the cayenne, and cook for 2 minutes, stirring a few times. Add the crawfish tails and cook, stirring, for 2 minutes. Add the green onions, garlic, and 2 tablespoons of the parsley and cook, stirring, for 1 minute.

Pour the mixture into a medium-size mixing bowl and let cool for about 2 minutes. Add the egg and bread crumbs and mix well. Set aside.

Season the flesh of the fish with the remaining 1/4 teaspoon salt and the black pepper. Stuff each fish with 1/2 cup of the dressing mixture. Rub the skin of each fish with 1/4 teaspoon of the olive oil.

Bake the fish on a baking sheet until it flakes easily with a fork, about 15 minutes. To serve, place the fish on plates and spoon the lemon sauce over it and garnish with the remaining 2 teaspoons parsley.

MAKES 4 SERVINGS

june

J UNE IS easy living down here in the South. ■ School's out and families flock to their camps or summer cottages for some fishing, crabbing, sailing, and lounging around on the piers that jut out over the water. There's no set time to do anything—eat when and what you want, take a nap under a whirring ceiling fan, float in an inner tube, lie in a hammock with a trashy novel, drink a cold beer for breakfast. ■ The landscape is a sweeping rainbow of crape myrtles, magnolias, yellow jasmine, oleanders, and hydrangeas under canopies of moss-draped live oaks. In the evenings, crickets and frogs chirp away, and fireflies dart among the fragrant gardenia bushes. Squealing children frolic in the deepening shadows until first dark, when the sun finally drops over the horizon. ■ Summer gardens, filled with tomatoes, eggplant, bell peppers, corn, okra, and squash, are at their peak. Supper, more often than not, is taken leisurely on lush patios or terraces, by the pool, or on screened-in porches. Grills and barbecue pits send whiffs of intoxicating and stimulating aromas through the night air. If the food is not from the grill, then it's cold soups, boiled crabs, or a cool salad tossed with fresh herbs from the garden. No one wants to waste a moment of the first summer days cooking indoors. It's a carefree time, when everything should be spontaneous and casual. ■ In New Orleans, vegetable stands, loaded with those famous Creole tomatoes, pop up on just about every corner, and the French Market is teeming with shoppers searching for the fixings for a leisurely supper. ■ In the northern part of the state, in Ruston, the first of the peach crop is showing up at roadside stands, and blueberry farms are filled with customers picking and filling up their baskets with

the beautiful blue-black fruit. ■ Yep, it's the good old summertime, the time for sno-balls, ice-cold watermelons, cool cucum-

bers, and refreshing cocktails, for jogging on the levee, going barefoot, taking a midnight swim in the pool, and making plans for a getaway to the beaches of nearby Mississippi, Alabama, or Florida.

crab

june

festival

IN 1977, several community groups in Bayou LaCombe, located in St. Tammany Parish north of Lake Pontchartrain, got together to organize their first crab festival. Since then, it has been a yearly event that offers a wide variety of crab specialties, including the popular soft-shell crab poorboy. ■ In the shade of the hundred-year-old oak trees in this charming rural setting, thousands of locals and visitors enjoy music, food, and a crab race, with contestants speeding their crabs on to the finish line with water guns.

HOT JALAPEÑO CRAB DIP

SWEET LUMP CRABMEAT IN A HOT DIP TO BE SCOOPED UP WITH PARTY CRACKERS OR TOASTED CROUTONS IS A MUST AT INFORMAL GATHERINGS IN THE BACKYARD OR ON THE PATIO. FELICIA SAYS THIS IS BY FAR ONE OF THE BEST SHE'S TASTED. I THINK SHE'S RIGHT!

Preheat the oven to 350°F.

Combine the crabmeat, garlic, jalapeños, Monterey Jack, Worcestershire, hot sauce, salt, and mayonnaise in a medium-size mixing bowl. Toss gently to mix. Spoon the mixture into a medium-size shallow baking dish. Sprinkle the cheese evenly on the top of the crabmeat mixture.

Bake until golden brown and bubbly, about 25 minutes. Remove from the oven and let sit for about 5 minutes before serving with the croutons.

1 pound lump crabmeat, picked over for shells and cartilage
1 teaspoon chopped garlic
1/2 cup chopped pickled jalapeños
1/4 pound Monterey Jack cheese with jalapeños, grated
1 teaspoon Worcestershire sauce
1 teaspoon hot sauce
1/2 teaspoon salt
1/2 cup Mayonnaise (page 129)
2 ounces Parmigiano-Reggiano cheese, grated
1 recipe Toasted Croutons (page 81)

MAKES 8 APPETIZER SERVINGS

MARINATED CRAB CLAWS

YOU KNOW, THERE ARE OTHER PARTS OF THE CRAB BESIDES THE LUMP CRABMEAT, BUT THEY DON'T GET AS MUCH ATTENTION. THE CRAB CLAWS CONTAIN VERY SWEET MEAT AND SOME COOKS LIKE TO THROW THEM IN THEIR POTS OF SEAFOOD GUMBO TO INTENSIFY THE FLAVOR, BUT WHAT I LIKE IS TO MARINATE THE COOKED CLAWS IN A SPICY OLIVE OIL–BASED MIXTURE FOR SEVERAL HOURS. THEN YOU CAN EITHER ARRANGE THEM ON A BED OF BUTTERHEAD LETTUCE OR PASS THEM AROUND FOR APPETIZERS AT A MORE INFORMAL GATHERING. BE SURE TO ACCOMPANY THEM WITH TOASTED CROUTONS TO SOP UP THE MARINADE.

1/2 cup extra-virgin olive oil
3 tablespoons fresh lemon juice
1 teaspoon Dijon mustard
1/4 cup assorted chopped fresh
  herb leaves, such as parsley,
  basil, and tarragon
1/2 teaspoon chopped garlic
1 teaspoon salt
1/4 teaspoon freshly ground black
  pepper
1/2 teaspoon sugar
1/2 cup small-diced red onion
1/2 cup small-diced Roma
  tomatoes
1 cup drained and thinly sliced
  canned artichoke hearts
  packed in water
16 Kalamata olives, pitted and
  halved
1 pound cooked crab claws
1 recipe Toasted Croutons
  (page 81)

Combine all of the ingredients except the croutons in a large mixing bowl. Toss to mix. Cover and chill for at least 4 hours before serving with the croutons.

MAKES 8 TO 10 APPETIZER SERVINGS

father's day

ON MOTHER'S Day, mothers get taken out for dinner, but on Father's Day, the men like to drag out their barbecue pits or big black cast-iron pots. At least that's what goes on here, because that's what Louisiana men like to do—cook. It's not unusual for a gentleman to have a separate kitchen, sometimes housed in a building set apart from the main house. There he is king of his domain, where he can putter to his heart's desire. There no one will tell him how to cook, what to cook, or how much to cook. He is the master, who thinks nothing of boiling hundreds of pounds of crawfish, stirring up a gumbo for fifty, or barbecuing twenty-five chickens for his friends and family. ■ Here's to my father, Mr. John, and all the fathers of Louisiana who are generous to a fault!

Notes on Roasted Pig

PORK IS VERY POPULAR in the rural communities of Louisiana simply because a great number of pigs are raised on farms throughout the area. A farmer may send most of his hogs to market, but he usually keeps one or two for personal consumption. Some families choose to roast their pig for Easter or Thanksgiving, while others may keep it for an occasion such as Father's Day. ■ *Cochon de lait* (koe-shon do lay) is the French term meaning suckling pig, and it once referred to a special springtime ritual of cooking the pig and serving it on Easter Sunday. The pig is slow-cooked, sometimes taking as much as twelve to eighteen hours over an open fire. (This is not to be confused with a *boucherie,* at which a whole hog is slaughtered and butchered and the entire day is spent making sausages, hogshead cheese, and *grattons* (fried pork skins) and preparing meats for pickling, smoking, and otherwise preserving the meat. Fresh cuts are taken home to cook immediately.) Sometimes the pig is put on a large spit that fits over a large barbecue pit and family members take turns during the night, feeding the fire and brushing the pig with a basting sauce. ■ A more popular method is to roast the pig in what is called a Cajun microwave. This huge smoker is a wooden boxlike affair, about 6 feet long, 3 to 4 feet wide, and about 20 inches deep, and sometimes, but not always, mounted on four legs. The inside can be lined with metal, but some cooks claim that the metal can produce too much heat and make it difficult to roast the pig at an even temperature. A wood-framed metal lid sits on top to hold the charcoal. ■ The pig can be injected with the same marinade that is used for the fried turkey featured on page 288. The pig is coated with a dry rub prior to roasting and the basting sauce is the same as the marinade. ■ I like to season the pig and store it in a large bag overnight before putting it on the pit or in a large oven, which we often do at Emeril's Restaurant.

CRUNCHY SLAW

DID YOU KNOW THAT *COLESLAW* COMES FROM THE DUTCH *KOOLSLA*, MEANING "COOL CABBAGE"? AND HERE I THOUGHT IT WAS A SOUTHERN THING, SINCE I SEE IT A LOT AT BARBECUES, FISH FRIES, AND OTHER SUCH OCCASIONS DOWN HERE. I'VE SEEN COLESLAWS MADE WITH A VARIETY OF INGREDIENTS, SOME TOSSED WITH A VINAIGRETTE AND OTHERS WITH A MAYONNAISE-BASED DRESSING. I'VE HAD SOME GOOD ONES AND SOME BAD, BUT THIS ONE IS SENSATIONAL. IT'S VIETNAMESE-INSPIRED AND I THINK IT'S GREAT TO SERVE WITH PORK. ■ OH, AND I GUESS IT'S BEST TO TELL YOU EITHER TO FIND A VERY LARGE SALAD BOWL IN WHICH TO TOSS IT, OR DO IT IN BATCHES—IT MAKES A LOT.

3 tablespoons olive oil
2 cups unsalted roasted peanuts
1 cup rice wine vinegar
1/2 cup sesame oil
1/4 cup honey
4 teaspoons salt
1 teaspoon freshly ground black
  pepper
1 large head white cabbage
  (about 3 1/2 pounds), cored
  and shredded
1 head red cabbage (about 1 1/2
  pounds), cored and shredded
2 cups sliced red onions
1 cup chopped green onions or
  scallions (green part only)
1 cup loosely packed fresh
  cilantro leaves
1/2 teaspoon cayenne

MAKES ABOUT 20 SERVINGS

In a large, heavy skillet, heat the olive oil over medium heat. Add the peanuts and, stirring often, toast them for 5 minutes. Remove from the heat and set aside.

In a medium-size mixing bowl, combine the vinegar, sesame oil, honey, 1 teaspoon of the salt, and 1/2 teaspoon of the black pepper.

Put the cabbage, red onions, green onions, and cilantro in a very large mixing bowl and season with the remaining 1 tablespoon salt, remaining 1/2 teaspoon black pepper, and the cayenne. Add the dressing mixture and toss to mix well and evenly. Store in large storage bags and refrigerate for at least 4 hours before serving. Keeps 1 day before getting soggy.

FRIED SWEET POTATOES

BECAUSE A LOT OF SWEET POTATOES ARE GROWN IN THE STATE, IN AN AREA AROUND OPELOUSAS IN SOUTH LOUISIANA, YOU'LL FIND SWEET POTATOES AT JUST ABOUT EVERY FESTIVE MEAL. SOMETIMES THEY'RE SERVED MASHED WITH BUTTER, OR IN CASSEROLES, AND SOMETIMES THEY'RE FRIED, LIKE THESE, AND SPRINKLED WITH SUGAR AND CINNAMON. THE SWEET TASTE IS GREAT WITH SALTY PORK. ■ IN LOUISIANA, WHEN WE HAVE LARGE PARTIES AND HAVE TO COOK FOR A CROWD, IT'S SOMETIMES EASIER TO DRAIN FRIED FOODS ON BIG BROWN GROCERY BAGS. I SUGGEST PUTTING ONE BAG INSIDE ANOTHER SO THAT THEY'RE MORE ABSORBENT, THEN SPREADING THEM OUT ON A LARGE TABLE NEAR YOUR FRYING STATION. WORKS LIKE A CHARM!

Combine the sugar and cinnamon in a small bowl and mix well. Set aside.

Heat the vegetable oil in a very large, heavy, deep pot or an electric deep-fryer to 360°F.

Fry the sweet potatoes, in batches, until golden, about 8 minutes. Drain on paper bags or on paper towels, sprinkle with the cinnamon sugar and serve hot.

1/2 cup sugar

2 teaspoons ground cinnamon

8 cups vegetable oil

5 pounds sweet potatoes, peeled and cut crosswise into 1/8-inch-thick slices

MAKES ABOUT 20 SERVINGS

ANGEL FOOD CAKE WITH MARINATED PEACHES

NO MAN I KNOW DISLIKES A SPONGY ANGEL FOOD CAKE, AND THIS ONE SERVED WITH PEACHES FROM RUSTON, LOUISIANA, IN SEASON DURING THE SUMMER MONTHS, WILL CERTAINLY BE A WINNER WITH FATHERS ON THEIR SPECIAL DAY!

2¹/₂ pounds fresh, ripe peaches, pitted and cut into ¹/₄-inch-thick slices

2 cups sugar

¹/₄ cup peach liqueur

¹/₄ cup dark rum

10 large egg whites, at room temperature

1 teaspoon cream of tartar

¹/₄ teaspoon salt

1 teaspoon pure vanilla extract

1 cup bleached all-purpose flour, sifted

¹/₈ teaspoon ground cinnamon

2 cups Sweetened Whipped Cream (page 49)

12 fresh mint sprigs

Preheat the oven to 375°F.

In a large bowl, combine the peach slices with 1 cup of the sugar, the peach liqueur, and the rum. Stir to mix. Cover and refrigerate for at least 1 hour. (This can be done a day ahead.)

Using an electric mixer fitted with a wire whip, beat the egg whites on medium speed with the cream of tartar and the salt until soft peaks form, about 2 minutes. Add the remaining cup sugar and the vanilla and beat until stiff peaks form, about 1 minute. Add the flour and the cinnamon and beat for 2 minutes, scraping down the sides of the bowl as needed. Pour the batter into an ungreased angel food cake pan. Bake until golden brown and springy when touched, 30 to 35 minutes. (The top of the cake may crack a little.) Remove the pan from the oven and turn it upside down over the neck of a bottle. Let cool completely.

Remove the cake from the pan and slice into 12 equal pieces. To serve, place the slices of cake on dessert plates, spoon some of the peaches over, and garnish with whipped cream and a sprig of mint.

MAKES 1 CAKE TO SERVE 12

french market
tomato
june
festival

THE GREAT French Market Tomato Festival began in 1986, with the idea of celebrating a local product, the Creole tomato. Initially, the French Market Corporation auctioned off the first Creole tomatoes grown in Louisiana within the Farmers' Market in the French Quarter to kick off the festival. Now the French Market kicks it off with a Battle of the Bands, a concert performed the last Friday in May, and the festival is held each year on the first Sunday in June. ■ The Creole tomato is locally grown in the rich Mississippi Delta soil, where the favorable weather conditions produce the Creole tomato's characteristic flavor. ■ Those Creole babies rule! You will never taste anything better than thickly sliced Creoles sprinkled with just a bit of salt and freshly cracked black pepper and drizzled with good olive oil; or try dabbing them with a lemony mayonnaise. Even better, enjoy them slightly chilled and topped with a cold crab or shrimp salad. Or, thick slices can be lightly grilled and plopped on a thick, juicy hamburger!

CREOLE TOMATO SALSA

WHEN THE CREOLE BABIES SHOW UP AT THE MARKETS, ROADSIDE STANDS, AND GROCERY STORES, THERE'S A MAD DASH TO GET A CASE OR TWO TO BRING HOME. THESE TOMATOES ARE SOME OF THE BEST THAT HAVE PASSED MY LIPS AND ARE SUPER IN A SALSA. MAKE A BATCH, SERVE IT WITH HOMEMADE TORTILLA CHIPS, AND YOU'LL BE SURPRISED HOW QUICKLY IT'S ALL GONE. BETTER YET, MAKE A COUPLE OF BATCHES.

Combine all of the ingredients except the chips in a large bowl and mix well. Cover and chill for at least 2 hours before serving with the chips.

4 cups chopped vine-ripened
    tomatoes
1 cup small-diced red onions
1 large fresh jalapeño, seeded
    and cut into small dice
1/2 cup loosely packed chopped
    fresh cilantro leaves
1 tablespoon chopped fresh
    parsley leaves
1 tablespoon chopped garlic
1 1/2 teaspoons salt
1/4 teaspoon freshly ground black
    pepper
1 teaspoon Worcestershire sauce
1 teaspoon hot sauce
6 tablespoons fresh lime juice
1 tablespoon extra-virgin olive oil
1 recipe Tortilla Chips
    (recipe follows)

MAKES ABOUT 5 CUPS

Tortilla Chips

Ten 6-inch corn tortillas
4 cups vegetable oil
½ teaspoon salt

Cut each tortilla into 8 triangles.

In a large, heavy, deep pot or an electric deep-fryer, heat the vegetable oil to 360°F. Deep-fry the tortilla chips, in batches, until lightly golden and crispy, 3 to 4 minutes. Drain on paper towels and season with the salt. Eat immediately!

MAKES 80 CHIPS

WARM PIMIENTO CHEESE-STUFFED TOMATOES

FELICIA INSISTED WE USE THIS RECIPE IN THIS CHAPTER. HER STEPMOM BRENDA HESTER HAS MADE THESE ON VISITS TO FLORIDA FOR SUMMER VACATION SINCE SHE WAS A CHILD. ALONG THE WAY, THEY STOPPED TO PICK UP VINE-RIPENED TOMATOES IN MISSISSIPPI AND ALABAMA. ONCE THEY ARRIVED AT THEIR DESTINATION, BRENDA IMMEDIATELY MADE A BATCH OF PIMIENTO CHEESE. THE CHEESE IS SPOONED ONTO THE QUARTERED TOMATOES, THEN BAKED. ■ IF YOUR TASTES LEAN TO RICH, HERE YOU GO! ■ OH, YOU HAVE TO GRATE THE CHEESE YOUR-SELF—NONE OF THAT PREGRATED STUFF WILL WORK.

½ pound sharp cheddar cheese, grated
½ pound Monterey Jack cheese, grated
3 tablespoons chopped pimientos
½ cup Mayonnaise (page 129)
1 teaspoon hot sauce
½ teaspoon salt
½ teaspoon freshly ground black pepper
4 large vine-ripened tomatoes (about 2 pounds), cored and quartered to the base (don't cut all the way through!)
1 recipe Toasted Croutons (page 81)

In a medium-size mixing bowl, combine the cheeses, pimientos, mayonnaise, hot sauce, ¼ teaspoon of the salt, and ¼ teaspoon of the black pepper. Mix well. Cover and refrigerate for 1 hour.

Preheat the oven to 400°F. Line a baking sheet with parchment paper.

Sprinkle the tomatoes with the remaining ¼ tea-spoon each salt and pepper. Spoon ½ cup of the cheese mixture into the center of each tomato. Put on the pre-pared baking sheet and bake until the cheese melts, about 6 minutes. Remove from the oven.

Place the tomatoes in the center of serving plates and serve warm with the croutons.

MAKES 4 SERVINGS

CHUNKY GARDEN GAZPACHO

GAZPACHO, A COLD TOMATO-BASED SOUP, ORIGINATED IN THE ANDALUSIA REGION OF SOUTHERN SPAIN. CREOLE TOMATOES GIVE IT AN EXTRA ZIP AND SOMETIMES I ADD BOILED SHRIMP OR CHUNKS OF COOKED LOBSTER TO IT WHEN SERVING. ■ MARCELLE TELLS ME THAT SHE SERVES THE SOUP OFTEN DURING THE SUMMER IN BIG WINE GLASSES AND SPLASHES IN VODKA RIGHT BEFORE SHE BRINGS IT OUT— A KIND OF BLOODY MARY SOUP, IF YOU WILL. ■ GAZPACHO WILL KEEP IN THE REFRIGERATOR FOR AS LONG AS A WEEK.

One 46-ounce can tomato juice
4 cups chopped vine-ripened
    tomatoes
2 cups chopped yellow onions
2 cups chopped celery
2 tablespoons chopped garlic
2 cups chopped assorted green,
    red, and yellow bell peppers
2 cups peeled, seeded, and
    chopped cucumbers
1/4 cup loosely packed chopped
    fresh cilantro leaves
2 tablespoons chopped fresh
    parsley leaves
1/2 cup chopped scallions
    (green part only)
2 tablespoons prepared
    horseradish
2 tablespoons Worcestershire
    sauce
2 teaspoons hot sauce
1/4 cup fresh lime juice
2 tablespoons fresh lemon juice
1 teaspoon salt
1/4 teaspoon freshly ground
    black pepper

Combine all of the ingredients in a large mixing bowl and stir to mix well. Chill for at least 6 hours before serving.

MAKES ABOUT 14 SERVINGS

July

THE LONG, lazy sun-drenched days of July are meant for seafood boils, softball games, moonlight sails, wiener roasts, and sipping long tall drinks while lounging by the pool. ■ It's also the month for figs. Fig trees grow well in Louisiana—mostly in backyards. Picked right off the tree, the figs are a real treat. Plunked in fresh, sweet cream, they're heavenly, or in homemade fig and Grand Marnier ice cream! ■ Because the fig season is short, most of the fruit is made into fig preserves, and that is downright fabulous on homemade biscuits, corn bread, or French toast. ■ If hot and humid days don't bother you, July is also a great time for long-weekend getaways. Visit the gardens of Avery Island or Jefferson Island in the south central part of the state. Take in the Pecan Ridge Bluegrass Festival in Jackson, north of Baton Rouge. Pack up your fishing gear and head out to Grand Isle on the Gulf of Mexico for the International Grand Isle Tarpon Rodeo. Visit the Folklife Festival in Natchitoches. Or maybe a relaxed weekend at any of the bed-and-breakfast inns or plantation homes across the state is more your style. ■ But perhaps the most outstanding event of the month is what is billed as "Coca-Cola Presents the *Essence* Music Festival." Initially held in celebration of the twenty-fifth anniversary of *Essence* magazine, the event has gained a title sponsor and consistently sets a new attendance record each year. Crowd size has increased from 142,000 in 1995 to 171,000 in 1998. Entertainment has included Grammy sensations such as Lauryn Hill, Patti LaBelle, Monica with Brian McKnight, the Temptations, and many others. The Superdome rocks! Visitors can find blues, classic soul, jazz, zydeco, and even brass bands. You want it, they have it! In

addition, there are empowerment seminars that feature popular authors, lecturers, and business, religious, social, and political leaders.

■ The month of July is also a time for the great getaway for thousands of natives, who flock to the beaches of Mississippi, Alabama, and Florida for a long week or two in condominiums or beach houses. The story goes that so many

july

Louisianians leave the state during the summer, they wonder who's taking care of things back home. Large groups of extended families have been known to stake out whole sections of the beaches so they can spend the day, from sunrise to sundown, enjoying the sand and sun, playing volleyball, building sand castles, and munching on an endless feast of fried shrimp, hamburgers, potato salad, hot dogs, chicken salad, ice cream sandwiches, and whatever else can be purchased at the refreshment stands. When the sun finally sets, the weary beach bums are eager to cool down under ceiling fans on broad verandahs overlooking the Gulf, or settle in with a good book in their air-conditioned bedrooms. ■ Even Emeril's and NOLA close down for two weeks so the staffs can get out of town. Some opt for lazy days tubing or canoeing on the rivers of nearby Mississippi, others head home, wherever it may be, to see their folks. ■ But if you're a homebody, plan a backyard party for the Fourth of July and enjoy.

july

fourth

of july

SMACK DAB in the middle of summer is the Fourth of July, the quintessential American holiday that commemorates the nation's Day of Independence. ■ Out in the country, celebrations are likely to be informal family gatherings in the backyard featuring a barbecue or hot dogs and hamburgers, potato salad, brownies, and cakes. Others might take to the water for an all-day sail around the bay, with a late-afternoon picnic in the harbor while watching a fireworks display. It's so hot, a pool-side party is a possibility, with water volleyball games and watermelon-eating contests. ■ City folks who live in high-rise apartment buildings often party at the penthouse—as my guests and I did at a recent July Fourth bash—with a panoramic view of downtown New Orleans and the ideal spot from which to chow down on barbecue ribs and all the trimmings and watch the fireworks in the French Quarter soon after dusk.

CLAMBAKE

I KNOW, I KNOW, THERE ARE NO CLAMBAKES IN LOUISIANA, BUT WHEN I LIVED UP IN THE NORTHEAST, WE HAD 'EM OFTEN AND ESPECIALLY FOR JULY 4 SHINDIGS, MUCH LIKE THEY HAVE CRAW-FISH AND CRAB BOILS HERE. I JUST HAD TO INCLUDE ONE IN THIS MENU. (YOU CAN SUBSTITUTE CRABS OR SHRIMP OR MUSSELS.) ■ AROUND HERE, JUST ABOUT EVERY SERIOUS COOK HAS A BOILING "RIG" COMPOSED OF A LARGE BOILING POT THAT SITS ON A BUTANE BURNER. THESE RIGS MUST BE USED ONLY OUTDOORS.

Fill a 4-gallon stockpot fitted with a strainer insert two-thirds full with water. Add the crab boil, onions, and garlic. Season the water with the salt and black pepper. Add the sweet corn and potatoes. Bring to a boil, then reduce the heat to a simmer. Add the hot dogs and sausage, and cook, covered, until the potatoes are almost fork-tender, about 8 minutes. Add the clams, cover, and cook until the shells pop open, about 5 minutes. Discard any clams that do not open.

Remove the strainer insert from the pot and drain the boil. Serve the clam boil on paper bags or newspapers. Pass the melted butter and bread.

1 tablespoon liquid Zatarain's Concentrated Crab & Shrimp Boil

4 medium-size yellow onions, quartered

3 heads garlic, halved

1 tablespoon salt

$1/2$ teaspoon freshly ground black pepper

4 ears fresh sweet corn, husked, cleaned, and cut into thirds

$1^{1}/2$ pounds new potatoes

$1/2$ pound all-beef hot dogs

1 pound andouille or other smoked sausage, cut into 2-inch lengths

4 quarts steamer clams, scrubbed

$1/2$ pound (2 sticks) unsalted butter, melted

1 loaf crusty French bread

MAKES 4 TO 6 SERVINGS

DUO BBQ RIBS

FOR ME, THERE'S SOMETHING THERAPEUTIC ABOUT BARBECUING. I LIKE THE WHOLE EXERCISE OF MARINATING THE MEAT, PREPARING THE FIRE, HANGING AROUND THE SMOKING PIT WHILE SIPPING ON SOME SUDS, AND, OF COURSE, ENJOYING THE RESULT. SINCE I LIKE A VERY INTENSE FLAVOR, I MARINATE THE RIBS FOR SEVERAL HOURS, OR EVEN OVERNIGHT, BEFORE SLAPPING THEM ON THE PIT. ■ NOW, FOR A QUICK REVIEW OF THE TYPES OF PORK RIBS AVAILABLE OUT THERE: ■ *BACK RIBS*, ALSO CALLED BABY BACK RIBS, ARE CUT FROM THE PORK LOIN. THEY'RE REALLY NO BETTER THAN SPARERIBS AS FAR AS FLAVOR AND TENDERNESS, BUT THEY'RE ALWAYS MORE EXPENSIVE, SINCE EVERY PIG THAT COMES TO THE MARKET SUPPLIES ONLY ONE SLAB OF BACK RIBS FOR EVERY TWO SLABS OF SPARERIBS. ■ *SPARERIBS* ARE THE MOST COMMON AND LEAST EXPENSIVE. THEY VARY ACCORDING TO THE SIZE OF THE PIG FROM WHICH THEY ARE CUT. ASK YOUR BUTCHER FOR "THREE AND UNDER," WHICH MEANS THE SLAB SHOULD WEIGH NO MORE THAN 3 POUNDS.■ *ST. LOUIS-STYLE RIBS* ARE THE RIBS FROM THE BREASTBONE OR "BRISKET BONE." ALL THE RAGGED EDGES ARE TRIMMED, LEAVING A UNIFORM SLAB OF RIB BONES WITH MEAT IN BETWEEN. THEY ARE AS TENDER AND MEATY AS BACK RIBS, BUT LESS EXPENSIVE. ■ *COUNTRY-STYLE RIBS* COME FROM THE BLADE LOIN END. THEY HAVE MORE MEAT ON THEM AND ARE POPULAR IN THE SOUTH.■ YOU WILL HAVE TO PLAY AROUND WITH THE DIFFERENT KINDS OF RIBS TO FIND WHICH ONES SUIT YOUR TASTE. THINK HOW MUCH FUN THAT CAN BE! OH, I SUGGEST YOU USE GOOD CHARRED HARDWOOD OR LUMP CHARCOAL RATHER THAN ORDINARY BRIQUETTES. IT BURNS CLEANER AND HOTTER AND GIVES OFF A GREAT AROMA. AND REMEMBER, FOOD COOKS MORE EVENLY WHEN THE LID OF THE BARBECUE IS CLOSED.

One 3-pound slab country-style
     pork ribs
One 3½-pound slab pork
     spareribs
2 teaspoons salt
2 cups Steen's 100% Pure Cane
     Syrup or other cane syrup
¼ cup soy sauce
¼ cup apple cider vinegar
½ cup water
2 tablespoons sesame oil
¼ cup minced yellow onion
2 tablespoons chopped garlic
2 tablespoons peeled and grated
     fresh ginger
½ teaspoon cayenne
¼ teaspoon freshly ground black
     pepper

Put the ribs in a very large soup pot or kettle. Add the salt and enough water to cover them. Bring to a boil and let boil for 30 minutes. Remove from the heat and drain.

Whisk the remaining ingredients together in a medium-size mixing bowl, blending well. Put the ribs in a large, deep braising pan or plastic container and pour the marinade over them. Cover and refrigerate for 8 to 12 hours, turning the ribs in the marinade about every 4 hours.

Prepare the pit or grill. You should have a glowing red fire with light ash, and the temperature of the pit or grill should be between 225° and 275°F.

Put the ribs on the pit away from the fire. Cook, basting with the marinade and turning the ribs every 15 minutes, for about 2 hours. You may have to feed the fire every 30 minutes or so.

Remove the ribs from the pit and let cool for several minutes before slicing to serve.

MAKES ABOUT 6 SERVINGS

BARBECUE BEANS

I SUPPOSE EVERYONE HAS HEARD OF BOSTON BAKED BEANS, BUT AS FAR AS I CAN RECALL, I NEVER SAW ANYBODY UP THERE COOKING BEANS FROM SCRATCH; THE BEANS ALWAYS CAME IN A CAN, ALREADY COOKED. FOR MY FOURTH OF JULY PARTY, I DECIDED IT WAS TIME TO MAKE MY OWN BEANS. I STARTED OFF WITH NAVY BEANS (ALSO CALLED WHITE PEA BEANS), WHICH ARE ABOUT AS BLAND A BEAN AS THERE IS. THEN I ADDED ALL THE STUFF THAT I THOUGHT MAKES BAKED BEANS TASTE GOOD—BITS OF BACON, ONIONS, BROWN SUGAR AND CANE SYRUP, MUSTARD, KETCHUP, AND SOME SPICES—AND COOKED IT ALL LONG AND SLOW, UNTIL THE BEANS WERE SOFT AND TENDER. MAN, WERE THEY GOOD AND, YOU KNOW, I NEVER PUT THEM IN THE OVEN. SO MUCH FOR "BAKED" BEANS. MAKE THEM A DAY AHEAD, AND THE FLAVOR WILL BE OUT OF THIS WORLD!

In a large pot over medium heat, fry the bacon until crispy, 8 to 10 minutes. Add the onions, jalapeño, and black pepper and cook, stirring, until the onions are soft, 3 to 4 minutes. Add the garlic and beans and cook for 1 minute. Add the cane syrup, brown sugar, ketchup, and mustard and mix well. Stir in the broth, add the bay leaves, and bring to a boil, then reduce the heat to medium-low. Cook, uncovered, until the beans are tender, about 4 hours, stirring occasionally. Remove the bay leaves before serving.

1 pound sliced bacon, chopped
2 cups chopped yellow onions
1 medium-size fresh jalapeño, seeded and chopped
1/2 teaspoon freshly ground black pepper
2 teaspoons chopped garlic
1 pound dried navy (white) beans, picked over and rinsed
1/2 cup Steen's 100% Pure Cane Syrup or other cane syrup
1/2 cup firmly packed light brown sugar
2 cups ketchup
1/4 cup yellow mustard
9 cups chicken broth
2 bay leaves

MAKES ABOUT 8 SERVINGS

LOUISIANA GARLIC BREAD

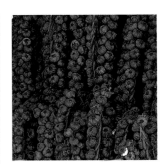

THERE AREN'T MANY MEALS SERVED IN LOUISIANA THAT DON'T INCLUDE FRENCH BREAD. ALTHOUGH IT'S USUALLY EATEN WARM AND TOASTY FROM THE OVEN AND SPREAD WITH BUTTER, THE LOCALS ALSO PUT AWAY A LOT OF GARLIC BREAD. YOU TAKE A REGULAR LOAF OF FRENCH BREAD, CUT IT IN HALF LENGTHWISE, LATHER IT WITH A GARLIC-BUTTER MIXTURE, AND THEN WARM IT IN THE OVEN OR ON THE OLD BARBECUE PIT. THERE HAVE BEEN TIMES I'VE DEVOURED A WHOLE LOAF BY MYSELF WHILE BARBECUING.

¼ pound (1 stick) unsalted butter, at room temperature
2 teaspoons chopped garlic
2 tablespoons fresh lemon juice
2 tablespoons chopped fresh parsley leaves
1 teaspoon freshly ground black pepper
1 large loaf French bread, split lengthwise in half

Combine the butter, garlic, lemon juice, parsley, and black pepper in a small mixing bowl. Stir to blend well. Spread both halves of the bread with the mixture. Put the halves together, wrap in a sheet of aluminum foil, and place on the barbecue pit or in an oven at 350°F to heat.

MAKES 1 LARGE LOAF; 6 TO 8 SERVINGS

SCALLOPED POTATOES

SCALLOPED POTATOES USUALLY APPEAR AT CASUAL OUTDOOR PARTIES, ESPECIALLY AT BARBECUES. THEY'RE PRETTY SIMPLE, SINCE ALL YOU DO IS LAYER SLICES OF POTATOES WITH BUTTER, FLOUR, CHEESE, AND MILK, THEN BAKE IN THE OVEN. HERE IS A VERSION THAT MARCELLE'S MAMA TAUGHT HER. THE TRICK IS TO BAKE IT AT THE LAST MINUTE AND BRING IT TO THE TABLE PIPING HOT!

Preheat the oven to 350°F. Grease a 2-quart baking dish with 1 teaspoon of the butter.

Put the potatoes in a large mixing bowl and add the salt and white pepper. Toss to season evenly. Arrange a layer of potatoes on the bottom of the prepared baking dish and sprinkle with 2 teaspoons of the flour. Dot with a tablespoon of the remaining butter, then sprinkle with ½ cup of each of the cheeses. Repeat the process until all the potatoes, butter, flour, and cheeses are used, ending with the cheeses. Pour in the milk.

Bake until golden brown and bubbly, about 1 hour. Remove from the oven and serve hot.

1 teaspoon plus ¼ cup (½ stick) unsalted butter

2½ pounds red potatoes, peeled and sliced ¼ inch thick

1½ teaspoons salt

1 teaspoon freshly ground white pepper

2 tablespoons plus 2 teaspoons bleached all-purpose flour

½ pound sharp cheddar cheese, grated

½ pound Monterey Jack cheese, grated

2 cups milk

MAKES ABOUT 8 SERVINGS

SHREDDED PORK FLAUTAS WITH CORN AND GOAT QUESO

A *FLAUTA* IS A CORN TORTILLA ROLLED UP AROUND SHREDDED MEAT, THEN FRIED UNTIL CRISP. OKAY, SO IT'S NOT A NATIVE DISH. BUT I LIKE THEM AND IT'S MY PARTY AND I'LL DO WHAT I WANT TO.

3½ pounds pork shoulder, trimmed of fat
¾ teaspoon salt
½ teaspoon freshly ground black pepper
1 teaspoon olive oil
½ cup chopped yellow onion
½ cup chopped and seeded vine-ripened tomato
1 teaspoon chopped garlic
½ cup beef broth
2 ripe Hass avocados, peeled, pitted, and diced
2 tablespoons fresh lime juice
8 cups vegetable oil
16 small flour tortillas
1 recipe Corn and Goat Queso (recipe follows)
1 recipe Creole Tomato Salsa (page 184)

Preheat the oven to 400°F.

Season the pork with ½ teaspoon of the salt and the black pepper. Put it in a shallow roasting pan and roast for 1½ hours. Reduce the oven temperature to 350°F and roast until very tender, about another 2½ hours. Remove from the oven and let cool. Remove the fat, then shred.

In a large nonstick skillet, heat the olive oil over medium heat. Add the onion and cook, stirring, for 3 minutes. Add the tomato, garlic, and beef broth and cook for 3 minutes. Add the pork and cook for 2 minutes. Remove from the heat and let cool for about 5 minutes.

In a small mixing bowl, toss the avocados with the lime juice and the remaining ¼ teaspoon salt.

In a large, heavy pot or an electric deep-fryer, heat the vegetable oil to 360°F.

To assemble the flautas, spoon about 2 tablespoons of the filling into the center of each tortilla. Roll up tightly and secure with 2 toothpicks. Fry the filled tortillas, 4 at a time, in the hot oil until golden brown, 2 to 3 minutes. Drain on paper towels.

To serve, spoon the queso over the bottom on a large serving platter. Arrange the flautas over the sauce, spoon the salsa over the flautas, and garnish with the avocados.

MAKES 8 SERVINGS

continued

Corn and Goat Queso

In a medium-size saucepan over medium heat, melt the butter. Add the onion, corn, salt, and cayenne and cook, stirring, for 6 minutes. Add the garlic and jalapeño, stir to mix, and cook for 2 minutes. Add the cheese and cream and stir until the cheese melts completely. Keep warm until ready to serve.

2 tablespoons unsalted butter
1/2 cup chopped yellow onion
2 cups fresh sweet corn kernels
   (from 2 medium-size ears)
1 teaspoon salt
1/2 teaspoon cayenne
1 tablespoon chopped garlic
1 medium-size fresh jalapeño,
   seeded and chopped
1/2 pound goat cheese, crumbled
1/2 cup heavy cream

MAKES ABOUT 2 1/2 CUPS

PEANUT BUTTER AND CHOCOLATE PRALINE ICE CREAM SANDWICHES

SINCE THE FOURTH OF JULY IS SUCH A GLORIOUS CELEBRATION OF THE BIRTHDAY OF OUR NATION, I THINK IT CALLS FOR ONE HECK OF A DESSERT, LIKE THIS ONE. I GUARANTEE THAT CHILDREN OF ALL AGES WILL LOVE THESE ICE CREAM SANDWICHES.

1/2 teaspoon plus 1/2 pound (2 sticks) unsalted butter, at room temperature

1/2 teaspoon plus 11/2 cups bleached all-purpose flour

11/4 cups sugar

4 large eggs

1 teaspoon pure vanilla extract

1/2 cup unsweetened cocoa powder

1 teaspoon baking powder

Pinch of salt

1 recipe Vanilla-Praline Ice Cream (recipe follows)

Peanut Butter and Chocolate Pralines (recipe follows)

Preheat the oven to 350°F. Butter and flour a 9 × 5 × 3-inch loaf pan with 1/2 teaspoon of the butter and 1/2 teaspoon of the flour

In a large mixing bowl, cream the remaining 1/2 pound (2 sticks) butter and the sugar together with an electric mixer until smooth. Add the eggs one at a time, beating after each addition. Beat in the vanilla.

Into a medium-size mixing bowl, sift the remaining 11/2 cups flour, the cocoa, baking powder, and salt together. Add one third of the flour mixture at a time to the butter-and-sugar mixture, beating after each addition. Spoon the batter into the prepared pan and bake until it springs back when touched, about 50 minutes. Remove from the oven and let cool in the pan on a wire rack for 10 minutes, then remove it from the pan and let cool completely on the rack.

After the ice cream is firm, remove it from the pan. Cut the ice cream into 16 slices. Place one slice of ice cream between two slices of pound cake, forming a sandwich. Repeat the process until all of the cake is used. Wrap each sandwich in plastic wrap and freeze until ready to serve.

To serve, unwrap the sandwiches and serve each with a praline on the side.

MAKES 8 SANDWICHES

Vanilla-Praline Ice Cream

2 cups milk
2 cups heavy cream
1 cup sugar
1 vanilla bean, split and scraped
6 large egg yolks
8 Peanut Butter and Chocolate Pralines (recipe follows), crumbled

In a medium-size nonreactive saucepan over medium heat, combine the milk, cream, sugar, and vanilla bean and pulp. Whisk to dissolve as the mixture heats. Heat the mixture to the scalding point (when bubbles form around the edges of the pan); do not let it boil. Remove from the heat.

Beat the egg yolks in a large mixing bowl. Add the hot cream mixture about ¼ cup at a time to the beaten yolks, whisking well after each addition. Pour the mixture back into the saucepan and cook, stirring, over medium heat until the mixture becomes thick enough to lightly coat the back of a spoon, 2 to 3 minutes; do not let it boil.

Remove from the heat and strain through a fine-mesh strainer into a glass bowl. Cover the top of the mixture with plastic wrap (this will keep a skin from forming) and let cool. Place the mixture in the refrigerator and chill completely.

Pour the mixture into an ice cream machine and follow the manufacturer's instructions for the churning time. Once the ice cream is almost ready, about 5 minutes before the churning time is complete, add the crumbled pralines through the ingredients spout. Continue to churn until the ice cream freezes.

Line an 8½ × 4½ × 2½-inch loaf pan with plastic wrap. Scoop the ice cream into the pan, smooth the top, cover, and freeze until firm, about 4 hours.

When ready to assemble the ice cream sandwiches, lift the ice cream out with the plastic wrap.

MAKES ABOUT 1 QUART

Peanut Butter and Chocolate Pralines

1 pound light brown sugar
(about 3 firmly packed cups)
3/4 cup evaporated milk
1/8 teaspoon salt
1 tablespoon unsalted butter
3 tablespoons creamy peanut
butter
2 teaspoons unsweetened cocoa
powder
2 cups pecan pieces

Combine the brown sugar, milk, salt, butter, peanut butter, and cocoa in a large saucepan over medium-high heat. Stir to dissolve as the mixture heats. Continue to cook, stirring, until the mixture begins to bubble around the edges of the pan and reaches 234° to 240°F on a candy thermometer, or the soft ball stage (that is, when a bit of the mixture is dropped into cold water, it forms a soft ball that flattens), about 12 minutes.

Remove from the heat and stir in the pecans. Drop the mixture by the tablespoonful onto waxed or parchment paper on a baking sheet and let cool completely. Lift the pralines off the paper with a thin knife.

Pralines can be stored in an airtight container at room temperature for up to 2 weeks.

MAKES ABOUT 1 1/2 DOZEN PRALINES

august

AUGUST IN New Orleans is sizzling-hot! Why, it's hot enough to fry an egg on the sidewalk, and the air is as thick and wet as a gumbo, and almost suffocating. Late-afternoon thunder showers that rumble in from the Gulf of Mexico sometimes offer a respite from the heat, making life bearable for an hour or two before dusk. These are the dog days of summer, and there's nothing to do but endure them. ■ Life moves more slowly, if that's possible, and cooking is best done early in the day or late in the evening. Entertaining is very informal, and the days are planned not by the clock, but rather by the position of the sun. ■ The old ice cream machines drone on in the afternoons, and pitchers of lemonade or ice tea flavored with fresh mint leaves from the garden are refreshing after a long, hot day. ■ The night air is

heavy, and stargazing is possibly the only recreation that can be enjoyed when the heat has abated. Sapped of energy, the locals may climb up to their widow's walks to catch a soft breeze and sip on a tall, cold gin and tonic. ■ As the

month progresses, it's time for some to close down the summer camps and cottages, for school will soon be commencing. Hammocks are cleaned, rolled, and stored in the shed. The outdoor furniture is gathered and covered with tarpaulins. Watercraft are retrieved from the slips and stored in boathouses. ■ Farmers are gearing up for the fall harvests. Rice combines are brought out from the barns to be cleaned and overhauled, as are gigantic sugarcane cutting tractors. ■ It's time to bid *au revoir* to summer, but it's like a lull before a storm for once fall arrives and a cool front blows through, everyone will be energized and ready for another round of parties and festivals.

boat

party

IT'S HOT, hot, hot, and an outing on the water is in order. Tommy Dantin and the crew of the *Wyoming* welcome us aboard their beautifully restored oyster lugger, in which we will motor down Bayou Lafouche, then into the open waters of the Gulf of Mexico. ■ Noisy seagulls and snow-white egrets fly overhead, following us down the busy bayou, looking for a bit of breakfast from the discards of the shrimp boats. We have our own stash of goodies to enjoy while we watch the steady flow of traffic of oceangoing tugs, oil field workboats, and graceful Lafitte skiffs. ■ Ice chests and picnic baskets hold summer fruit, assorted cheeses, cold drinks, wine, crusty breads, party crackers, and, of course, our picnic lunch. ■ We are more than prepared for a day in the sun!

COUNTRY PÂTÉ, MY WAY

TRADITIONALLY, A COUNTRY PÂTÉ IS MADE WITH CHUNKY PIECES OF MEATS THAT ARE MARINATED WITH HERBS AND SPICES FOR ABOUT TWENTY-FOUR HOURS, THEN GROUND COARSELY, BUT I'VE MADE THE PREPARATION A LITTLE SIMPLER. SERVE WITH TOASTED CROUTONS, MUSTARD, CHOPPED RED ONIONS, AND CORNICHONS.

Put the chicken livers, onion, celery, and carrot in a food processor and pulse two or three times to combine. Transfer the mixture to a large mixing bowl. Add the pork, veal, pork fat, salt, cayenne, oregano, thyme, basil, brandy and mix well. Cover and refrigerate for 24 hours.

Preheat the oven to 350°F.

Remove the pâté mixture from the refrigerator, add the pistachios, and mix well. Line the bottom and sides of a 1½-quart earthenware terrine or pâté mold with the bacon slices, leaving enough of the bacon overlapping on all sides of the dish so that the bacon will cover the top of the pâté mixture when folded over. Put the pâté mixture in the terrine and press it down firmly with your fingers. Fold the overlapping bacon slices over the mixture to encase it. Top with the bay leaves.

Place the terrine on a baking sheet and bake until the internal temperature reaches 170°F on a meat thermometer, about 2 hours. Remove from the oven and cover with a sheet of aluminum foil, then place a 2- to 3-pound weight or a brick wrapped in aluminum foil on top of the pâté. (Do not use a can.) Let cool completely.

Remove the weight and unmold the pâté. Wrap tightly in plastic wrap and refrigerate for at least 8 hours before slicing to serve with the croutons.

½ pound chicken livers, trimmed of membranes
½ cup finely chopped yellow onion
¼ cup finely chopped celery
¼ cup finely chopped carrot
1 pound ground pork
1½ pounds ground veal
¼ pound ground pork fat
2 teaspoons salt
¾ teaspoon cayenne
½ teaspoon dried oregano
½ teaspoon dried thyme
½ teaspoon dried basil
½ cup brandy
1½ cups shelled pistachios
12 slices bacon
6 bay leaves
1 recipe Toasted Croutons (page 81)

MAKES ABOUT 20 APPETIZER SERVINGS

PLANTER'S PUNCH

WHEN IT'S HOT AND HUMID LIKE IT IS HERE, ESPECIALLY DURING THE SUMMER, A COLD PLANTER'S PUNCH IS JUST WHAT YOU NEED TO COOL YOU DOWN. MARCELLE AND HER FRIENDS MAKE SEVERAL BATCHES EACH YEAR TO CELEBRATE THE ARRIVAL OF SUMMER. WHIP UP THE PUNCH AS MUCH AS TWO WEEKS AHEAD OF TIME AND STORE IT IN THE REFRIGERATOR. TO TAKE IT ON THE BOAT, PUT IT IN QUART OR HALF-GALLON CONTAINERS AND BURY THEM IN CRUSHED ICE TO KEEP THEM ICE-COLD.

1 fifth dark rum
One 6-ounce can frozen orange
    juice concentrate
One 6-ounce can frozen pink
    lemonade concentrate
3 tablespoons fresh lemon juice
3 tablespoons grenadine
4 cups water

In a large container, combine all of the ingredients and stir to dissolve the concentrates. Refrigerate until ready to serve.

MAKES ABOUT 16 SERVINGS

MUFFULETTA SALAD

A MUFFULETTA IS A SANDWICH UNLIKE ANY OTHER. MEATS, CHEESES, AND OLIVE SALAD ARE STUFFED IN BETWEEN GREAT THICK SLICES OF ITALIAN BREAD. AFICIONADOS ARGUE ABOUT WHETHER IT SHOULD BE SERVED COLD OR WARM—I LIKE IT BOTH WAYS. ■ HERE WE'VE MADE A MUF-FULETTA SALAD TO TOTE ALONG FOR OUR PARTY ON THE WATER. MAKE IT A DAY AHEAD TO ALLOW THE FLAVORS TO MINGLE. PACK IT INTO AN AIRTIGHT CONTAINER AND STOW IN THE ICE CHEST TO KEEP IT COOL.

Put the water and 1 teaspoon of the salt in a large saucepan and bring to a boil over high heat. Add the pasta and cook, uncovered, stirring occasionally, until tender, 6 to 8 minutes. Remove from the heat and drain. Rinse with cool water and drain again.

In a large mixing bowl, combine the pasta, salami, pro-volone, mortadella, ham, olives, onion, garlic, celery, parsley, and thyme. In a small bowl, whisk together the oil, vinegar, Worcestershire, hot sauce, ½ teaspoon of the salt, and the pepper. Pour over the salad mixture. Add the remaining 1 teaspoon salt. Toss to mix well. Store in an airtight container and refrigerate for at least 8 hours before serving.

6 cups water
2½ teaspoons salt
1 pound small shell pasta
½ pound salami, cut into ¼-inch cubes
1 pound provolone cheese, cut into ¼-inch cubes
½ pound mortadella, cut into ¼-inch cubes
½ pound boiled ham, cut into ¼-inch cubes
20 pitted jumbo black olives, sliced
20 green Queen olives stuffed with pimientos, sliced
½ cup minced yellow onion
1 tablespoon minced garlic
½ cup chopped celery
½ cup chopped fresh parsley leaves
¼ cup fresh thyme leaves
1 cup extra-virgin olive oil
6 tablespoons apple cider vinegar
1 teaspoon Worcestershire sauce
½ teaspoon hot sauce
1 teaspoon freshly ground black pepper

MAKES 8 TO 10 SERVINGS

SHRIMP AND CORN SALAD

DOWN ON BAYOU LAFOURCHE, THERE'S RARELY A SHORTAGE OF FRESH
SEAFOOD. SHRIMP COMBINED WITH LOCAL GARDEN-GROWN SWEET CORN
MAKES A GREAT SALAD TO MUNCH ON WHILE WE CRUISE THE WATERS.

8 cups water
1 lemon, halved
1 tablespoon liquid Zatarain's
   Concentrated Shrimp & Crab
   Boil
2 bay leaves
1 tablespoon plus 1/2 teaspoon
   salt
2 cups fresh sweet corn kernels
   (from 2 medium-size ears)
11/2 pounds medium-size shrimp,
   peeled and deveined
1/2 cup olive oil
2 tablespoons Dijon mustard
1 tablespoon fresh lemon juice
1 teaspoon hot sauce
1/2 teaspoon freshly ground black
   pepper
1/2 teaspoon minced garlic
2 tablespoons chopped fresh
   basil leaves
1/2 cup chopped red onion
1 pint cherry tomatoes, halved
1/2 cup chopped red bell pepper
1/2 cup chopped yellow bell
   pepper

In a large pot, combine the water, the juice from the
lemon halves, the shells, the boil, bay leaves, and 1 tablespoon of the salt. Bring to a boil, add the corn, and cook
for 5 minutes. With a skimmer, remove the corn from
the boiling liquid, put it in a shallow bowl, and let cool
completely.

Meanwhile, bring the water back to a boil and add
the shrimp. Cook for 5 minutes. Remove from the heat
and drain. Remove the bay leaves, put the shrimp in a
shallow bowl, and let cool completely.

In a small mixing bowl, combine the olive oil, mustard, lemon juice, hot sauce, the remaining 1/2 teaspoon
salt, the black pepper, and garlic. Whisk to blend well.

In a large salad bowl, combine the corn, shrimp, basil,
onion, tomatoes, and bell pepper. Add the dressing and
toss to mix. Cover and chill for at least 2 hours before
serving.

MAKES ABOUT 10 SERVINGS

LIZZIE'S CHOCOLATE BROWNIES

LIZZIE, THE WIFE OF MY GOOD FRIEND TONY CRUZ, WHO'S BEEN WITH ME IN MY BUSINESS PRACTICALLY SINCE THE BEGINNING, LOVES BROWNIES AND SUGGESTED THESE TO BRING ALONG ON THE BOAT PARTY.

Preheat the oven to 350°F. Grease a 17 x 12-inch baking pan with 1 teaspoon of the shortening.

In a large, heavy saucepan over medium heat, melt the remaining 1 cup shortening. Remove from the heat and let cool slightly. Add the sugar and blend. Add the eggs one at a time, whisking after each addition. Add the water and vanilla and whisk to mix well. Add the flour, cocoa, baking powder, and salt and stir to blend. Fold in the walnuts and chopped chocolate, then spread the batter evenly in the prepared pan.

Bake until the cake springs back when touched, about 25 minutes. Remove from the oven and let cool for 30 minutes.

Spread the icing over the cake with a rubber spatula. Let cool completely before cutting into squares to serve.

1 teaspoon plus 1 cup vegetable shortening
2 cups sugar
4 large eggs
$1/2$ cup water
1 teaspoon pure vanilla extract
1 cup bleached all-purpose flour
$3/4$ cup unsweetened cocoa powder
1 teaspoon baking powder
$1/2$ teaspoon salt
1 cup chopped walnuts
4 ounces semisweet chocolate, chopped
1 recipe Chocolate Icing (recipe follows)

MAKES ABOUT 20 BROWNIES

214

Chocolate Icing

1 pound confectioners' sugar

1/2 cup unsweetened cocoa powder

1/4 pound (1 stick) unsalted butter, at room temperature

1/3 cup boiling water

Sift together the confectioners' sugar and cocoa powder into a large mixing bowl. Add the butter and use an electric mixer to combine. Add the water and mix until smooth. Let cool, then use.

MAKES ABOUT 2 CUPS

shrimp

festival

THE DELCAMBRE Shrimp Festival is one of several of its kind held in the port towns along Vermilion Bay. Like many other festivals, there are rides, food, bands, and dancing. What is unique, though, is that the shrimp fleet, in anticipation of the opening of the shrimp season, is blessed by the local priest. For days prior to the festival, the captains and crews along with family members decorate the boats with flags and bunting; then the ritual calls for the priest to sprinkle holy water over the gaily festooned boats before they set out to sea. The occasion is marked by the people of the town offering popular Louisiana shrimp dishes to those who gather to pray and to party.

SHRIMP CLEMENCEAU

GEORGE BENJAMIN EUGENE CLEMENCEAU BECAME THE PREMIER OF FRANCE IN 1906 AND A CHICKEN DISH WAS CREATED IN NEW ORLEANS TO HONOR HIM, I BELIEVE AT GALATOIRE'S, THE REVERED RESTAURANT THAT OPENED IN 1905. I'VE TAKEN A LITTLE LIBERTY AND SUBSTITUTED SHRIMP FOR THE CHICKEN TO CELEBRATE THE SHRIMP FESTIVAL.

In a heavy, deep pot or an electric deep-fryer, heat the vegetable oil to 360°F. Add the potatoes, in batches, and fry until golden brown, 8 to 10 minutes. Remove with a slotted spoon and drain on paper towels.

In a large, nonstick skillet over medium-high heat, heat the olive oil. Add the onion and season with ¼ teaspoon of the salt and ¼ teaspoon of the black pepper. Cook for 2 minutes. Season the shrimp with ¼ teaspoon of the salt and the cayenne and add to the skillet. Cook, stirring, for 2 minutes. Add the ham, green peas, garlic, and the potatoes. Add the remaining ½ teaspoon salt and ¼ teaspoon black pepper. Cook for 3 minutes, then add the butter and cook, stirring, for 1 minute.

To serve, divide the mixture into 4 equal portions on serving plates and drizzle with the hollandaise.

3 cups vegetable oil

2 large Idaho potatoes, peeled and cut into small dice (about 3 cups)

2 teaspoons olive oil

½ cup chopped yellow onion

1 teaspoon salt

½ teaspoon freshly ground black pepper

1 pound medium-size shrimp, peeled and deveined

⅛ teaspoon cayenne

6 ounces boiled ham, cut into small dice

½ cup fresh sweet baby green peas

1 teaspoon chopped garlic

2 tablespoons unsalted butter

1 recipe Hollandaise Sauce (page 15)

MAKES 4 SERVINGS

SHRIMP STEW

SHRIMP STEW IS PRACTICALLY A STAPLE DISH IN THE AREA OF LOUISIANA KNOWN AS ACADIANA, IN THE SOUTHERN PART OF THE STATE, AND, OF COURSE, IS A POPULAR ITEM SERVED AT THE SHRIMP FESTIVAL. OLD-TIME COOKS GARNISHED THE STEW WITH CHOPPED HARD-BOILED EGGS, WHICH I THINK IS A NICE TOUCH. ■ IF YOU CAN, PURCHASE SHRIMP WITH THE HEADS AND SHELLS INTACT SO THAT YOU CAN USE THEM TO MAKE A STOCK, BUT IN A PINCH YOU CAN SUBSTITUTE 1 QUART CHICKEN BROTH.

2 pounds medium-size shrimp, shells and heads on

6 cups water

1 medium-size yellow onion, quartered

2 bay leaves

1 tablespoon plus 1/2 teaspoon salt

1/2 cup vegetable oil

1/2 cup bleached all-purpose flour

1 cup chopped yellow onion

1/2 cup chopped green bell pepper

1/2 cup chopped celery

1/4 teaspoon cayenne

2 tablespoons chopped fresh parsley leaves

2 hard-boiled eggs, shelled and finely chopped

Peel the shrimp and reserve the shells and heads. Refrigerate the shrimp and put the shells and heads in a large saucepan. Add the water, quartered onion, bay leaves, and 1 tablespoon of the salt. Bring to a boil, then reduce the heat to medium and simmer, uncovered, for 30 minutes. Remove from the heat and strain through a fine-mesh strainer. Discard the peelings and set aside the shrimp stock.

Combine the oil and flour in a large cast-iron pot or enameled cast-iron Dutch oven over medium heat. Stirring slowly and constantly, make a roux the color of peanut butter, 15 to 20 minutes. Add the chopped onion, bell pepper, and celery and cook, stirring, until soft, 6 to 8 minutes. Add the shrimp stock and whisk to blend with the roux. Bring to a boil, then reduce the heat to medium-low and simmer, uncovered, for 1½ hours.

Add the shrimp, the remaining ½ teaspoon salt, and the cayenne and cook for 20 minutes. Remove from the heat and stir in the parsley. Ladle into individual soup bowls, garnish with the chopped eggs, and serve hot.

The stew can also be served over white rice.

MAKES ABOUT 6 SERVINGS

SHRIMP TOAST

SHRIMP TOAST IS GREAT FOOD TO EAT WHILE YOU STROLL AROUND THE FESTIVAL GROUNDS. YOU CAN SUBSTITUTE SCALLOPS, CRAWFISH, OR LOBSTER FOR THE SHRIMP.

Put the shrimp, egg white, onion, cilantro, salt, cayenne, and ½ teaspoon of the sesame oil in a food processor and pulse two or three times to finely chop. Do not puree.

Put the egg yolks, the remaining 2 tablespoons sesame oil, and the water in a shallow bowl and whisk to blend.

Spread equal amounts of the shrimp mixture onto 8 slices of the bread. Top with the remaining 8 slices of bread. Press together gently but firmly.

Heat 3 tablespoons of the vegetable oil in a large non-stick skillet over medium-high heat. Dip 4 of the sandwiches in the egg mixture, coating them evenly on both sides. Fry until golden brown, about 4 minutes on each side. Remove from the skillet. Repeat the process with the remaining 3 tablespoons vegetable oil and sandwiches. Slice each sandwich into 4 triangles to serve.

½ pound medium-size shrimp, peeled and deveined
1 large egg white
2 tablespoons chopped yellow onion
1 tablespoon chopped fresh cilantro leaves
¼ teaspoon salt
⅛ teaspoon cayenne
½ teaspoon plus 2 tablespoons sesame oil
2 large egg yolks
¼ cup water
16 slices white bread, crusts removed
6 tablespoons vegetable oil

MAKES 4 SERVINGS

AFTER LABOR DAY, all the locals can talk about is when will the first cold front swing through from the west. Long before the brisk winds move into the precious lowlands of southern Louisiana, avid hunters are busy preparing for the coming hunting season. Camps are opened and refreshed, duck blinds are rebuilt, and by the time flocks of green-winged teal, mallards, and pintails arrive, all is at the ready. ■ On the other hand, farmers

closely watch the weather forecasts, hoping and praying that hurricanes that spawn in the Caribbean will pass them by. If the howling winds head this way, thousands of acres of sugarcane could be damaged or lost entirely. ■ From late summer through autumn, a hurricane can rise out of the sea and overwhelm the land, its winds sometimes reaching up to 150 miles an hour or more. The winds and rains are sometimes accompanied by huge tidal waves that can flood the low-lying coastal areas, sending a deluge of saltwater more than 15 feet deep. Because of the possibility of massive destruction, when a hurricane

threatens, the inhabitants along the coast make a beeline for safer regions. Sometimes, to relieve them of their fear, they hold a hurricane party with their fellow evacuees. ■ In the Big Easy, we brace for another kind of barrage. September heralds the opening of the social and cultural season, which is marked by gala parties, symphony performances, operas, and ballets. And for the sports fans, there's always the high school, college, and professional football games. ■ After the slow summer season, restaurants wind up for the busy months of the fall and winter, when large convention groups besiege the city. ■ Deep in the swamps and marshlands and along the bayous, the leaves of the bald cypress trees are turning an earthy sienna and spindly

pecan trees are beginning to shed their brittle leaves. Autumn is moving in, the days are getting shorter, and the weather is changing,

imperceptibly so, but changing nonetheless. ■ As if on cue, once the weather turns cooler, there're many festivals to honor the fall crops. ■ It's also the month we honor our friendly frogs (yep, frogs) as well as music and wooden boats—something for just about everyone.

festivals acadiens

FESTIVALS ACADIENS, held in Lafayette, is billed as the festival that celebrates everything uniquely Cajun. It actually is a combination of festivals that includes the Festival de Musique Acadienne, the Bayou Food Festival, the Louisiana Native & Contemporary Crafts Festival, Downtown Alive!, Kids Alive!, the Heritage Pavilion, and La Vie Cadienne Wetlands Folklife Festival. ■ The food booths serve up goodies like alligator sausage poorboys, homemade boudin, bread pudding with rum sauce, jambalaya, crawfish fettuccine, bloomin' onions, gator-on-a-stick, bite-size fried catfish—all made for enjoying while walking around.■ Louisiana's best Cajun and zydeco bands draw thousands of people from across the country and around the world to the festival. Hunters, fishermen, shrimpers, craftsmen, and wetlands specialists share their knowledge, skills, inventions, and stories. More than seventy-five booths are filled with traditional native crafts, and young visitors can enjoy hands-on activities such as butter churning, and making corncob dolls and pottery. ■ This is one of the best "catch-all" festivals in the state.

EGGPLANT AND SEAFOOD AU GRATIN

AT FESTIVALS IN LAFAYETTE, THE COOKS GO ALL OUT. I'M ALWAYS AMAZED AT WHAT THEY CAN PRODUCE IN BOOTHS SET UP ON THE STREETS OR IN PARKS, WHERE THEY HAVE TO BRING COOKTOPS, BUTANE BURNERS, GRILLS, AND WARMERS TO KEEP THEIR FOOD FRESH AND HOT. THE FOOD IS SERVED ON SMALL DISPOSABLE PLATES AND EVERYONE PASSES THEIR SELECTIONS AROUND FOR THE FESTIVAL GOERS TO TASTE. THIS IS ONE THAT I ESPECIALLY LIKE.

6 tablespoons (3/4 stick) unsalted
    butter
1 medium-size eggplant (about
    12 ounces), peeled and cubed
1 cup chopped yellow onions
1 1/4 teaspoons salt
1/2 teaspoon cayenne
1/4 cup bleached all-purpose
    flour
2 1/2 cups milk
1/2 pound medium-size shrimp,
    peeled and deveined
1/2 pound lump crabmeat, picked
    over for shells and cartilage
1 dozen freshly shucked oysters,
    with their liquor
1/4 cup freshly grated
    Parmigiano-Reggiano cheese
1/4 cup chopped green onions or
    scallions (green part only)

In a large skillet, melt 2 tablespoons of the butter over medium–high heat. Add the eggplant, onions, salt, and cayenne and cook, stirring, until the vegetables are soft, 6 to 8 minutes.

Add the remaining 4 tablespoons butter and the flour and cook, stirring, for 3 minutes. Stream in the milk, stirring constantly, and cook until the mixture thickens, about 4 minutes.

Reduce the heat to medium and add the shrimp. Simmer for 4 minutes. Remove from the heat. Add the crabmeat, oysters, cheese, and green onions and stir gently to mix. Serve hot.

MAKES ABOUT 8 SERVINGS

CRISPY SHRIMP BURGERS

I TELL YOU, THOSE ACADIANS IN SOUTH LOUISIANA ARE CLEVER. AT SOME OF THE LOCAL SANDWICH SHOPS, YOU'LL FIND THESE SHRIMP BURGERS ON THE MENU. THEY ARE SOMETIMES SERVED AT FESTIVALS SUCH AS FESTIVALS ACADIENS. MARCELLE SAYS THEY WERE CREATED FOR FRIDAY MEALS, THE DAY WHEN CATHOLICS CANNOT EAT MEAT. GOOD IDEA! GOOD BURGERS! YOU CAN ALSO MAKE THEM WITH CRAWFISH OR CRABMEAT.

In a large skillet, melt the butter over medium heat. Add the onions, celery, bell pepper, salt, and cayenne. Cook, stirring, until soft for about 6 minutes. Add the shrimp and cook, stirring, for 3 minutes. Transfer the mixture to a large mixing bowl and let cool slightly. Add the garlic, green onions, 2 of the eggs, and 1 cup of the bread crumbs. Stir to mix well. Divide into 8 equal portions and form into patties.

Put the flour in a shallow bowl and season with 1 teaspoon of the Creole seasoning. Put the remaining 1 cup bread crumbs in another shallow bowl and season with the remaining 1 teaspoon Creole seasoning. Put the beaten egg in yet another shallow bowl, add the water, and beat lightly.

Heat the vegetable oil in a large skillet over medium heat. Dredge each patty first in the flour, then in the egg mixture, then in the bread crumbs, turning to coat completely and shaking off any excess. Cook 4 patties at a time until lightly browned, 5 to 6 minutes on each side. Drain on paper towels.

To serve, spread both sides of each toasted bun with some of the tartar sauce, place a patty on the bottom half of the bun, dress with lettuce and tomatoes, and top with the other bun half.

1 tablespoon unsalted butter
3/4 cup chopped yellow onions
1/4 cup chopped celery
1/4 cup chopped green bell
  pepper
1 1/2 teaspoons salt
3/4 teaspoon cayenne
2 pounds medium-size shrimp,
  peeled, deveined, and chopped
2 teaspoons chopped garlic
1/4 cup chopped green onions or
  scallions (green part only)
2 large eggs plus 1 egg, beaten
2 cups fine dried bread crumbs
1/2 cup unbleached all-purpose
  flour
2 teaspoons Creole Seasoning
  (page 13)
2 tablespoons water
1/4 cup vegetable oil
8 hamburger buns, toasted
1 recipe Tartar Sauce
  (recipe follows)
Shredded lettuce
Sliced vine-ripened tomatoes

MAKES 8 SERVINGS

Tartar Sauce

Put the egg, garlic, lemon juice, parsley, green onions, and relish in a food processor or blender and process for 15 seconds. With the motor running, pour the oil through the feed tube in a slow steady stream. Add the cayenne, mustard, and salt and pulse once or twice to blend.

Cover and let sit for 1 hour in the refrigerator before using. Best if used within 24 hours.

1 large egg (see Note on
    page 13)
1 tablespoon minced garlic
2 tablespoons fresh lemon juice
1 tablespoon chopped fresh
    parsley leaves
2 tablespoons chopped green
    onions or scallions
    (green part only)
2 teaspoons drained sweet
    pickle relish
1 cup vegetable oil
¼ teaspoon cayenne
1 tablespoon Creole or
    whole-grain mustard
1 teaspoon salt

MAKES ABOUT 1 ¼ CUPS

FRIED CATFISH ON A STICK

JUST ABOUT EVERY FESTIVAL FEATURES SOMETHING ON A STICK. MARCELLE'S HUSBAND, ROCK, FAVORS BOUDIN ON A STICK, ANDOUILLE ON A STICK, AND THIS CATFISH ON A STICK. YOU MAY HAVE TO TRIM THE BAMBOO SKEWERS SO THEY FIT IN YOUR SKILLET.

Cut each fillet lengthwise into 3 strips, each about 1½ inches wide. Thread each strip onto a skewer. Lay them in a shallow bowl.

Combine 1 teaspoon of the Creole seasoning, the salt, cayenne, mustard, and buttermilk in a small mixing bowl and stir to blend. Pour the mixture over the catfish, cover, and refrigerate for 8 hours.

4 catfish fillets (about 4 ounces
    each)
Twelve 10-inch bamboo skewers
1 tablespoon Creole Seasoning
    (page 13)
½ teaspoon salt
⅛ teaspoon cayenne

Remove the fish from the refrigerator. Heat the oil to 360°F in a large deep cast-iron skillet. In a large mixing bowl, combine the flour and the remaining 2 teaspoons Creole seasoning. Dredge 2 to 3 skewers at a time in the flour, shaking off any excess. Fry them in batches until golden brown, about 4 minutes on each side. Drain on paper towels. Serve hot with the rémoulade sauce.

2 tablespoons Creole or
    whole-grain mustard
1 cup buttermilk
4 cups vegetable oil
2 cups bleached all-purpose flour
1 recipe Rémoulade Sauce
    (recipe follows)

MAKES 6 SERVINGS (2 SKEWERS PER PERSON)

Rémoulade Sauce

Put the green onions, garlic, horseradish, mustards, ketchup, hot sauce, Worcestershire, lemon juice, egg, salt, and cayenne in a food processor or blender and process until smooth, about 30 seconds. With the motor running, slowly pour in the vegetable oil through the feed tube. The mixture will thicken.

Transfer to a container, cover, and refrigerate for 1 hour before using. Best if used within 24 hours.

1/4 cup chopped green onions or
    scallions (green part only)
2 teaspoons chopped garlic
1 tablespoon prepared horseradish
2 tablespoons Creole or whole-
    grain mustard
2 teaspoons yellow mustard
3 tablespoons ketchup
1 teaspoon hot sauce
1 teaspoon Worcestershire sauce
2 tablespoons fresh lemon juice
1 large egg (see Note on
    page 13)
1/2 teaspoon salt
1/4 teaspoon cayenne
3/4 cup vegetable oil

MAKES ABOUT 2 CUPS

september

sugarcane
festival

IN 1937, a group of New Iberia civic and community leaders, sugar planters, and the New Iberia Chamber of Commerce joined forces and created the Sugar Cane Festival to honor the ever-growing industry that, in 1995, celebrated two hundred years of raising cane. Over 380,000 acres of land are planted in sugarcane, and in the last few years, production has exceeded over nine million tons of cane, worth about $400 million to cane growers and raw-sugar factories in the state. ■ *La Roulaison*, the harvest of the cane, begins in September and usually ends around the first of the year. During the harvest, farmers and field workers labor from early morning until dusk, cutting the cane, burning off the shafts, and hauling it to the sugar mills for processing into raw sugar, which is then sold to refineries, processed again, and packaged for the consumer markets. ■ The festival began as a one-day event, but it is now one of the largest in the state, and is packed with activities, including a livestock show, a spectacular boat parade on Bayou Teche, several street parades, and the coronation of Queen Sugar and King Sucrose. ■ Hi, Sugar!

DIVINE DIVINITY FUDGE

BOTH MARCELLE AND FELICIA REMEMBER THIS DIVINITY FUDGE FROM THEIR CHILDHOOD. MARCELLE TALKED TO HER AUNT TAYE AND FELICIA QUERIED HER GRANDMOTHER LOVIS TO GET THE LOW-DOWN ON THIS INCREDIBLE SWEET. IT'S A FLUFFY BUT CREAMY CANDY MADE WITH SUGAR, CORN SYRUP, AND STIFFLY BEATEN EGG WHITES AND IT HAS TO BE MADE ON A CLEAR, COOL, DRY DAY FOR IT TO TURN OUT JUST RIGHT. ANY HUMIDITY WILL PREVENT IT FROM REACHING THE FINAL STAGE. ■ IT CAN BE BEATEN BY HAND, BUT IT'LL WEAR YOU OUT. WE DID IT IN A HEAVY-DUTY ELECTRIC MIXER, BUT YOU MIGHT BURN OUT A HAND-HELD ONE. THE RESULT IS, WELL, LIKE ITS NAME, DIVINE! ■ THE CANDY CAN BE DROPPED IN INDIVIDUAL PEAKS ONTO WAXED PAPER OR SPREAD IN A BUTTERED PAN AND CUT INTO 1-INCH SQUARES WHEN FIRM.

Beat the egg whites with an electric mixer until stiff. Line a baking sheet with parchment or waxed paper.

Put the sugar, corn syrup, and water in a medium-size heavy saucepan over medium-high heat. Stir to dissolve the sugar, bring to a boil and cook until the temperature reaches 260°F on a candy thermometer, or the hard-ball stage, when a bit of the mixture dropped into cold water holds its shape, 10 to 15 minutes.

Remove from the heat. Pour in a thin steady stream into the beaten egg whites and beat with an electric mixer on high for about 3 minutes, scraping down the sides of the bowl. Add the vanilla, and continue beating on high just until the candy starts to lose its gloss, 5 to 6 minutes.

2 large egg whites
2 cups sugar
1/2 cup light corn syrup
1/2 cup water
1 teaspoon pure vanilla extract
1/2 cup chopped pecans

When the beaters are lifted, the mixture should fall in a ribbon that mounds on itself. Add the pecans, stir to mix, and quickly drop the mixture by tablespoons onto the prepared sheet. If the mixture flattens out, beat again for 1 minute more. If the mixture is too thick to drop, beat in a few drops of hot water until the candy is a softer consistency.

NOTE

If the candy is poured into a pan and cut into squares, you should have about 48 pieces.

MAKES ABOUT 24 PIECES

SUGARED POPCORN

WHEN MARCELLE WAS A SMALL CHILD, HER TANTE BELLE MADE THIS SUGARED TREAT FOR ALL TO ENJOY TOGETHER WHILE THEY PLAYED DOMINOS. MARCELLE TELLS ME THAT TANTE BELLE SOMETIMES ADDED FOOD COLORING TO THE SUGAR MIXTURE—RED DURING THE CHRISTMAS HOLIDAYS, GREEN FOR MARDI GRAS, AND YELLOW OR PINK FOR EASTER. THEY MADE CONES OUT OF COLORED PAPER IN WHICH TO SERVE IT. SOUNDS LIKE FUN TO ME!

1 cup sugar
1 tablespoon unsalted butter
3 tablespoons water
6 cups popped butter-flavored popcorn

In a large, heavy pot over medium heat, combine the sugar, butter, and water. Stirring constantly, cook until thick like syrup, about 5 minutes. Remove from the heat, add the popcorn, and stir to coat evenly. Turn onto a sheet of parchment or waxed paper to cool. Serve in a basket or paper cones.

MAKES 6 SERVINGS

pirogue race
picnic

A PIROGUE is a boat, but not an ordinary one. Because travel in the swamps was almost impossible, the early settlers invented the pirogue, a hollowed-out cypress log that, the locals say, can ride on a heavy dew. Trappers, hunters, and fishermen cut silently between trees and glide easily over swamp grass, leaving only a slim trail behind, like a crease in the water. ■ Maneuvering such a vessel is an art form. The strength and grace of a pirogue in the hands of a man who knows how to maneuver it is something to marvel at. Waterways two feet wide can be negotiated; almost as if the boat were weightless, it can be poled across mud flats from lake to lake. It's the only way to travel in the swamps and marshes of south Louisiana. ■ To honor this vessel, the townspeople of Jean Lafitte, south of New Orleans, hold the World Championship Pirogue Race each year in September. Throughout the day, there are different divisions of races, and if the weather is clear and cool, enjoying a picnic on the banks of the bayou is the way to take it all in.

BEEF TENDERLOIN SANDWICHES WITH HORSERADISH SPREAD

FOOD EATEN OUTDOORS ALWAYS TASTES BETTER AS FAR AS I'M CON-
CERNED, AND THEREFORE I PACK MY BASKET WITH LOTS OF GOOD
THINGS—NO BALONEY SANDWICHES ON *MY* PICNIC. BRING ALONG
THE TENDERLOIN ALREADY PREPARED, AND FINISH UP THE SAND-
WICHES RIGHT BEFORE SERVING.

Preheat the oven to 350°F.

In a small mixing bowl, mix together the olive oil and Creole seasoning. Spread this evenly over the tenderloin. Heat a large ovenproof skillet over medium-high heat, then sear the tenderloin for 5 minutes on each side in the skillet. Transfer the skillet to the oven and roast for 25 minutes for medium-rare. Remove from the oven and let rest for 30 minutes.

Cut the tenderloin into thin slices.

In a small mixing bowl, combine the mayonnaise, horseradish, salt, and black pepper and whisk to mix. Cover and refrigerate until ready to use.

In a medium-size mixing bowl, toss the arugula with the olive oil, salt, and pepper.

Spread about ½ teaspoon of the horseradish mixture on each slice of toast. Top with a slice of beef and a few cheese shavings, then finish with a little of the arugula. Top each sandwich with a slice of toast. Pass on a platter to serve.

FOR THE TENDERLOIN
2 tablespoons olive oil
1 tablespoon Creole Seasoning (page 13)
One 2-pound beef tenderloin, trimmed of fat

FOR THE HORSERADISH SPREAD
3 tablespoons Mayonnaise (page 129)
1 tablespoon prepared horseradish
⅛ teaspoon salt
⅛ teaspoon cracked black peppercorns

TO ASSEMBLE
2 cups baby arugula, rinsed and patted dry
1 tablespoon extra-virgin olive oil
¼ teaspoon salt
⅛ teaspoon freshly ground black pepper
1 loaf French bread (about 15 inches long), cut crosswise into ¼-inch-thick slices and lightly toasted
½ pound Parmigiano-Reggiano cheese, shaved with a vegetable peeler

MAKES 6 TO 8 SERVINGS

CAPRESE SALAD

TORRE, THE WIFE OF MAURICIO ANDRADE, ONE OF THE TOP PEOPLE IN OUR ORGANIZATION, FIRST TASTED THIS SALAD WHILE VISITING THE PIZZA ROLANDI RESTAURANT IN COZUMEL AND THOUGHT IT WAS MARVELOUS. I AGREE. IT CAN BE MADE SEVERAL HOURS AHEAD OF TIME RIGHT IN A PLASTIC CONTAINER THAT CAN BE PACKED IN THE ICE CHEST TO BRING TO THE PICNIC. JUST BE SURE TO USE THE BEST TOMATOES YOU CAN FIND AND GOOD FRESH MOZZARELLA.

Cut each tomato crosswise into twelve ½-inch-thick slices. Cut the mozzarella crosswise into twelve ½-inch-thick slices. Season both sides of each slice of tomato and mozzarella with the salt and pepper.

Arrange half of the tomato slices in the bottom of a shallow plastic or glass bowl. Top each with 2 basil leaves. Place a slice of the mozzarella on top of the basil leaves, then top with the remaining tomato slices and repeat the process using up the remaining mozzarella and basil. Drizzle with the olive oil, cover, and refrigerate for at least 2 hours before serving.

2 large vine-ripened tomatoes (about 1 pound), cored
1 pound fresh buffalo or cow's milk mozzarella cheese
1 teaspoon salt
1 teaspoon freshly ground black pepper
About 48 large fresh basil leaves
¼ cup extra-virgin olive oil

MAKES 6 SERVINGS

FLO'S POTATO SALAD

JUST SO YOU'LL KNOW, FELICIA'S NICKNAME IS FLO, AND THIS IS HER POTATO SALAD, ONE OF THE BEST I'VE TASTED. IT'S GREAT TO BRING ALONG ON PICNICS; JUST BE SURE TO KEEP IT WELL CHILLED.

6 large eggs

A pinch plus 2 teaspoons salt

3 pounds new potatoes, washed and quartered

1/2 pound sliced bacon, cut into small dice

3/4 cup Mayonnaise (page 129)

1/4 cup Creole or whole-grain mustard

3 tablespoons fresh lemon juice

1 teaspoon hot sauce

3/4 cup finely chopped red onions

1/2 cup chopped green onions or scallions (green part only)

1 tablespoon chopped garlic

1/2 teaspoon freshly ground black pepper

Put the eggs in a saucepan and cover with water, add the pinch of salt. Bring to a boil and boil for 2 minutes. Turn off the heat, cover, and let stand for 10 minutes. Drain, then cool in a bowl of ice water. Peel and chop.

Put the potatoes in a large saucepan with 1 teaspoon of the salt and enough water to cover. Bring to a boil, then reduce the heat to medium and cook until fork-tender, about 12 minutes. Remove from the heat and drain. Let cool to room temperature.

Fry the bacon until crisp, remove from the pan with a slotted spoon, and drain on paper towels. Set aside to cool to room temperature.

In a large salad bowl, combine the mayonnaise, mustard, lemon juice, hot sauce, red onions, green onions, garlic, the remaining 1 teaspoon salt, and the black pepper. Whisk to blend. Add the eggs, potatoes, and bacon and toss to coat evenly. Keep refrigerated until ready to serve.

MAKES 6 TO 8 SERVINGS

HOT-SAUCED FRIED CHICKEN

A PICNIC IN LOUISIANA WOULDN'T BE A PICNIC WITHOUT CRISPY FRIED CHICKEN. THIS RENDITION WILL KNOCK YOUR SOCKS OFF. THE CHICKEN IS SOAKED IN A HOT SAUCE AND BUTTERMILK MIXTURE OVERNIGHT BEFORE IT'S FRIED. DON'T BE UNEASY ABOUT THE AMOUNT OF HOT SAUCE. I PROMISE A LOT OF THE HEAT IS COOKED OFF DURING FRYING AND THE FLAVOR IS GREAT.

Put the chicken in a large mixing bowl, add the hot sauce, buttermilk, salt, and pepper, and stir to coat evenly. Cover and refrigerate for 8 hours, turning the chicken pieces several times.

Remove the chicken from the refrigerator. In a deep cast-iron skillet, heat the vegetable oil to 360°F.

Combine the flour and 2 teaspoons of the Creole seasoning in a large mixing bowl. Dredge several pieces of chicken at a time in the flour, coating evenly and shaking off any excess. Fry the chicken, 4 to 5 pieces at a time, in the hot oil until golden brown, about 6 minutes on each side. Drain on paper towels and sprinkle with the remaining 1 teaspoon Creole seasoning. Serve hot or at room temperature.

1 fryer (about 4 1/2 pounds), cut into 10 pieces
1/2 cup hot sauce
1/2 cup buttermilk
3/4 teaspoon salt
1/2 teaspoon freshly ground black pepper
4 cups vegetable oil
2 cups bleached all-purpose flour
1 tablespoon Creole Seasoning (page 13)

MAKES 6 TO 8 SERVINGS

CHOCOLATE BUNDT CAKES WITH PEANUT BUTTER FILLING AND CHOCOLATE GLAZE

BUNDT PANS ARE TUBE PANS WITH FLUTED SIDES. FELICIA FOUND SOME 1-CUP BUNDT PANS TO MAKE THESE CHOCOLATE CAKES SO THAT PICNIC GUESTS COULD HAVE THEIR VERY OWN. THEY CAN BE PACKED IN AN AIRTIGHT CONTAINER TO PUT IN THE PICNIC BASKET.

2 tablespoons plus ¼ pound (1 stick) unsalted butter
2 cups bleached all-purpose flour
1 teaspoon baking powder
1 teaspoon baking soda
Pinch of salt
2 cups granulated sugar
2 large eggs
4 ounces unsweetened baking chocolate, melted
1 teaspoon pure vanilla extract
1 cup plus 6 tablespoons milk
2 cups peanut butter chips

FOR THE GLAZE
½ cup unsweetened cocoa powder
2 cups confectioners' sugar

Preheat the oven to 350°F. Grease 12 individual 1-cup Bundt pans with 2 tablespoons of the butter.

Into a small mixing bowl, sift the flour, baking powder, baking soda, and salt together. Set aside.

In a large mixing bowl, cream together the remaining butter and the granulated sugar using an electric mixer fitted with the paddle attachment set on medium speed. Add the eggs one at a time, beating well after each addition. Add the melted chocolate and vanilla and beat to mix. Add the flour mixture ½ cup at a time, alternating with the milk, beating until everything is incorporated.

Fill each tin with ¼ cup of the batter. Place some of the peanut butter chips in the center of the batter in each cup, then pour in the remaining batter to fill the tins. Bake until the cakes set, 18 to 20 minutes. Remove from the oven and let cool in the pans for 5 minutes, on wire racks, then flip out of the tins and cool for 5 minutes more.

In a small mixing bowl, combine the cocoa powder, confectioners' sugar, and as much of the remaining milk as needed to whisk into a smooth glaze. Set the cakes on a wire rack and spoon equal amounts of the glaze over them. Allow the glaze to set before serving.

MAKES 12 INDIVIDUAL CAKES

october

THE ARRIVAL of cool, crisp weather is a welcome change after the hot months of summer. The air is refreshed and the piney woods in the northern part of the state are blanketed with an enchanting fragrance. ■ To the south, in the swamps, Spanish moss hangs thickly from the bare limbs and trunks of swamp trees. In the west, the wind howls on the flat prairies. Raccoons, nutria, and river otters seek shelter in moldering tree stumps or sunken tree trunks. The swamps are ghostly and quiet, save for the lonely wail of a brown owl or the quack of a wood duck. The flat coastal salt marshes are punctuated only by ridge-like chênières (mounds or ridges in the marsh supporting oak trees, called *chênes* in French) that are much like elongated islands. It is here that the migratory waterfowl and marsh birds—geese, ducks, coots, gallinules, and rails—land in the natural ponds and along the mud flats. It is here that the hunters hide and wait in their camouflaged hunting blinds. ■ In the central part of the state, the cotton fields are a sea of white puffs on the brittle brown plants that flutter in the wind, and fall vegetables like squash, carrots, cabbage, and beans are gathered and put by for winter meals. ■ The landscape

becomes dismal save for the intermittent appearance of the bright red leaves of swamp maples, but the cold

winds give a gush of energy to the people who gather for the inaugural gumbo of the cold-weather season. ■ And it's in October that, after a cold front rushes in and the dark rain-filled skies move through, there will be what is known down here as bluebird days, with bright blue skies and a snap in the air. Because of this delightful time, there are probably more weddings now than there are in June. The churches and reception halls are booked solid. ■ And also because of this wonderfully cool weather, the fishing in the bays along the southern coast and in the Gulf is at its best. Yes, sir, there's hardly a man on the streets on weekends—they are fishing, hunting, or at the football stadium. What a life!

annie and tom's
toasting
october
party

ANNE KEARNEY, a native of Ohio, came to work at Emeril's in New Orleans and became a personal friend of mine. When she began dating Tom Sands, also from Ohio, I curiously followed their relationship. ■ She admits that she had a secret crush on Tom years ago when they were in high school together, but nothing came of it, until, while she was visiting her family during a Thanksgiving holiday, they renewed their acquaintance. Bing went the strings as Cupid fired his arrows. ■ Tom moved to New Orleans to court Anne and on November 28, 1997, while hiking through Yellow Spring National Park in Ohio, he popped the question. ■ They were married on October 10, 1998, a cloudless cool fall day, at the venerable St. Louis Cathedral on Jackson Square. When they left the church and proceeded to the gala reception at Gallier House in the French Quarter, a group of gospel singers led the guests through the narrow streets. ■ Under a billowing white tent erected on the terrace, an over-the-top array of food, a dance band, and flowing Champagne made for a joyous all-day affair.

GOUGÈRE

A GOUGÈRE IS MADE OF CHOUX PASTRY (A DOUGH CREATED BY COM-BINING FLOUR WITH HOT LIQUID AND BUTTER, THEN BEATING EGGS INTO THE MIXTURE) FLAVORED WITH GRUYÈRE CHEESE THAT IS EITHER PIPED OR SPOONED INTO A RING AND BAKED. IT CAN BE SERVED HOT FROM THE OVEN OR AT ROOM TEMPERATURE. EITHER WAY, IT'S A DELICIOUS HORS D'OEUVRE TO OFFER AT COCKTAIL PARTIES.

Preheat the oven to 400°F. Line a baking sheet with parchment paper.

In a large saucepan, combine the milk, butter, salt, and black pepper over medium-high heat. Bring to a boil, then remove from the heat, add the flour, and, with a wooden spoon, stir briskly for about 1 minute to incor-porate. Return to the heat and continue stirring for 1 minute over medium-high heat. Remove from the heat and add the eggs one at a time, beating after each addi-tion. Add the cheese and beat until it is incorporated and a slightly soft dough forms.

Drop the dough by the spoonful onto the prepared baking sheet to form a ring (about 12 to 14 spoon-fuls). Bake for 10 minutes, then reduce the oven tem-perature to 350°F and bake until golden brown, about 25 minutes.

1 cup milk
1/4 cup (1/2 stick) unsalted butter
1/4 teaspoon salt
1/8 teaspoon freshly ground black pepper
1 cup bleached all-purpose flour
4 large eggs, at room temperature
1/4 pound Gruyère cheese, grated

MAKES ABOUT 12 SERVINGS

CARAMELIZED SALMON IN NEW POTATOES

FOR A TOASTING PARTY OR ANY KIND OF SMALL COCKTAIL RECEPTION, I LIKE TO SERVE FINGER FOOD—THAT IS JUST WHAT IT'S CALLED, TIDBITS YOU CAN PICK UP WITH YOUR FINGERS. ■ BE SURE TO FIND THE SMALL-EST OF NEW POTATOES TO USE FOR THIS DISH. OH, THE POTATOES SHOULD BE SERVED AT ROOM TEMPERATURE.

24 very small new potatoes
(about 3 pounds)
2 teaspoons salt
One 8-ounce fresh salmon fillet
3/4 teaspoon freshly ground
black pepper
1 tablespoon sugar
3 tablespoons minced red onion
1 tablespoon chopped fresh
chervil leaves
3 tablespoons extra-virgin
olive oil

Put the potatoes in a large pot and add water to cover and 1 teaspoon of the salt. Bring to a boil, reduce the heat to medium-high, and cook until fork-tender, about 12 minutes. Remove from the heat, drain, and let cool to room temperature.

Trim about ¼ inch off each end of the potatoes. Using a paring knife or a small spoon, scoop out about three-quarters of the flesh of each potato from one end and reserve in a bowl. Place the potato shells on a parch-ment paper–lined baking sheet or work surface.

Season the salmon on the flesh side with ¼ teaspoon of the salt, ⅛ teaspoon of the black pepper, and the sugar. Heat a medium-size nonstick skillet over medium-high heat. Place the salmon flesh side down in the hot skillet and cook for 3 minutes, then flip it over and cook on the other side for 2 minutes. Remove from the heat and let cool to room temperature, then flake the salmon with a fork.

With a fork, mash the reserved potato flesh. Add the onion, chervil, olive oil, ½ teaspoon of the salt, and the remaining ½ teaspoon black pepper. Add the flaked fish and stir to mix.

Sprinkle the potato shells with the remaining ¼ tea-spoon salt and ⅛ teaspoon pepper. Spoon the mixture into the shells and serve at room temperature.

MAKES 12 SERVINGS (2 POTATOES PER PERSON)

new iberia gumbo cook-off

ABOUT TEN years ago, the Greater Iberia Chamber of Commerce organized a World Championship Gumbo Cook-off to be held in the historic downtown of the city, right on the banks of Bayou Teche. The first year, there were three or four judges, and only about ten entries. It took no time at all to pick the winner. Onlookers numbered about three hundred. ■ Now the gumbo cook-off attracts more than ten thousand people and there are over sixty-five teams, amateurs and professionals, who hunker down in a huge parking lot to put together the best gumbo they can. The teams are not allowed to use electricity and have to prepare the roux, the basis of the gumbo, on site. (Roux in Louisiana serves as a base and thickening agent for bisques, gumbos, stews, and some gravies. Equal parts flour and oil are slowly cooked and constantly stirred until the mixture is brown and has a nutlike aroma and taste.) The Gumbo Police inspect each team's ingredients before they begin the cook-off to ensure that everyone abides by the "Gumbo Code of Ethics," and they continue their patrol throughout the day.

GUMBO YA-YA

THE TERM "GUMBO YA-YA" LOOSELY TRANSLATES TO "EVERYBODY TALKING AT ONCE" AND REFERS TO THE MÉLANGE OF PEOPLE—FRENCH, SPANISH, INDIAN, ACADIAN, AND AFRICAN AMERICAN—WHO SETTLED IN THE BAYOU COUNTRY OF LOUISIANA AND IN AND AROUND NEW ORLEANS, AND THEIR VARIOUS TRADITIONS, WHICH MELDED TOGETHER TO FORM WHAT IS NOW A UNIQUE COMMUNITY. ■ GUMBO IS THE QUINTESSENTIAL DISH OF THE STATE. IT IS MADE WITH A ROUX AND INCLUDES MEATS LIKE FOWL, GAME, SAUSAGE, AND SEAFOOD. *GUMBO* IS ALSO THE AFRICAN-AMERICAN WORD FOR OKRA, WHICH IS OFTEN ADDED TO THE POT FOR THICKENING. ■ WHEN THE BRENNAN FAMILY OPENED MR. B'S BISTRO IN THE FRENCH QUARTER, GUMBO YA-YA APPEARED ON THE FIRST MENU. CREATED BY CHEF PAUL PRUDHOMME, IT WAS A RICH, THICK GUMBO, INTENSELY FLAVORED WITH SMOKY ANDOUILLE SAUSAGE, AND I MUST ADMIT IT IS ONE OF MY FAVORITE VERSIONS OF THE LOCAL DISH. THIS IS MY INTERPRETATION OF THE GUMBO. THE SECRET IS TO MAKE THE STOCK WITH A BIG HEN, THEN TAKE THE MEAT OFF THE BONES AND ADD IT TO THE GUMBO WITH SAUSAGE.

Put the hen, water, quartered onions, celery pieces, bay leaves, 1 tablespoon of the salt, and 1 teaspoon of the cayenne in a large, heavy pot. Bring to a boil over high heat, then reduce the heat to medium and cook, partially covered, until the hen is tender, about 2 hours. Remove the hen, strain and reserve the broth.

In a large, heavy pot or a Dutch oven over medium heat, combine the oil and flour. Stirring slowly and constantly, make a dark brown roux, the color of chocolate, 20 to 25 minutes. Add the chopped onions, bell peppers, chopped celery, and chopped sausage.

1 hen (about 6 pounds)
8 cups water
2 medium-size yellow onions, quartered
2 ribs celery, each cut into 6 pieces
2 bay leaves
1 tablespoon plus 1 1/2 teaspoons salt
1 1/2 teaspoons cayenne
1 1/2 cups vegetable oil

1½ cups bleached all-purpose
    flour
2 cups chopped yellow onions
1 cup chopped green bell peppers
1 cup chopped celery
½ pound andouille or other
    smoked sausage, finely
    chopped, plus 1 pound smoked
    sausage, cut crosswise into
    ¼-inch-thick slices
2 tablespoons chopped green
    onions or scallions
    (green part only)
2 tablespoons chopped fresh
    parsley leaves

Cook, stirring, until the vegetables are very soft, 8 to 10 minutes. Add the reserved broth and stir until the roux mixture and broth are well combined. Bring to a boil, then reduce the heat to medium–low and cook, uncovered, stirring occasionally, for 1½ hours.

Meanwhile, remove the skin from the hen and pick the meat off the bones, discarding the skin and bones. Coarsely chop the chicken meat. Add the chicken and the sliced sausage to the gumbo. Cook for 15 minutes. Remove from the heat and let sit for 5 minutes before skimming off the fat that has risen to the surface.

Stir in the green onions and parsley and serve the gumbo in individual soup or gumbo bowls.

MAKES 8 TO 10 SERVINGS

DUCK AND ANDOUILLE SAUSAGE GUMBO

Season the duck with the Creole seasoning.

Heat the oil in a large Dutch oven or heavy pot over medium-high heat. Add the duck and brown, 3 to 5 minutes on each side. Transfer to a platter and set aside.

Reduce the heat to medium and add the flour. Stir slowly and constantly to make a dark brown roux, the color of chocolate, 20 to 25 minutes. Add the onions, celery, bell peppers, salt, and cayenne. Cook, stirring constantly until the vegetables are wilted, about 10 minutes. Add the sausage and bay leaves and continue to cook, stirring, for 3 minutes. Stir in the broth and bring to a gentle boil, then simmer, uncovered, for 1 hour. Add the duck and simmer for another hour.

Remove the bay leaves and skim off any oil that has risen to the surface. Serve in deep bowls with the rice. Garnish with the green onions.

1 domestic duck (4$\frac{1}{2}$ to 5 pounds), cut into 8 pieces
2 teaspoons Creole Seasoning (page 13)
1 cup vegetable oil
1 cup bleached all-purpose flour
2 cups chopped yellow onions
1 cup chopped celery
1 cup chopped green bell peppers
$\frac{1}{2}$ teaspoon salt
$\frac{1}{4}$ teaspoon cayenne
1 pound andouille or other smoked sausage, cut crosswise into $\frac{1}{4}$-inch-thick slices
2 bay leaves
3 quarts chicken broth
2 cups cooked long-grain rice
2 tablespoons chopped green onions or scallions (green part only)

MAKES ABOUT 6 SERVINGS

SEAFOOD GUMBO

IN LOUISIANA, THERE ARE ALL KINDS OF GUMBO, A SPICY, THICK SOUP THAT CAN CONTAIN ANY NUMBER OF INGREDIENTS SUCH AS FISH OR SHELLFISH, POULTRY, GAME, AND MEAT. ALONG THE BAYOUS AND THE COAST WHERE SEAFOOD IS READILY AT HAND, YOU'LL OFTEN FIND A GUMBO MADE WITH A VARIETY OF SEAFOOD LIKE THIS ONE WITH SHRIMP, CRABMEAT, AND OYSTERS.

3/4 cup vegetable oil
3/4 cup bleached all-purpose
  flour
2 cups chopped yellow onions
1 cup chopped green bell peppers
1 cup chopped celery
1 tablespoon salt
1 teaspoon cayenne
5 bay leaves
8 cups water
1 pound medium shrimp, peeled
  and deveined
1 pound lump crabmeat, picked
  over for shells and cartilage
2 dozen oysters, shucked,
  with their liquor
2 tablespoons chopped green
  onions or scallions
  (green part only)
2 tablespoons chopped fresh
  parsley leaves

MAKES 6 SERVINGS

Combine the oil and flour in a large cast-iron or enameled cast-iron Dutch oven over medium heat. Stirring slowly and constantly, make a dark brown roux, the color of chocolate, 20 to 25 minutes. Add the onions, bell peppers, celery, salt, cayenne, and bay leaves. Cook, stirring occasionally, until very soft, about 10 minutes. Add the water and stir to blend with the roux. Reduce the heat to medium-low and simmer for 1½ hours.

Add the shrimp and crabmeat and cook for 15 minutes. Add the oysters, green onions, and parsley and cook until the edges of the oysters curl, 2 to 3 minutes. Remove the bay leaves.

Serve immediately over steamed long-grain rice in soup bowls.

october

halloween

To most everyone, Halloween means wandering around the neighborhood on a crisp fall night in costume and mask, with crunching leaves underfoot. ■ In New Orleans, especially in the French Quarter, costumed maskers take to the streets not unlike the way they do during Mardi Gras. The balconies and storefronts are decorated with make-believe spider webs, garish masks, swaths of black fabric, and drapes of gray moss, creating a perfectly ghastly and eerie stage for the maskers. ■ At the Farmers' Market, also in the French Quarter, hundreds and hundreds of bright orange pumpkins arrive in time for the pumpkin-carving contest held each year. ■ Local author Anne Rice, who has written seventeen popular novels, including the Vampire Chronicles series and the saga of the Mayfair Witches, throws a ghoulishly great Halloween bash at her home in the Garden District, and there's an annual Ghostly Galavant at the 1850 House on Jackson Square in the French Quarter. But the most fun is to have your own Halloween party for friends and relatives at your house. ■ Halloween is the eve of All Saints' Day, the day when those who have died are commemorated in special ceremonies by the Catholic Church.

EMERIL'S WEDGIE SALAD

I DECIDED I NEEDED A BREAK FROM SALADS MADE WITH MESCLUN, THE COMBINATION OF SMALL, YOUNG, SALAD GREENS, AND WENT FOR ONE MADE WITH ICEBERG LETTUCE DRESSED WITH A CREAMY BLUE CHEESE DRESSING, A FAVORITE OF MINE. IT GOES WELL WITH BOTH THE BEAN SOUP AND THE RISOTTO.

In a medium-size mixing bowl, combine the blue cheese, lemon juice, Worcestershire, hot sauce, salt, and black pepper. Using the back of a fork, mash the mixture together to form a thick paste. Drizzle in the olive oil, stirring continuously with the fork until the mixture is creamy. Add the buttermilk and mix well. Cover and refrigerate for 1 hour.

Cut the heads of lettuce into 4 wedges each. Spoon about ¼ cup of the dressing over each wedge. Serve immediately.

1/2 pound blue cheese, crumbled
1/4 cup fresh lemon juice
1 teaspoon Worcestershire sauce
1/2 teaspoon hot sauce
1/2 teaspoon salt
3/4 teaspoon freshly ground
    black pepper
1 cup olive oil
1/4 cup buttermilk
2 large heads iceberg lettuce,
    cored, washed, and patted dry

MAKES 8 SERVINGS

BEEF AND MUSHROOM RISOTTO

MAKE A POT OF THIS BEEF AND MUSHROOM RISOTTO AND ALL THE GOBLINS AND WITCHES WILL FLOCK TO YOUR HOUSE, WHETHER YOU WANT THEM TO OR NOT! IT'S ONE OF THOSE WARM AND COZY DISHES THAT I LIKE TO SERVE AT INFORMAL PARTIES LIKE THIS ONE.

One 1-pound beef tenderloin, trimmed of fat
1 teaspoon salt
$1/2$ teaspoon freshly ground black pepper
2 tablespoons olive oil
2 cups chopped yellow onions
$1/2$ pound white button mushrooms, wiped clean, stems trimmed, and thinly sliced
2 teaspoons chopped garlic
1 pound (2 cups) Arborio rice
6 cups beef broth
$1/2$ cup heavy cream
1 tablespoon butter
$1/4$ pound Parmigiano-Reggiano cheese, grated
$1/2$ cup chopped green onions or scallions (green part only)

Cut the beef crosswise into $1/4$-inch-slices, then into $1/2$-inch-wide strips. Season with the salt and black pepper.

Heat the olive oil in a large, heavy pot over medium-high heat. Add the beef and cook, stirring occasionally, until lightly browned, about 4 minutes. Add the onions and cook, stirring occasionally, until slightly soft, about 4 minutes. Add the mushrooms, garlic, and rice and stir for 2 minutes, then add the beef broth and bring to a boil. Reduce the heat to medium and stir constantly until the mixture is creamy and bubbly and the rice is tender, 15 to 18 minutes. Add the cream and continue to stir for 2 minutes, then remove from the heat.

Add the cheese and green onions and stir until the cheese melts. Serve hot.

MAKES 8 SERVINGS

DUCK AND WHITE BEAN SOUP

I LIKE WHITE BEANS AND I LIKE DUCK, A GREAT COMBINATION FOR THIS SOUP, WHICH REMINDS ME A BIT OF THE FRENCH CASSOULET. SOUPS ARE VERY INVITING ON A COLD, SCARY, WINDY NIGHT. BOO!

Put the duck in a large, heavy pot and cover with water. Add the quartered onion, garlic cloves, 2 teaspoons of the salt, and the red pepper flakes. Bring to a boil, then reduce the heat to medium, partially cover, and cook for 2 hours. Remove the duck, transfer to a platter, and let cool.

Remove the skin from the duck and pick the meat off the bones, discarding the skin and bones. Shred the meat and set aside.

Strain the duck broth through a fine-mesh sieve. You should have about 2½ quarts. Add enough water to make 3 quarts. Set aside.

In a large, heavy pot over medium-high heat, fry the bacon until slightly crisp, about 7 minutes. Add the chopped onions, celery, carrots, the remaining 1 teaspoon salt, the black pepper, and bay leaves. Cook, stirring, until the vegetables are slightly soft, about 3 minutes. Add the chopped garlic and beans and cook, stirring, for 2 minutes.

Add the reserved duck broth and bring to a boil. Reduce the heat to medium and simmer, uncovered, until the beans are tender, about 1½ hours.

Remove and discard the bay leaves. Add the duck meat and heat for about 2 minutes. Serve hot in soup bowls.

1 duck (4 to 5 pounds), trimmed of excess fat
1 medium-size yellow onion, quartered
4 cloves garlic, peeled
1 tablespoon salt
1 teaspoon red pepper flakes
1/2 pound sliced bacon, chopped
2 cups chopped yellow onions
1 cup chopped celery
1 cup chopped carrots
1/2 teaspoon freshly ground black pepper
2 bay leaves
2 teaspoons chopped garlic
1 pound dried navy beans, picked over and rinsed

MAKES ABOUT 8 SERVINGS

BEEF TARTARE

FELICIA AND MARCELLE VOTED FOR THIS BEEF TARTARE, BECAUSE THEY SAID IT REMINDED THEM OF CHILDHOOD HALLOWEEN PARTIES, WHEN GROUND BEEF WAS PASSED OFF AS BRAINS. ■ YOU WILL NEED A CHILLED WOODEN OR GLASS BOWL; PUT IT IN THE FREEZER THIRTY MINUTES BEFORE YOU NEED IT. ALSO, PLEASE BE SURE TO TELL YOUR BUTCHER TO GIVE YOU THE FRESHEST GROUND BEEF TENDERLOIN, AND USE IT THE DAY YOU PURCHASE IT. DISCARD ANY TARTARE THAT IS LEFT OVER BECAUSE YOU SHOULDN'T KEEP THE MIXTURE FOR LONGER THAN A FEW HOURS AFTER PREPARING IT. REFRIGERATE THE MIXTURE UNTIL SERVING TIME.

2 anchovy fillets
2 cloves garlic, chopped
³/4 teaspoon salt
1 teaspoon capers, drained
1 large egg (see Note on
    page 13)
2 tablespoons Dijon mustard
¹/4 cup olive oil
¹/2 teaspoon freshly ground black
    pepper
1 teaspoon Worcestershire sauce
¹/4 cup minced shallots
1 pound freshly ground beef
    tenderloin

FOR THE GARNISHES
16 slices white bread, crusts
    removed, cut into triangles,
    and toasted
2 hard-boiled eggs, shelled, yolks
    and whites separated, and
    each finely chopped
¹/4 cup finely chopped red onion
¹/4 cup chopped fresh parsley
    leaves

Put the anchovies, garlic, and ¼ teaspoon of the salt in a chilled medium-size mixing bowl and, with a fork, mash to make a paste. Add the capers and mash them into the anchovy paste. Add the egg and whisk it into the anchovy paste with the fork. Whisk in the mustard. Slowly drizzle in the olive oil, whisking constantly until incorporated. Whisk in the remaining ½ teaspoon salt, the black pepper, and Worcestershire. Add the beef and mix well with a wooden spoon.

To serve, mound the beef tartare in the center of a large cold serving platter, arrange the toast points around it, and mound the garnishes around the rim of the platter.

MAKES ABOUT 8 APPETIZER SERVINGS

SWEET POTATO CHOCOLATE BARS

AS IF YOU NEED A DESSERT FOR A HALLOWEEN PARTY, WHAT WITH ALL THE TRICK-OR-TREAT CANDY THAT ENDS UP AT THE HOUSE. BUT MR. LOU, THE PASTRY CHEF AT EMERIL'S, SAYS THESE CHOCOLATE AND SWEET POTATO BARS ARE A MUST.

Preheat the oven to 375°F.

Rub the sweet potatoes with the vegetable oil and place on a baking sheet lined with parchment paper. Bake until fork-tender, 1 to 1½ hours. Remove from the oven and let cool, then peel and mash in a large bowl.

Add to the mashed potatoes the brown sugar, cinnamon, nutmeg, salt, vanilla, eggs, and 2½ cups of the milk and mix well. Set aside.

Lower the oven temperature to 350°F.

Combine the graham cracker crumbs and pecan pieces in a food processor and process for about 1 minute, to make a fine meal. With the motor running, gradually pour the melted butter through the feed tube and process for 1 minute. Transfer the crumb mixture to a 13 × 18-inch baking pan and, using your fingers, firmly press the crumbs evenly onto the bottom and up the sides of the pan.

Pour the sweet potato mixture into the crust and spread evenly with a rubber spatula.

1½ pounds medium-size sweet potatoes
1 tablespoon vegetable oil
3/4 cup firmly packed light brown sugar
1/2 teaspoon ground cinnamon
1/4 teaspoon freshly grated nutmeg
Pinch of salt
1 teaspoon pure vanilla extract
3 large eggs
3 cups milk
2½ cups graham cracker crumbs
2 cups pecan pieces
3/4 cup (1½ sticks) unsalted butter, melted
8 ounces semisweet chocolate morsels

Put the chocolate morsels and the remaining ½ cup milk in a medium-size saucepan over medium heat and stir constantly until the chocolate melts and the mixture is smooth. Spoon the chocolate in three rows, about 2 inches apart, lengthwise over the sweet potato mixture. Then, with a knife, make a zigzag pattern to marbleize the chocolate and the sweet potato mixture.

Bake until the edges are browned and the filling is set, 20 to 25 minutes. Remove from the oven and let cool completely. To serve, cut into bars.

MAKES 2 DOZEN BARS

alessandro's christening

ALESSANDRO ERNESTO Andrade was born May 22, 1998, and what a grand day it was for the proud parents, my good friends Torre and Mauricio Andrade. The bouncing baby boy weighed in at 8 pounds, 14 ounces, and sported a shock of black hair and had beautiful brown eyes. ■ The christening, a very special event in the Catholic community, was at St. Rita's Catholic Church, where the Reverend Joel P. Cantones did the honors. The godparents, Eric Linquest and Tierney Walker, hovered over the baptismal font along with the grandparents, Terrence and Joan Walker and Luis and Jeannette Andrade. ■ After the ceremony, the family and close friends gathered at Torre and Mo's home for a joyful celebration, with much dancing to the music of an Italian band and, of course, a grand feast!

CRABMEAT DEVILED EGGS

FOR GATHERINGS SUCH AS THIS, IT'S BEST TO HAVE SOME "PICK-UP" FOOD, AND THESE DEVILED EGGS FIT THE BILL. BE SURE TO KEEP THEM CHILLED UNTIL YOU'RE READY TO SERVE.

Remove the yolks from the whites and put in a medium-size mixing bowl. Using the back of a fork, mash the yolks, then add the mayonnaise, lemon juice, salt, white pepper, and hot sauce. Stir with the fork to mix. Add the crabmeat and stir gently to mix. Spoon equal amounts of the mixture into the egg white halves. Chill the eggs for 2 hours before serving.

To serve, garnish with the caviar.

12 hard-boiled eggs, shelled and
   cut lengthwise in half
3 tablespoons Mayonnaise
   (page 129)
2 tablespoons fresh lemon juice
1/4 teaspoon salt
1/8 teaspoon freshly ground
   white pepper
1/4 teaspoon hot sauce
1/2 pound lump crabmeat, picked
   over for shells and cartilage
1 ounce caviar, such as beluga,
   osetra, or sevruga

MAKES 12 SERVINGS (2 DEVILED EGG HALVES PER PERSON)

SPINACH AND CHEESE QUICHE

QUICHE, WHICH ORIGINATED IN THE REGION OF ALSACE-LORRAINE IN NORTHEASTERN FRANCE, IS SO VERSATILE, SINCE IT CAN BE MADE WITH ANY NUMBER OF INGREDIENTS, SUCH AS HAM, ONIONS, MUSHROOMS, OR WHATEVER FRESH GARDEN VEGETABLES ARE AVAILABLE. I PARTICULARLY LIKE THIS ONE MADE WITH FRESH SPINACH AND, OF COURSE, CHEESE.

Combine the flour, ½ teaspoon of the salt, and ¼ teaspoon of the cayenne in a medium-size mixing bowl. Cut in the shortening with a pastry blender or two knives until the mixture resembles coarse meal. Add 4 tablespoons of the ice water and mix until the dough come away from the sides of the bowl, adding the remaining tablespoon of water, if necessary. Form into a ball, cover with plastic wrap, and refrigerate for at least 1 hour.

2 cups bleached all-purpose flour
1¼ teaspoons salt
¼ teaspoon plus ⅛ teaspoon cayenne
½ cup vegetable shortening
4 to 5 tablespoons ice water, as needed
1½ cups heavy cream

3 large eggs
1/8 teaspoon freshly grated
   nutmeg
1 tablespoon unsalted butter
1/2 cup chopped yellow onion
1/8 teaspoon freshly ground black
   pepper
2 teaspoons chopped garlic
3 cups tightly packed fresh
   spinach, stems removed,
   washed, and patted dry
2 ounces Gouda cheese, grated
2 ounces sharp white cheddar
   cheese, grated

Preheat the oven to 350°F.

Remove the dough from the refrigerator and let sit for 5 minutes. Lightly dust a work surface with flour. Roll the dough out into a 12-inch round about ¼ inch thick. Fold the dough into fourths, place it in a 10-inch quiche pan, and unfold it. Press the dough into the bottom and up the sides of the pan. Roll a rolling pin over the pan to cut off the excess dough. Prick the bottom of the crust all over with a fork.

In a large mixing bowl, combine the cream, eggs, ½ teaspoon of the salt, the remaining ⅛ teaspoon cayenne, and the nutmeg. Whisk to blend.

In a large skillet over medium heat, melt the butter. Add the onion, the remaining ¼ teaspoon salt, and the black pepper and cook, stirring, until the onion is soft, about 3 minutes. Add the garlic and spinach and cook until the spinach wilts, about 2 minutes. Remove from the heat and set aside.

Arrange the spinach mixture evenly over the bottom of the crust. Sprinkle the cheeses evenly over the spinach. Pour the cream mixture over the top.

Bake until the center is set and the top is golden, about 45 minutes. Serve warm or at room temperature.

MAKES ONE 10-INCH QUICHE; 8 SERVINGS

RASPBERRY CRUMB COFFEE CAKE

CELEBRATIONS SUCH AS THIS DEMAND A SCRUMPTIOUS SWEET DELIGHT AND THIS CRUMB CAKE FITS THE BILL PERFECTLY. OF COURSE, YOU CAN SERVE IT AT BRUNCHES OR AFTERNOON TEAS. HECK, SERVE IT TO YOUR FAMILY NEXT SUNDAY.

Preheat the oven to 350°F. Grease a 10 × 2-inch round cake pan with 1 teaspoon of the butter.

In a medium-size nonreactive saucepan, combine the raspberries, ½ cup of the granulated sugar, and the lemon juice. Bring the mixture to a boil and cook at a boil for 3 minutes.

In a small bowl, dissolve the cornstarch in the water. Add to the raspberry mixture and cook, stirring, until it thickens, about for 2 minutes. Remove from the heat and let cool completely.

In a large mixing bowl, cream ¼ pound (1 stick) of the butter with the remaining 1 cup granulated sugar with an electric mixer. Add the eggs one at a time, beating well after each addition.

Into a medium-size mixing bowl, sift 3½ cups of the flour, the baking powder, baking soda, ½ teaspoon of the cinnamon, and the salt. Add the flour mixture, buttermilk, and vanilla to the butter mixture and beat with the electric mixer until everything is incorporated.

In another medium-size mixing bowl, combine the remaining ¼ cup (½ stick) butter, the remaining ½ cup flour, the brown sugar, and the remaining ¼ teaspoon cinnamon. Using your hands, combine the mixture until it resembles fine crumbs.

1 teaspoon plus ¾ cup (1½ sticks) unsalted butter, at room temperature
2 pints fresh raspberries, picked over
1½ cups granulated sugar
3 tablespoons fresh lemon juice
2 tablespoons cornstarch
¼ cup water
3 large eggs
4 cups bleached all-purpose flour
1 teaspoon baking powder
1 teaspoon baking soda
¾ teaspoon ground cinnamon
¼ teaspoon salt
1½ cups buttermilk
1 teaspoon pure vanilla extract
½ cup firmly packed light brown sugar
1 cup confectioners' sugar
2 tablespoons Steen's 100% Pure Cane Syrup or other cane syrup
2 tablespoons milk

Spread half of the batter in the prepared pan. Spread the raspberry mixture over the batter. Drop heaping spoonfuls of the remaining batter over the raspberry mixture, about 1 inch apart. Sprinkle the crumb mixture evenly over the surface.

Put the cake pan on a baking sheet and bake until golden brown, about 40 minutes. Remove from the oven and let cool slightly.

In a medium-size mixing bowl, whisk together the confectioners' sugar, cane syrup, and milk until smooth. Drizzle the frosting over the top of the coffee cake. Cut into slices and serve warm.

MAKES ONE 10-INCH CAKE; 12 SERVINGS

PECAN STICKY BUNS

BRIOCHE, THAT WONDERFUL BUTTERY YEAST BREAD GIVEN TO THE WORLD BY THE FRENCH, IS THE DOUGH I USE FOR THESE STICKY BUNS. THEY'RE LIGHT BUT RICH, AND THE PECAN-BROWN SUGAR TOPPING IS JUST RIGHT FOR THEM. ■ EVERY TIME I MAKE BRIOCHE, I THINK OF MR. AMARILLO, A GREAT BAKER AND TEACHER OF MINE WHEN, AS A YOUNG BOY, I WORKED AS A BAKER IN FALL RIVER.

To make the dough, combine the yeast and warm milk in a medium-size mixing bowl and stir to dissolve the yeast. Add 1 cup of the flour and mix to blend well. Add the vanilla pulp (discard the bean) and let stand at room temperature in a warm, draft-free place for about 2 hours to allow fermentation.

Put 2 cups of the remaining flour in a large mixing bowl. Add 4 of the eggs one at a time, beating well with a wooden spoon after each addition. The dough will be sticky, thick, and spongy. Add the warm water, 3 tablespoons of the granulated sugar, and the salt and mix well, beating vigorously. Add the butter and work it into the dough with your hands until it is all incorporated. Add 2 more of the eggs and mix well. Add the remaining 2 cups flour and blend into the dough, breaking up any lumps with your fingers. Add the yeast mixture and using your hands, knead and fold it into the dough. Continue kneading and folding until everything is well mixed, about 5 minutes. The dough will be sticky and moist. Cover with a clean cloth and let rise in a warm, draft-free place until doubled in size, about 2 hours.

With your fingers, lightly punch down the dough. Cover and let rise again in a warm, draft-free place until doubled in size again, about 1 hour.

FOR THE BUNS

3 envelopes active dry yeast
1/2 cup warm milk (about 110°F)
5 cups bleached all-purpose flour
1 vanilla bean, split and scraped
7 large eggs
1/2 cup warm water
   (about 110°F)
3 tablespoons plus 1 cup
   granulated sugar
2 teaspoons salt
3/4 pound (3 sticks) unsalted
   butter, at room temperature
1 teaspoon ground cinnamon

FOR THE TOPPING

1/2 pound (2 sticks) unsalted
   butter, at room temperature
1 cup firmly packed light brown
   sugar
1/2 teaspoon ground cinnamon
2 cups pecan pieces

Remove the dough from the bowl and divide into two equal balls. Refrigerate one portion while working with the other.

Lightly dust the work surface with flour and roll out the dough into a rectangle about 14 inches long, 10 inches wide, and ¼ inch thick. In a small bowl, lightly beat the remaining egg. With a pastry brush, brush the edges of the dough with the beaten egg. In another small bowl, combine the remaining 1 cup granulated sugar and the cinnamon. Sprinkle half of the cinnamon sugar over three fourths of the dough. Roll the dough up tightly to form a log, starting from the long side. Wrap it in plastic wrap and freeze for 30 minutes. Repeat the process with the remaining dough.

For the topping, combine the butter, brown sugar, and cinnamon in a bowl and blend well. Spread the mixture over the bottom of two 10 × 2-inch round cake pans. Sprinkle both evenly with the pecans.

Remove the dough logs from the freezer and, with a sharp knife, cut crosswise into 1½-inch-thick slices. Lay the slices on top of the butter-and-pecan mixture, about ½ inch apart. Let the buns rise in a warm, draft-free place until doubled in size, about 1½ hours.

Preheat the oven to 400°F.

Bake until golden brown, about 35 minutes. Remove from the oven, let cool for about 5 minutes, and then flip onto a large serving platter and serve.

MAKES 18 BUNS

october
pepper
fest

WHEN THE Kiwanis Club of St. Martinville organized the first Pepper Fest, they hoped it would be a success. It was! Now, on the last weekend in October, the small community is bustling with activities. A pepper-eating contest is one of the highlights of the celebration, as is a round of bands that keep visitors and natives hopping on the blocked-off streets that run along the legendary Bayou Teche. ■ Booths, filled with pepper products and arts and crafts featuring pepper themes, do a hot business and well they should since St. Martinville is in the heart of the pepper-growing industry. Down the road is Avery Island where Tabasco sauce originated, and B. F. Trappey's Sons, Inc., was down the bayou until just a couple of years ago. Cajun Chef Products and Acadiana Pepper Company are located in the town, and some newcomers are springing up in the area. ■ There's nothing like a pepper sauce or a pepper-based dish to spike up anyone's day.

HOMEMADE PEPPER SAUCE

IF YOU'VE PERUSED THE CONDIMENT SECTION OF YOUR SUPERMAR-
KET LATELY, YOU'VE NOTICED THAT JUST ABOUT EVERYONE AND HIS
MOTHER HAS COME OUT WITH A HOT SAUCE. SOME ARE SO HOT,
THEY'LL BLOW THE TOP OF YOUR HEAD OFF. THAT'S NOT MY IDEA OF
A GOOD HOT SAUCE. A HOT SAUCE, IN MY OPINION, SHOULD HAVE
GOOD FLAVOR AND A FAIR AMOUNT OF HEAT, BUT NOT SO MUCH SO
THAT YOUR TASTE BUDS ARE RUINED FOR LIFE. I TEND TO USE
LOUISIANA-MADE HOT SAUCES BECAUSE MOST OF THEM HAVE BEEN
AROUND FOR A LONG TIME AND THE FAMILIES OR COMPANIES THAT
MAKE THEM KNOW WHAT THEY'RE DOING. PLUS, MOST HOT SAUCES
AROUND HERE ARE MADE WITH LOCALLY GROWN PEPPERS, LIKE
CAYENNES OR TABASCOS. (I SUPPOSE YOU KNOW THAT TABASCO HOT
SAUCE ORIGINATED IN LOUISIANA, SPECIFICALLY, ON AVERY ISLAND
IN SOUTH LOUISIANA, MADE BY EDMUND MCILHENNY, WHO BOTTLED
HIS FIRST BATCH IN 1868.) ■ BUT SOMETIMES I GET A HANKERING TO
MAKE MY OWN PEPPER SAUCE. THIS ONE'S MADE WITH ANAHEIMS AND
SERRANOS. ■ SINCE THE OILS IN THE FLESH AND SEEDS OF HOT PEP-
PERS ARE QUITE VOLATILE, YOU SHOULD WEAR RUBBER GLOVES
WHEN HANDLING THEM. BE CAREFUL NOT TO TOUCH YOUR FACE OR
EYES WHILE WORKING WITH THE PEPPERS.

Remove the stems from the peppers, cut them lengthwise in half, and remove the seeds. Cut crosswise into
½-inch-thick slices.

Put the peppers, vinegar, water, and salt in a medium-
size nonreactive saucepan over medium-high heat.
Bring to a boil, reduce the heat to medium, and simmer for 20 minutes. Remove from the heat and let
steep until completely cool.

6 large red Anaheim peppers
   (about 12 ounces)
4 serrano peppers
   (about 1/2 ounce)
2 1/4 cups distilled white vinegar
1 cup water
1 tablespoon salt

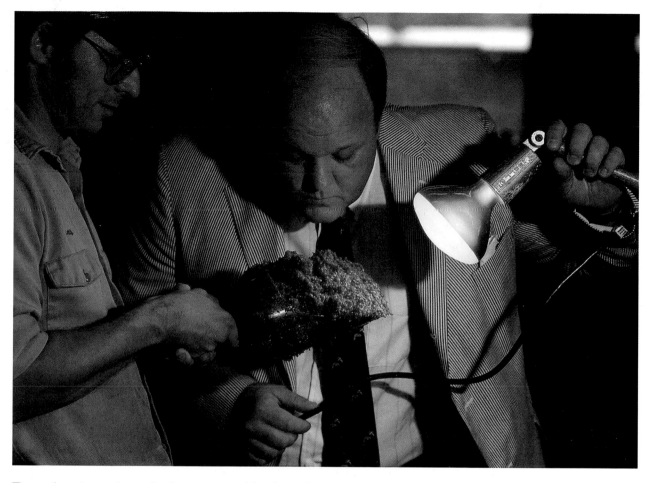

Pour the mixture into a food processor or blender and process until smooth. Strain through a fine-mesh strainer, pour into sterilized bottles, and secure with airtight lids. Refrigerate and let age for at least 2 weeks before using. The sauce can be stored in the refrigerator for up to 6 months.

MAKES 1 PINT

NOVEMBER is a month of variables. It begins solemnly with the observance of All Saints' Day, which coincides with the Day of the Dead, celebrated throughout Mexico. In Louisiana, and especially in New Orleans and the Catholic communities of southern Louisiana, November 1 is when families visit the graves of loved ones. ■ During the week preceding All Saints' Day, people trek to the cemeteries to scrub, clean, and whitewash the aboveground tombs. Because of the water-saturated soil and the heavy annual rainfall, Louisianians adopted the Spanish custom of building these structures. Old cemeteries are surrounded with brick walls honeycombed with vaults, inexpensive burial places for families of modest means. Affluent families usually had their own tombs. The private burial places, some very ornate, were built to accommodate multiple burials and look like small houses, thus giving the large walled graveyards the aspect of a city. They are, in fact, often called "Cities of the Dead." ■ It is tradi-

tionally the duty of the women of the family, oftentimes accompanied by young children, to tend to the gravesites. Once the tombs are cleaned, the ladies often weed and trim around them in preparation for the pilgrimage that takes place on November 1. ■ Bearing armloads of flowers, sometimes simple handmade wreaths of mums or a large spray of expensive blossoms, entire families visit the houses of their dead, some bringing lunch and spending the day in the cemetery, where there is often a mass celebrated. Years ago, it was a tradition to light blessed candles on the tombs. Sometimes members of the family would stay the night, replacing the candles as they burned out. Unfortunately, I think, this practice is no longer observed. ■ Since November is a

cooler month, family *boucheries*, or slaughters, were always held in the rural areas. The host would be a farmer, and his guests would be

friends and relatives as well as farmworkers. Early in the day, a hog was slaughtered, and the rest of the day was spent butchering it, making cracklings, sausages, boudin, and backbone stew, and dividing up the better cuts for everyone to take

november

home. Many times there were an accordionist and a fiddler to keep the workers entertained. Now, because of modern refrigeration, boucheries are getting harder and harder to find, but there are still several communities that continue the tradition to this day. ■ As Thanksgiving approaches, it's time to turn to turkey. The gobblers are stuffed, then roasted, or deep-fried—and that's a really big procedure down here! It's the first of the holiday gatherings that will continue until New Year's, and a lot of cooking is going on around the state.

 ■ In Abbeville, they're not talking turkey, they're talking eggs, lots of eggs, about five thousand, if truth be told. Thousands of visitors gather on the square in this quaint town on the Vermilion River to get a taste of an omelette that is cooked in a huge specially made skillet right on the street!

november

omelette

festival

THE STORY goes that when Napoleon and his army were traveling through the South of France, they decided to rest for the night near the town of Bessières. Napoleon feasted on an omelette prepared by a local innkeeper that was such a culinary delight, he ordered the townspeople to gather all the eggs in the village and to prepare a huge omelette for his army the next day.■ Since 1985, Abbeville has been hosting the Giant Omelette Celebration, during which the egg feast is prepared in a huge skillet over an open wood fire, tended by *chevaliers* from French-speaking countries around the world. The eggs are carried in large baskets. The rest of the ingredients, a gallon and a half of cooking oil, 50 pounds of onions, 75 bell peppers, 4 pounds of green onions, 2 pounds of parsley, 6½ gallons of milk, 52 pounds of butter, 3 boxes of salt, 2 boxes of black pepper, and Tabasco sauce to taste, are transported as well. ■ Once the eggs are beaten with the other ingredients, and stirred by large paddles, and cooked, festival goers are given samples to taste. Eggsactly what they came for!

PORK SAUSAGE AND CHEESE OMELETTE

ONE OF THE FIRST THINGS I LEARNED TO MAKE WAS AN OMELETTE, AND I LIKE THE FACT THAT IT IS SO VERSATILE. YOU CAN PUT JUST ABOUT ANYTHING IN IT—HAM, CHEESE, HERBS, CHOPPED TOMATOES, PEPPERS, CRABMEAT—WHATEVER YOUR HEART DESIRES. SAVORY ONES ARE MORE COMMON, BUT THE FRENCH ALSO MAKE SWEET OMELETTES, FILLING THEM WITH JAM OR POACHED FRUIT FLAVORED WITH LIQUEUR, THEN SPRINKLING THEM WITH SUGAR AND BROWNING THEM UNDER THE BROILER. ■ FOR MY ODE TO THE OMELETTE FESTIVAL, I OFFER THIS ONE COMPOSED OF SAUSAGE AND CHEESE. THERE'S SOME CONTROVERSY OVER WHETHER TO ADD CREAM OR MILK TO THE BEATEN EGGS, BUT I FIND THAT ADDING A LITTLE WATER MAKES THE OMELETTE PUFF UP A BIT, MAKING IT LIGHT AND AIRY.

In a large skillet over high heat, cook the sausage and onion, stirring often, until the meat is browned and the onion is lightly golden, about 6 minutes. Remove from the pan and drain on paper towels. Set aside.

Combine the eggs, salt, black pepper, and water in a medium-size mixing bowl and whisk to mix.

In a medium-size nonstick skillet over medium heat, melt 1 tablespoon of the butter. Pour half of the egg mixture into the skillet and stir it around with a spatula, then swirl it around until it begins to set, about 3 minutes. Add half of the sausage-and-onion mixture, half the cheese, and half of the green onions, spreading them evenly over the eggs. Cook for 2 minutes. With

1 pound breakfast sausage, removed from the casings and crumbled
1/2 cup chopped yellow onion
12 large eggs
1 teaspoon salt
1/2 teaspoon freshly ground black pepper
1/2 cup water
2 tablespoons unsalted butter
1 cup grated cheddar cheese
1/2 cup chopped green onion or scallion (green part only)

a spatula, carefully fold the omelette in half and cook for 1 minute more. Carefully slide the omelette onto a serving plate, flipping it over as you do; keep warm.

Repeat the process with the remaining 1 tablespoon butter and the remaining egg mixture, sausage and onion, cheese, and green onion.

To serve, cut each omelette in half.

MAKES 2 OMELETTES; 4 SERVINGS

thanksgiving

THANKSGIVING, turkey day, is about family and friends gathering to enjoy a meal together and to give thanks for all that we have. Naturally, there are traditions each family develops over the years. Turkey is the national symbol of Thanksgiving, and cranberries in some form and pumpkin pie are usual accompaniments, but around the country, the other dishes on the menu may vary. ■ In Louisiana, a lot of gobblers end up on the dinner table, but you can also expect to see roasted wild duck or venison on the menu. The happy hunters around here are more than pleased to use whatever they bag for the family meal. What's fun too is that just about everyone gets to bring a family favorite to the table— sweet potatoes prepared in some fashion usually show up, as do corn bread, oysters, and seasonal vegetables. ■ Thanksgiving has also come to mean football, beginning in the morning and running until the late afternoon, and there's always the question of when dinner should be served, at halftime, or after the game. Some households make it simple—they eat all day.

JALAPEÑO CORN BREAD

CORN BREAD IS ONE OF THOSE SOUTHERN THINGS THAT APPEARS ON JUST ABOUT EVERY HOLIDAY TABLE. THESE CORN BREAD MUFFINS ARE JAZZED UP WITH JALAPEÑOS, WHICH GIVE THEM A GOOD KICK, JUST HOW I LIKE MY CORN BREAD. THE FRESH CORN KERNELS GIVE THEM A GOOD TEXTURE. SPREAD SOME BUTTER ON THEM FOR GOOD MEASURE.

Preheat the oven to 425°F. Grease a 12-mold muffin tin with 1 tablespoon of the vegetable oil.

In a large saucepan over medium-high heat, combine 1 cup of the milk, the corn, and ½ teaspoon of the salt. Bring to a boil, reduce the heat to medium, and cook, stirring occasionally, for 15 minutes. Remove from the heat. Add the bell pepper and jalapeño.

In a large mixing bowl, combine the sugar, cornmeal, flour, the remaining 1 teaspoon salt, and the baking powder. Mix well. Add the remaining ¼ cup vegetable oil, the remaining ½ cup milk, the eggs, and the corn mixture. Mix well.

Spoon a heaping ¼ cup of batter into each muffin tin and bake until lightly golden, 20 to 25 minutes or until golden brown. Remove from the oven and cool for 3 minutes, then remove from the muffin tins and serve warm.

1 tablespoon plus ¼ cup vegetable oil
1 cup fresh sweet corn kernels (from 1 small ear)
1½ cups milk
1½ teaspoons salt
¼ cup minced red bell pepper
2 tablespoons minced seeded fresh jalapeño
2 tablespoons sugar
1 cup yellow cornmeal
1 cup bleached all-purpose flour
2 teaspoons baking powder
2 large eggs

MAKES 1 DOZEN MUFFINS

PUMPKIN SOUP

DURING THE FALL, THOUSANDS OF PUMPKINS IN ALL SHAPES AND SIZES ARRIVE AT THE FRENCH MARKET. IT'S A SIGHT TO BEHOLD! FAMILIES WANDER AROUND, PICKING OUT JUST THE RIGHT PUMPKIN OR PUMPKINS TO TAKE HOME TO MAKE JACK-O'-LANTERNS OR TO SET OUT FOR DECORATION DURING THE THANKSGIVING HOLIDAYS. ■ AND, AS USUAL, EVERYONE WANTS TO KNOW WHAT TO DO WITH THE PUMPKIN FLESH. HERE'S ONE SOLUTION—A HEARTY SOUP THAT'S FULL OF FLAVOR, AND TALK ABOUT THE GREAT AROMA THAT FILTERS THROUGH THE HOUSE WHILE IT'S COOKING! HILDA, MY MAMA, SAVES THE SEEDS AND TOASTS THEM WITH A LITTLE SALT AND CRUSHED RED PEPPER TO USE AS A GARNISH FOR THE SOUP.

4 pounds fresh pumpkin flesh, peeled, seeded, and chopped
2 teaspoons salt
2 tablespoons unsalted butter
2 cups chopped yellow onions
3 bay leaves
1/2 teaspoon freshly ground white pepper
2 teaspoons sugar
8 cups chicken broth
4 cups water
2 tablespoons smooth peanut butter
1/4 teaspoon ground cinnamon
1/8 teaspoon freshly grated nutmeg
1/8 teaspoon ground allspice

Put the chopped pumpkin in a large saucepan, cover with water, and add 1 teaspoon of the salt. Bring to a boil and cook until fork-tender, about 15 minutes. Drain, let cool, and mash. You should have about 4 cups.

In a large, heavy pot or Dutch oven, melt the butter over medium-high heat. Add the onions, bay leaves, the remaining 1 teaspoon salt, the white pepper, and sugar. Cook, stirring, until the onions are soft and lightly golden, about 10 minutes. Add the chicken broth, water, pumpkin puree, and peanut butter. Stir to mix. Bring to a boil, then reduce the heat to medium and cook, uncovered, until it coats a spoon, about 1 hour and 15 minutes.

Stir in the cinnamon, nutmeg, and allspice. Remove and discard the bay leaves and serve hot in soup bowls.

MAKES 10 TO 12 SERVINGS

EMERIL'S FRIED TURKEY

FIRST OF ALL, YOU MUST UNDERSTAND THAT WE'RE FRYING THE WHOLE TURKEY HERE, NOT PIECES. DON'T ATTEMPT TO DO THIS IN YOUR KITCHEN. IF YOU'RE GOING TO TAKE THIS ON, YOU NEED ONE OF THOSE RIGS THAT WE USE AROUND HERE TO COOK EVERYTHING FROM BOILED SEAFOOD TO GUMBOS AND STEWS FOR A LARGE CROWD. THE RIG CONSISTS OF A PROPANE BURNER, A PROPANE TANK, AND A HEAVY FORTY- TO SIXTY-QUART POT FITTED WITH A METAL BASKET. ■ THE RIG CAN BE SET UP ON A PATIO OR IN THE BACKYARD, AND NEWSPAPERS OR THICK CARDBOARD SHOULD BE SPREAD AROUND THE BURNER TO PROTECT THE AREA FROM GREASE SPLATTERS. HAVE ON HAND TWO LARGE PAPER BAGS, AND ARM YOURSELF WITH TWO LONG-HANDLED BARBECUE FORKS (SOME COOKS USE METAL COAT HANGERS TO FASHION A GADGET WITH WHICH TO LIFT THE TURKEY OUT OF THE HOT OIL) AND A BROOM HANDLE; ALSO I STRONGLY SUGGEST THAT YOU HAVE BARBECUE MITTENS OR LARGE INSULATED POT HOLDERS. YOU SHOULD HAVE A THERMOMETER TO MEASURE THE HEAT OF THE OIL AS WELL AS A MEAT THERMOMETER TO TEST THE TURKEY'S DONENESS. YOU'LL ALSO NEED A THINGAMAJIG CALLED A CAJUN INJECTOR, WHICH IS NOTHING MORE THAN A LARGE SYRINGE, TO INJECT THE TURKEY WITH THE MARINADE (SEE THE SOURCE GUIDE). ■ REMEMBER TO KEEP THE KIDS AWAY FROM THE HOT OIL! ■ LAST YEAR, FOR *GOOD MORNING AMERICA*, I AND ONE OF THE CHEFS FROM EMERIL'S, MY GOOD BUDDY TOM WOLFE, FRIED SIX TURKEYS AT FIVE A.M. WE HAD A BLAST COOKING AND EATING THOSE WONDERFUL BIRDS. ■ THERE'S SOME DEBATE ABOUT WHAT SIZE TURKEYS SHOULD BE USED WHEN FRYING THEM WHOLE. I BELIEVE ONE WEIGHING EIGHT TO TEN POUNDS IS EASIER TO HANDLE THAN A LARGER ONE, PLUS SMALLER ONES TAKE LESS TIME TO COOK. ■ IT'S BEST TO INJECT THE TURKEYS WITH THE MARINADE, THEN SEASON THE OUTSIDE. THEY CAN THEN CAN BE STORED IN LARGE PLASTIC BAGS AND ICED DOWN IN AN ICE CHEST FOR SEVERAL HOURS OR OVERNIGHT.

FOR THE MARINADE

2 tablespoons Worcestershire
    sauce
1 tablespoon liquid Zatarain's
    Concentrated Crab & Shrimp
    Boil (optional)
1/4 cup apple cider
3/4 cup honey
One 12-ounce bottle beer
1 tablespoon salt
1 tablespoon ground allspice
1/2 cup Creole Seasoning
    (page 13)
1/4 teaspoon cayenne
Pinch of ground cloves

FOR THE SEASONING MIX

1 cup salt
1 tablespoon cayenne
1 tablespoon freshly ground
    black pepper

TO FRY

2 turkeys (8 to 10 pounds each)
About 10 gallons peanut oil

Make the marinade.

Combine all of the ingredients in a food processor or blender and process for about 5 minutes. Fill the syringe and inject each turkey in the breast and thigh area, as well as the back, wings, and legs. You will have to fill the syringe several times.

Next, combine the seasoning ingredients and rub the mixture evenly all over each turkey. Place them in large plastic bags and secure before icing them down or refrigerating them for twenty-four hours.

To fry each turkey, fill the pot three quarters of the way full with the peanut oil and heat the oil to between 350° and 360°F. Place one turkey in the basket insert and carefully and slowly lower it into the hot oil. Turn the turkey every 10 minutes, using long-handled forks. A whole turkey will take 3 to 5 minutes per pound to cook. It is done when the internal temperature reaches 170° to 180°F on an instant read meat thermometer.

Carefully lift the basket out of the hot oil. This can be done by inserting a broomstick through the handles and having two strong people lift the basket out of the pot. Using the long-handled forks, transfer the turkey to a large brown paper bag and let stand for about 15 minutes before removing to carve.

Repeat the procedure for the second turkey.

MAKES ABOUT 20 SERVINGS (10 PER TURKEY)

SUZANNE'S CARROT RING

THIS CARROT RING IS A STANDARD DISH SERVED AT FELICIA'S THANKSGIVING DINNER. HER MOTHER, SUZANNE, TELLS ME THAT IT'S BEEN IN THE FAMILY FOR A LONG TIME. IT'S KIND OF LIKE A SAVORY AND SWEET CARROT CAKE THAT'S MADE IN A TUBE PAN, THEN GARNISHED WITH COOKED CAULIFLOWER, PEAS, AND TURNIPS. HERE I'VE USED MIRLITON, WHICH IS VERY POPULAR IN THE SOUTH. MIRLITON, ALSO KNOWN AS CHAYOTE, VEGETABLE PEAR, CHRISTOPHINE, OR CHO-CHO IS GROWN ALL OVER LOUISIANA. THE FIRM, CRISP FLESH, SURROUNDING A SINGLE FLAT SEED, HAS A DELICATE FLAVOR. YOU CAN SUBSTITUTE SQUASH OR EGGPLANT FOR THE MIRLITON. IT'S AN INTERESTING DISH.

Preheat the oven to 350°F. Grease a 10-inch Bundt or tube pan with the vegetable oil. Dust the bottom and sides of the pan evenly with the bread crumbs.

With an electric mixer in a medium-size mixing bowl, beat the egg whites until stiff peaks form. Set aside.

With the mixer fitted with a paddle attachment, in a large mixing bowl, cream ¾ pound (3 sticks) of the butter and the sugar together. Add the egg yolks one at a time, beating after each addition. Add the carrots, milk, and lemon juice and beat until well mixed. Add 1 teaspoon of the salt, the baking powder, baking soda, and flour and beat again until well mixed. Fold in the beaten egg whites until no white streaks remain and pour into the prepared pan.

1 tablespoon vegetable oil
¼ cup fine dried bread crumbs
4 large eggs, separated
¾ pound (3 sticks) plus
    2 tablespoons unsalted butter,
    at room temperature
¾ pound carrots, grated
    (about 3 cups)
2 tablespoons milk
2 tablespoons fresh lemon juice
1½ teaspoons salt
2 teaspoons baking powder
1 teaspoon baking soda
2 cups bleached all-purpose flour
2 medium-size mirliton, boiled in
    water until fork-tender,
    drained, peeled, and cut into
    small dice

1 pound English (sweet) peas (fresh or frozen), blanched in boiling water for 2 minutes and drained

½ teaspoon freshly ground black pepper

Bake until golden brown and the top springs back when touched, about 1 hour. Remove from the oven and let cool for about 5 minutes. With a thin knife, loosen the sides of the cake and remove it from the pan, turning it, bottom side up, onto a serving platter.

Melt the remaining 2 tablespoons butter in a large skillet over medium heat. Add the mirliton and peas, season with the remaining ½ teaspoon salt and the black pepper, and cook for about 5 minutes.

Spoon the mixture into the hole of the carrot ring. Slice the ring and serve with the vegetables.

MAKES ABOUT 12 SERVINGS

HOLIDAY CRANBERRY PIE

PIES MADE WITH PECANS, SWEET POTATOES, OR PUMPKIN ARE COMMON
FARE FOR THE LOUISIANA THANKSGIVING TABLE AND THEY'RE ALL GOOD,
BUT I LIKE CRANBERRIES AND THOUGHT ABOUT HOW I COULD MAKE A
PIE WITH THEM. HERE'S WHAT I CAME UP WITH! ■ OH, BY THE WAY, THE
CRANBERRY TOPPING CAN ALSO DOUBLE AS A GARNISH FOR THE TURKEY.

MAKE THE PIECRUST

Combine the flour and salt in a large mixing bowl.
Cut in the shortening with a pastry blender or two
knives until the mixture resembles coarse meal. Add 4
tablespoons of the ice water and mix until the dough
comes away from the sides of the bowl, adding the
remaining water, if necessary. Form into a ball, cover
with plastic wrap, and refrigerate for at least 1 hour.

Preheat the oven to 350°F.

Remove the dough from the refrigerator and let sit
for 5 minutes. Lightly dust a work surface with flour.
Roll the dough out into a 12-inch round about ¼ inch
thick. Fold the dough into quarters, place it in a 9-inch
deep-dish pie pan, unfold it, and fit it into the pan.
Crimp the edges and prick the bottom of the crust with
a fork. Bake until lightly golden, 20 to 22 minutes.
Remove from the oven and let cool completely.

FOR THE PIECRUST

2 cups bleached all-purpose flour
1/2 teaspoon salt
1/2 cup vegetable shortening
4 to 5 tablespoons ice water, as
   needed

FOR THE CRANBERRIES

1/2 pound fresh cranberries
1 tablespoon grated orange zest
1 teaspoon grated lemon zest
1/4 cup fresh orange juice
3 tablespoons fresh lemon juice
1/2 cup sugar
1 teaspoon pure vanilla extract
2 cups water
3 tablespoons cornstarch

FOR THE PASTRY CREAM

2¹/₂ cups milk

³/₄ cup sugar

2 large egg yolks

¹/₂ teaspoon pure vanilla extract

¹/₄ cup cornstarch

TO FINISH

Double recipe Sweetened
    Whipped Cream (page 49)

MAKE THE CRANBERRIES

Put the cranberries, orange and lemon zests, orange and lemon juices, sugar, vanilla, and 1½ cups of the water in a medium-size nonreactive saucepan over medium-high heat. Bring to a boil and cook at a boil for 8 minutes. Dissolve the cornstarch in the remaining ½ cup water and add to the pan. Reduce the heat to medium, then stir constantly until the mixture thickens, about 2 minutes. Remove from the heat and let cool completely.

Make the pastry cream. Combine 2 cups of the milk and the sugar in a medium-size saucepan over medium heat and stir to dissolve the sugar. Scald the milk—that is, heat it until small bubbles form around the edge of the pan, about 10 minutes; don't let it boil. Remove from the heat.

In a small bowl, combine ¼ cup of the hot milk with the egg yolks, whisking to mix, then return this mixture to the hot milk in the saucepan. Stir in the vanilla.

Dissolve the cornstarch in the remaining ½ cup milk, add to the pan, and cook, whisking constantly, until the mixture thickens, about 4 minutes. Pour the mixture into a glass bowl, cover the top of the mixture with plastic wrap (this will keep a skin from forming), and let cool completely.

Pour the cooled pastry cream into the pie shell, cover the cream with plastic wrap, and refrigerate for 1 hour. Remove from the refrigerator and spread the cranberry mixture evenly over the surface. Cover and refrigerate for 4 hours.

Remove the pie from the refrigerator and spread with the whipped cream before serving.

MAKES ONE 9-INCH PIE; 6 TO 8 SERVINGS

TO OUR NORTHERN neighbors, December usually means wondrous snow-filled landscapes. Not so down here in the South, though, to be sure, there is some bone-chilling weather. Like everywhere else, the month is filled with anticipation as the joyous holidays draw near. ■ There's the tree to be picked out and decorated, family get-togethers to be planned, and gifts to be selected with care and wrapped. Then there's all the food

for feasting to prepare—pâtés, pralines, bonbons, and dozens of other goodies. ■ Uptown, downtown, the French Quarter, Mid-City, and the Lakefront all sparkle with colored lights, evergreen boughs, holly, and mistletoe. The majestic oaks in City Park are strung with millions of lights for the Celebration of the Oaks. There's caroling by candlelight in Jackson Square in front of St. Louis Cathedral. ■ Elsewhere in the state, the Christmas spirit is celebrated with numerous events, like the barge parade and Christmas Festival of Lights in Natchitoches, the City Harbor Lights Parade and Festival in Morgan City, bonfires on the levees along the River Road, and the St. Lucy Fest in the historic town of St. Martinville. ■ Come Christmas Eve, the entire family will gather to attend the solemn Midnight Mass at the cathedral or neighborhood churches. It will be in the wee hours of the morning when they return home for a break-

fast of sweet rolls, jellied meats, molded desserts, and demitasses. Then it's to bed for a few hours before rising to greet the special day. ■ During the day, there is much visiting and toasting with eggnog, and, of course, there's the elaborate meal at the end of the day. ■ For many years, New Year's Day, rather than Christmas, was the day for exchanging lavish gifts. Then, after a leisurely breakfast, visits begin again. For the old Creoles of the city, the Christmas season is a holy one, and intensely personal and family-oriented. The day usually ends with a large meal attended by friends and relatives, while in other parts of the city football fans in town for the Sugar Bowl Classic are carousing in the streets or dining at local restaurants and cafés. ■ A new year and a new millennium have arrived, and they're met with the greeting *Bonne Année*, Happy New Year!

christmas tree
trimming

CHRISTMAS, AS far as I'm concerned, is simply the happiest and jolliest time of the year. It's certainly my favorite holiday. I'm like a child—I can't wait to open gifts, and I love cooking for my friends and spending as much time as I can with my daughters, Jill and Jessie, and with Hilda, Mr. John, and the rest of my family. ■ I can't imagine anyone not enjoying this special time of year, when friends and relatives come together to partake of good food and drink and help decorate the tree. ■ The tree, usually the focal point of the holiday, can be a tiny-needled balsam, a feathery white pine, or a sturdy Scotch pine, my personal favorite. But whatever it is, it's fun to have some people over to fill it out with lights, ornaments, and bows and to make a party of it. ■ My suggestion is to have food that has some substance to it, like the oyster stew and the truffle pizza that we have here, but you can also offer simpler items like toasted nuts and assorted cookies and candy. ■ Light a fire in the fireplace, put on some Christmas music, set out the food, and get into the spirit!

RED ROOSTER

WHEN GIGI LINQUEST, MY FRIEND ERIC'S WIFE, TOLD ME ABOUT THIS POTION THAT HER FAMILY ENJOYS DURING THE HOLIDAYS, I WAS INTRIGUED. THEN I LEARNED THAT THERE ARE MANY OTHERS AROUND THE STATE WHO ALSO WHIP UP THIS DRINK TO ENJOY WHILE FRIENDS AND RELATIONS BUSTLE AROUND DECORATING THE TREE OR AT IMPROMPTU GATHERINGS. ■ IT'S QUITE REFRESHING AND SLIDES DOWN EASILY, SO WATCH YOURSELF!

Combine all of the ingredients in a large plastic container. Freeze for several hours. It will not freeze solid, but rather achieve the consistency of a slushy.

Scoop into punch cups or wine glasses and serve.

1½ quarts cranberry juice cocktail
One 6-ounce can frozen orange juice concentrate, defrosted
2 cups vodka

MAKES 2 QUARTS

OYSTER STEW WITH ANDOUILLE POTATO MASH

WHEN WE HAVE THAT AWFUL BONE-CHILLING WEATHER DOWN HERE, I CRAVE THIS HEARTY OYSTER STEW. THE PLUMP OYSTERS ARE BURSTING WITH FLAVOR AND THE ANDOUILLE GIVES IT A GOOD TWEAK.

FOR THE POTATOES

6 ounces andouille or other
   smoked sausage, chopped
1½ pounds Idaho potatoes,
   peeled and cubed
½ teaspoon salt
½ cup heavy cream
⅛ teaspoon freshly ground black
   pepper

FOR THE STEW

1 tablespoon unsalted butter
½ cup finely chopped yellow
   onion
½ teaspoon salt
¼ teaspoon freshly ground black
   pepper
2 teaspoons chopped garlic
1 cup heavy cream
24 freshly shucked oysters, with
   their liquor
1 tablespoon chopped fresh
   parsley leaves
½ teaspoon Worcestershire
   sauce
½ teaspoon hot sauce

MAKES 8 TO 12 SERVINGS

MAKE THE POTATOES

In a large skillet over medium-high heat, brown the sausage, stirring, about 6 minutes, then drain on paper towels. Set aside.

Put the potatoes in a large saucepan, add enough water to cover and ¼ teaspoon of the salt, and bring to a boil. Reduce the heat to medium and simmer until fork-tender, about 12 minutes. Drain and return the potatoes to the saucepan over medium heat to dry for about 2 minutes. Mash the potatoes with a fork, add the andouille and cream, and stir to mix. Stir in the remaining ¼ teaspoon salt and the black pepper. Keep hot over very low heat.

MAKE THE STEW

In a large skillet over medium heat, melt the butter. Add the onion, salt, and black pepper and cook, stirring, for 3 minutes. Add the garlic and cream and simmer for 3 minutes. Add the oysters, and their liquor, the parsley, Worcestershire, and hot sauce and cook until the edges of the oysters curl, about 4 minutes.

To serve, spoon equal amounts of the mashed potatoes into small serving bowls and top each with a generous ladleful of the oyster stew. Pass on a tray.

TRUFFLE POTATO PIZZA

MY DAUGHTER JESSIE ADORES THIS DISH AND I DON'T BLAME HER. IT'S ALSO ONE OF MY PERSONAL FAVORITES AND IDEAL FOR PASSING AROUND DURING A PARTY. WHEN I OPENED NOLA IN THE FRENCH QUARTER, IT WAS ON THE MENU. IT'S BEEN SO POPULAR, IT REMAINS ON THE MENU.

MAKE THE CRUST

In the bowl of an electric mixer fitted with a dough hook, combine the yeast, water, and sugar. Mix to dissolve the yeast and sugar, about 2 minutes. Add the salt, pepper, and 2 tablespoons of the olive oil and blend. Add the flour and beat on low speed until the mixture comes up the paddle and pulls away from the side of the bowl.

Remove the dough and pat it into a smooth ball. Using the remaining ½ teaspoon olive oil, coat the inside of a large mixing bowl. Add the dough and turn to oil all sides. Cover with plastic wrap or a clean towel and put in a warm, draft-free place until it doubles in size, about 2 hours.

MAKE THE POTATOES

Put the potatoes in a medium-size saucepan and add enough water to cover and the salt. Bring to a boil over high heat, then reduce the heat to medium and cook until fork-tender, 10 to 12 minutes. Drain and rinse under cool water. Arrange in a shallow dish and let cool to room temperature.

Preheat the oven to 375°F. Lightly oil two baking sheets each with the olive oil.

FOR THE CRUST

1 envelope active dry yeast
1 cup warm water (about 110°F)
½ teaspoon sugar
¼ teaspoon salt
⅛ teaspoon freshly ground
   black pepper
2 tablespoons plus
   ½ teaspoon olive oil
2¾ cups bleached all-purpose
   flour

FOR THE POTATOES

1 pound new potatoes, cut
   crosswise into ¼-inch-thick
   slices
¼ teaspoon salt

TO ASSEMBLE

1 teaspoon olive oil

1 tablespoon truffle oil

$1/4$ teaspoon salt

$1/4$ teaspoon freshly ground
   black pepper

1 cup thinly sliced red onions

2 confit duck legs (about
   7 ounces each), shredded

$1/4$ pound Fontina cheese, grated

2 teaspoons chopped fresh
   parsley leaves

Remove the dough from the bowl and divide into four equal portions. With your fingers dusted with flour, pat the dough into free-form circles, each 8 to 10 inches in diameter, and put them on the prepared baking sheets. Prick each randomly with a fork.

Brush each dough circle with ½ teaspoon of the truffle oil and top each with equal amounts of the potatoes, salt, pepper, onions, shredded confit, and cheese. Drizzle the remaining teaspoon of truffle oil evenly over the pizzas.

Put one baking sheet on the middle rack of the oven and bake until the crust is golden brown, about 25 minutes. Remove from the oven and let cool for a few minutes before slicing each into 8 slices to serve. Repeat with the remaining baking sheet.

Garnish with the parsley and serve.

MAKES 32 SLICES, 8 TO 10 SERVINGS

christmas dinner

CHRISTMAS DINNER itself should be a grand but intimate occasion, one that includes the immediate family and maybe a few close friends. This is one of those affairs that I think you should pull out all the stops for. Use fine china and crystal, get out the good silverware, dress up the table with fresh flowers—camellias, winter roses, sasanquas and pansies—and fresh greenery, light the candles, and serve an exciting menu, but not one so complicated that it keeps you from enjoying yourself and your guests. ■ It's always been my philosophy that it's best to let your locale dictate your menu—use what's fresh and available. If you can't get shrimp, use lobster. Use regular chicken if you can't put your hands on squabs. You get what I mean. It's best not to allow the busyness of the season to overwhelm you. Make the meal one that is pleasant yet joyous, follow your own traditions, and create some new ones. Enjoy, and with that, I bid you the merriest of holiday seasons!

SHRIMP BISQUE

SINCE WE HAVE FRESH SHRIMP ALMOST YEAR-ROUND, I LIKE TO USE THEM WHEN I CAN, AND ESPECIALLY FOR FESTIVE OCCASIONS LIKE THIS. A GOOD BISQUE IS BUILT UPON A GOOD STOCK. HERE I USE SHRIMP SHELLS TO MAKE THE STOCK FOR THIS WONDERFULLY RICH SOUP. ■ TO THICKEN THE BISQUE, I ADDED A *BEURRE MANIÉ*, WHICH IS THE FRENCH TERM FOR KNEADED BUTTER, MEANING BUTTER KNEADED TOGETHER WITH FLOUR.

MAKE THE STOCK

In a large stockpot over medium-high heat, heat the olive oil. Add the onions, celery, carrots, salt, and black pepper. Cook, stirring, until the vegetables are soft, about 5 minutes. Squeeze the lemon halves over the pot and add the lemon shells. Add the water, shrimp shells, peppercorns, thyme, bay leaves, and garlic and bring to a boil, then reduce the heat to medium and simmer, uncovered, for 1 hour. Remove from the heat and strain through a fine-mesh sieve, reserving the stock. Set aside.

MAKE THE BISQUE

In a large, heavy Dutch oven or pot, heat the olive oil over medium-high heat. Add the onions, celery, carrots, 1 teaspoon of the salt, and ¼ teaspoon of the cayenne. Cook, stirring, until the vegetables are soft, about 6 minutes. Add the herbs, tomato paste, and brandy and cook, stirring, for 2 minutes. Add the shrimp stock and bring to a boil. Reduce the heat to medium and simmer for 1 hour.

FOR THE SHRIMP STOCK (MAKES ABOUT 3 QUARTS)

1 tablespoon olive oil
1 cup chopped yellow onions
1 cup chopped celery
1 cup chopped carrots
1 teaspoon salt
1/2 teaspoon freshly ground black pepper
1 medium-size lemon, halved
4 quarts water
Shrimp shells from 3 pounds medium-size shrimp (reserved)
1/2 teaspoon black peppercorns
5 sprigs fresh thyme
4 bay leaves
6 cloves garlic, peeled

FOR THE BISQUE

1 tablespoon olive oil
2 cups chopped yellow onions
1 cup chopped celery
1 cup chopped carrots
2 1/2 teaspoons salt
3/4 teaspoon cayenne

1 teaspoon chopped fresh
   oregano leaves
1 teaspoon chopped fresh thyme
   leaves
1 tablespoon chopped fresh basil
   leaves
2 teaspoons chopped fresh
   tarragon leaves
2 bay leaves
3 tablespoons tomato paste
1 cup brandy
$1/4$ cup ($1/2$ stick) unsalted butter,
   at room temperature
$1/4$ cup bleached all-purpose
   flour
$1/2$ cup heavy cream
3 pounds medium-size shrimp,
   peeled, deveined, and chopped
   (shells reserved for stock)
$1/2$ cup chopped green onions or
   scallions (green part only)
$1/2$ cup chopped fresh parsley
   leaves

MAKES ABOUT 12 SERVINGS

Make the *beurre manié* by combining the softened butter and flour in a small bowl and kneading it with your fingers until you have a smooth paste. Add the mixture a tablespoon at a time to the pot, whisking after each addition. Cook for 5 minutes, then slowly pour in the cream, whisking constantly. Add the shrimp and stir to mix. Bring to a gentle boil and cook for 15 minutes.

Remove from the heat and stir in the green onions and parsley. Ladle into soup bowls to serve.

OYSTERS BIENVILLE

JUST ABOUT EVERYONE KNOWS ABOUT OYSTERS ROCKEFELLER, MADE WITH A RICH SAUCE THAT WAS CREATED IN 1899 AT ANTOINE'S RESTAURANT IN NEW ORLEANS TO HONOR ONE OF THE RICHEST MEN IN AMERICA. ■ OYSTERS BIENVILLE, ANOTHER POPULAR OYSTER DISH, IS NAMED IN HONOR OF JEAN BAPTISTE LE MOYNE, SIEUR DE BIENVILLE, THE FRENCH COLONIAL GOVERNOR OF LOUISIANA, WHO FOUNDED NEW ORLEANS IN 1718. BRAVO FOR MONSIEUR BIENVILLE! ■ IT'S USUALLY SERVED AS AN APPETIZER, BUT I CAN MAKE A MEAL OUT OF IT ANYTIME.

In a large skillet over medium-high heat, fry the bacon until crisp, about 8 minutes. Add the onions, salt, and cayenne and cook, stirring, for 2 minutes. Add the garlic and butter, and cook, stirring, for 2 minutes until the butter melts. Add the flour and, stirring slowly and constantly, cook for 2 minutes. Add the milk and wine and stir to blend. Reduce the heat to medium, then add the mushrooms and shrimp. Stir and fold to mix and cook until the mixture is very thick, about 12 minutes. Add the lemon juice, green onions, and parsley and stir to mix well. Remove from the heat, add the beaten egg yolks, and blend well. Let cool to room temperature.

Preheat the oven to 400°F.

Arrange the reserved oyster shells on a bed of rock salt in four pie pans or on a large baking sheet. Put an oyster in each shell and top it with about 2 heaping tablespoons of the sauce. Or, the oysters can be put in a shallow pan (without the shells and rock salt) and topped with the sauce to bake. Bake until the sauce is delicately browned and the oysters begin to curl at the edges, about 20 minutes. Serve hot.

1/2 pound sliced bacon, chopped
1 cup chopped yellow onions
1 teaspoon salt
1/2 teaspoon cayenne
2 teaspoons chopped garlic
1/4 cup (1/2 stick) unsalted butter
1 cup bleached all-purpose flour
2 cups milk
1/2 cup dry white wine
1/4 pound white button mushrooms, wiped clean, stems trimmed, and sliced (about 2 cups)
1 pound medium-size shrimp, peeled, deveined, and chopped
3 tablespoons fresh lemon juice
1/2 cup chopped green onions or scallions (green part only)
3 tablespoons chopped fresh parsley leaves
4 large egg yolks, lightly beaten
3 dozen medium-size oysters, shucked and drained; reserve the deeper bottom shells
Rock salt (optional)

MAKES 12 SERVINGS (3 OYSTERS PER PERSON)

RELISH TRAY

IN THE LATE 1800S AND EARLY 1900S, RELISH TRAYS WERE QUITE POPULAR AT HOLIDAY GATHERINGS. SOMETIMES THE RELISHES WERE PASSED AROUND BEFORE THE MEAL TO WHET THE APPETITE, MUCH LIKE AN ANTIPASTO, BUT THEY WERE OFTEN A PART OF THE MEAL USED AS A GARNISH. NEW ORLEANIANS LIKE THIS LITTLE TOUCH, AND I OFFER YOU MY VERSION.

½ pound green beans, ends trimmed

1 pound baby carrots

1 head cauliflower, cut into florets

½ pound celery, cut into 3-inch pieces

One 1-pound jar Kalamata olives packed in vinegar brine and olive oil

One 11.5-ounce jar pickled peperoncini

One 16-ounce jar pickled hot cherry peppers

One 10-ounce jar pickled imported Spanish Queen olives stuffed with pimientos

One 8-ounce jar pickled Holland cocktail onions

20 fresh basil leaves

6 sprigs fresh thyme

6 sprigs fresh oregano

2 tablespoons chopped fresh parsley leaves

1 teaspoon red pepper flakes

1 cup olive oil

Blanch the green beans and carrots separately in a large pot of boiling salted water for 4 to 5 minutes. Drain, and shock in ice water to cool.

Put all of the ingredients in a large glass bowl. Toss to coat the vegetables evenly with the olive oil. Refrigerate for 8 hours before serving in shallow glass dishes.

MAKES ABOUT 12 SERVINGS

ROASTED SQUAB WITH ORANGE RICE

SQUAB ARE YOUNG AND EXTREMELY TENDER DOMESTICATED PIGEONS, AND YEARS AGO WERE OFTEN A PART OF THE HOLIDAY TABLE IN NEW ORLEANS. I REDISCOVERED THEM RECENTLY AND FIND THEY HAVE A DELICATE FLAVOR. THEY SHOULD NOT BE OVER-COOKED. I'VE CHOSEN TO SERVE THEM WITH RICE, A LOUISIANA STA-PLE, PREPARED WITH FRESH, DELECTABLE LOUISIANA NAVEL ORANGES. THE CITRUS TASTE ADDS A NICE TOUCH TO THE BIRDS.

Trim the birds, removing the heads, feet, and first joints of the wings. (If your birds come without heads and feet, ask for them from your butcher.) Remove the livers and hearts from the cavities and discard. Rinse the birds well under cool running water. Set the birds aside.

MAKE THE SAUCE

In a medium-size saucepan over medium-high heat, heat the olive oil. Add the bird trimmings along with the salt and black pepper and cook, stirring, until well browned, about 15 minutes. Add the onions, carrots, celery, bay leaves, and thyme and cook, stirring to loosen any brown bits from the bottom of the pan, for 5 minutes. Add the tomato paste, stir to mix, and cook for 2 minutes. Add the wine, stir, and cook for 2 minutes. Add the water, bring to a boil, reduce the heat to medium, and simmer for 1 hour. Strain through a fine-mesh sieve into another saucepan or a gravy boat. Skim off any fat that rises to the surface. Keep warm.

MAKE THE RICE

In a large saucepan over medium-high heat, heat the olive oil. Add the onions, salt, and cayenne and cook, stirring, for 4 minutes. Add the oranges and their juice, the bay leaves, and rice and cook, stirring, for 2 min-utes. Add the water and bring to a boil, then reduce the heat to medium-low, cover, and cook until all the

6 squab (about 1 pound each)

FOR THE SAUCE

1 tablespoon olive oil

1 teaspoon salt

1/2 teaspoon freshly ground black pepper

2 cups chopped yellow onions

1 cup chopped carrots

1 cup chopped celery

3 bay leaves

5 sprigs fresh thyme

2 tablespoons tomato paste

1 cup dry red wine

4 cups water

FOR THE RICE

1 tablespoon olive oil

2 cups chopped yellow onions

2 teaspoons salt

1/2 teaspoon cayenne

2 medium-size navel oranges, peeled, white pith removed, and chopped, with their juice (about 1 1/2 cups)

3 bay leaves

1 pound long-grain rice
  (about 2 cups)
4 cups water
1/4 cup chopped green onions or
  scallions (green part only)
2 tablespoons chopped fresh
  parsley leaves

FOR THE BIRDS
4 teaspoons olive oil
2 teaspoons salt
2 teaspoons freshly ground black
  pepper
1/2 cup chopped green onions or
  scallions (green part only)

water is absorbed, about 20 minutes. Remove from the heat, add the green onions and parsley, and stir gently to mix. Remove the bay leaves and let stand with the lid on for 10 minutes before serving.

Meanwhile, make the birds. Preheat the oven to 400°F. Rub the birds with the olive oil and season with the salt and black pepper. Put the birds breast side down on a rack fitted over a baking sheet. Bake until golden brown, about 25 minutes (and the internal temperature is 150°F). Remove from the oven and let sit for 10 minutes. To carve, cut each bird lengthwise, in half, then cut out the backbone.

To serve, arrange an equal portion of the rice in the center of each serving plate, put half a squab on top of the rice, and then drizzle with about 2 tablespoons of the sauce.

MAKES 12 SERVINGS

CELEBRATION CAKE

BECAUSE CHRISTMAS DINNER WAS SUCH A JOYOUS OCCASION FOR THE OLD CREOLE FAMILIES OF NEW ORLEANS, THERE WAS ALWAYS A SPECIAL DESSERT, MUCH LIKE THIS ONE, FOR THE CELEBRATION TABLE. AFTER READING SEVERAL NINETEENTH-CENTURY NEW ORLEANS COOKBOOKS, I WAS INSPIRED TO COMBINE A COUPLE OF RECIPES INTO THIS ONE FOR A WONDERFULLY MOIST CAKE MADE WITH CURRANTS, A RICH VANILLA-FLAVORED SAUCE, AND ALMONDS.

½ pound dried currants
1 cup sugar
1 cup water
1 cup dry sherry
1 recipe Basic Sponge Cake
   (recipe follows)
1 cup toasted slivered almonds
1 recipe Crème Anglaise
   (page 312)
1 cup Sweetened Whipped
   Cream (page 49)
12 fresh mint sprigs

In a medium-size saucepan over medium heat, combine the currants, sugar, and water. Bring to a boil and cook for 10 minutes. Remove from the heat and stir in the sherry. Let cool completely.

Spread the mixture evenly over the sponge cake, then sprinkle the almonds evenly over the currant mixture. Cut the cake horizontally into 1-inch-wide strips, then cut the strips into quarters. Spoon the crème anglaise into 12 dessert bowls, then in each bowl stack four pieces of the cake on top of each other. Spoon over the whipped cream, and garnish with a mint sprig. Serve immediately.

MAKES 1 CAKE TO SERVE 12

Basic Sponge Cake

Preheat the oven to 350°F.

In a small saucepan, warm the milk and 2 teaspoons butter together over medium-low heat. With an electric mixer fitted with a wire whip, beat the eggs and 1 cup of the sugar on medium-high speed until the mixture is pale yellow and thick, and has tripled in volume, about 8 minutes. With the mixer on low, beat in the warm milk mixture.

Sift the flour, baking powder, and salt into a medium-size mixing bowl. Fold the flour mixture into the egg mixture and blend thoroughly until smooth. Add the vanilla and mix gently.

Grease a 17 × 12-inch baking pan or jelly roll pan with 2 teaspoons butter. Sprinkle evenly with the remaining 2 tablespoons sugar. Pour the batter into the pan, spreading it evenly. Bake until the cake springs back when touched, about 15 minutes. Cool for about 2 minutes, then gently flip it out onto a large wire rack or a large sheet of parchment paper. Let cool completely.

¼ cup milk
2 tablespoons plus 2 teaspoons
  unsalted butter
8 large eggs
1 cup plus 2 tablespoons sugar
1 cup bleached all-purpose flour
1 teaspoon baking powder
⅛ teaspoon salt
1 teaspoon pure vanilla extract

MAKES 1 SPONGE CAKE

Crème Anglaise

5 large egg yolks
1/2 cup sugar
2 cups heavy cream
1 teaspoon pure vanilla extract

Put the yolks in a saucepan and add the sugar. Beat with a wire whisk until thick and lemon colored.

Put the cream in a nonreactive saucepan and heat to the scalding point (when bubbles form around the edge of the pan). Gradually add the cream to the yolk mixture, beating constantly. Cook over low heat until the mixture thickens slightly. Do not overcook or boil, as the sauce will curdle. Remove from the heat and stir in the vanilla.

Strain through a fine-mesh sieve into a cold bowl. Cover with plastic wrap, pressing it down on the surface to prevent a skin from forming if not using immediately. Will keep refrigerated for 24 hours. Before serving, warm over low heat.

MAKES ABOUT 2 1/2 CUPS

BONBONS

I HAVE AN INSATIABLE SWEET TOOTH AND DURING THE HOLIDAYS I CAN'T SEEM TO GET ENOUGH OF THESE SMALL CHOCOLATE CANDIES MADE WITH COCONUT. MAKE A COUPLE OF BATCHES OF THESE NOT ONLY FOR A PARTY BUT ALSO FOR UNANNOUNCED GUESTS WHO DROP IN DURING THE CHRISTMAS SEASON.

In a large mixing bowl, combine the coconut, milk, sugar, almonds, butter, and vanilla. Mix well. Cover and refrigerate for 1 hour.

Remove from the refrigerator and form into balls about the size of a pecan. Line a baking sheet with parchment paper.

In a bowl set over simmering water or in a double boiler, melt the chocolate. Using two toothpicks, dip each ball into the chocolate, covering them evenly. Place them on the prepared sheet. Using a fork, drizzle the tops of each ball with any remaining chocolate. Refrigerate until set.

2^2/3 cups (7 ounces) flaked coconut

1/2 cup sweetened condensed milk

2/3 cup confectioners' sugar

1/4 cup sliced almonds, finely chopped

2 tablespoons unsalted butter, at room temperature

1/4 teaspoon pure vanilla extract

8 ounces semisweet chocolate, coarsely chopped

MAKES 24 BONBONS

new year's eve

IT'S HARD to believe we are bidding farewell to the twentieth century and greeting not only a new year, but a new millennium. It's exciting, to say the least, but it's also mind-boggling. With all the advances and changes we have witnessed in this century, what is waiting for us in the next? ■ But only time will tell. *Que será, será.* ■ I do know what I'm planning for this very extraordinary event, and that is a gala I won't soon forget—and one that I hope my friends will be able to look back on and say, "What a blast we had!" ■ I'm sure that just about everyone has begun making plans for this New Year's Eve. Whether you're on an ocean cruise, lolling about on a sandy beach, at a bash in New York City, or traveling in a foreign country, I hope the New Year is all that you want it to be and more. ■ Happy New Year and welcome to the twenty-first century!

ROYAL CUP

A ROYAL CUP, JUST AS THE NAME IMPLIES, IS A VERY ELEGANT DRINK FOR A GRAND CELEBRATION, SUCH AS NEW YEAR'S. USE THE VERY BEST CHAMPAGNE YOU CAN AFFORD—AFTER ALL, WE'RE APPROACHING THE NEW MILLENNIUM! OH, AND BY THE WAY, I MUST TELL YOU ABOUT PEYCHAUD BITTERS. ■ THE STORY GOES THAT IN 1793, WHEN WEALTHY PLANTATION OWNERS WERE FORCED OUT OF SAN DOMINGO BECAUSE OF A SLAVE UPRISING, SOME WERE ABLE TO FLEE WITH THEIR PRECIOUS BELONGINGS, WHILE OTHERS HAD NOTHING BUT THE CLOTHES ON THEIR BACKS. ONE REFUGEE TOOK WITH HIM A RECIPE FOR A LIQUID TONIC CALLED BITTERS. EVIDENTLY THE RECIPE HAD BEEN A FAMILY SECRET FOR YEARS. THE GENTLEMAN, WHO FOUND HIS WAY TO NEW ORLEANS, WAS ONE ANTOINE AMÉDÉE PEYCHAUD, WHO HAD BEEN EDUCATED AS AN APOTHECARY. THE BITTERS MADE FROM THE SECRET RECIPE WERE DISPENSED TO HIS PATRONS TO CURE ALL SORTS OF MALADIES. THEY ALSO GAVE AN ADDED ZEST TO BRANDY HE SERVED TO HIS FRIENDS. WELL, THE REST IS HISTORY, AS WE SAY. HIS CONCOCTION BECAME QUITE POPULAR AND A DASH OR TWO OF IT WAS ADDED TO FRENCH BRANDY SERVED AT THE LOCAL WATERING HOLES, THEN CALLED COFFEE HOUSES. ■ *À VOTRE SANTÉ!*

Pour the Grand Marnier into a Champagne flute, a wine glass, or a large martini glass, add the bitters, and then slowly add the Champagne. Serve immediately.

1/2 ounce Grand Marnier
3 drops Peychaud bitters
4 ounces chilled Champagne

MAKES 1 SERVING

FOIE GRAS TERRINE

FOIE GRAS LITERALLY TRANSLATES AS "FAT LIVER," BUT FOIE GRAS GENERALLY REFERS TO GOOSE LIVER. IT IS THE ENLARGED LIVER FROM A GOOSE (OR DUCK) THAT HAS BEEN FORCE-FED AND FATTENED OVER A PERIOD OF SEVERAL MONTHS. THE GEESE ARE NOT ALLOWED TO EXERCISE, THUS CREATING A HUGE, FATTY LIVER. FOIE GRAS IS VERY EXPENSIVE, SO I CALL THIS MY OVER-THE-TOP TERRINE. I SUGGEST THAT YOU OPEN TWO CHRISTMAS CLUB SAVINGS ACCOUNTS AT YOUR BANK—ONE FOR YOUR CHRISTMAS GIFTS AND ONE FOR THE FOIE GRAS.

Season the foie gras with 2 teaspoons of the salt and 1 teaspoon of the cracked pepper. Put them in a large plastic storage bag or a large shallow plastic bowl. Pour in the port wine. Refrigerate for 12 hours, turning them about every 2 hours.

Remove the foie gras from the bags or bowl and discard the marinade.

Season the foie gras with the remaining 2 teaspoons salt and 1 teaspoon cracked pepper. Cut each diagonally into 4 pieces, each about 1 inch wide.

Line a classic terrine mold (12 × 4 × 2½ inches) with a sheet of plastic wrap, leaving enough to overlap the edges by about 3 inches.

In a large skillet over high heat, sear the foie gras, 4 to 5 pieces at a time, browning them evenly, 30 to 45 seconds per side. Drain the fat from the skillet after cooking each batch and strain it through a fine-mesh sieve into a bowl.

Arrange a layer of the seared foie gras in the bottom of the prepared terrine. Pour about ½ cup of the strained fat over the layer of foie gras. Arrange the next

3 foie gras (about 1½ pounds each)
4 teaspoons salt
2 teaspoons cracked black peppercorns
4 cups port wine
Toasted Croutons (page 81)
1 recipe Port Wine Reduction (recipe follows)

batch of foie gras in another layer, pressing it down gently but firmly so that there are no air pockets. Repeat the process until all the pieces are in the terrine. Reserve ½ cup of the remaining strained fat and discard the rest. Refrigerate the fat.

Fold the plastic wrap tightly over the foie gras. Wrap the entire terrine tightly with another large sheet of plastic wrap. Weight the top with a brick or two wrapped in aluminum foil. Refrigerate for 12 hours.

Remove the terrine from the refrigerator and briefly submerge the bottom in hot water, then carefully lift it out of the mold, grabbing the plastic wrap. Melt the reserved ½ cup fat and generously brush the sides, top, and bottom of the terrine. Wrap the terrine tightly in fresh plastic wrap, and refrigerate for 12 hours more.

To serve, cut into ¼-inch-thick slices. Serve with the croutons and drizzles of the port wine reduction.

MAKES 18 TO 20 SERVINGS

Port Wine Reduction

½ cup chopped onions
½ cup chopped carrots
2 bay leaves
3 cups port wine

Combine all of the ingredients in a medium-size saucepan over medium heat and bring to a boil. Continue to boil the mixture until it thickens and reduces to about ½ cup, about 45 minutes. Strain through a fine-mesh strainer and let cool. Use at room temperature.

MAKES ABOUT ½ CUP

CAVIAR PARFAIT

NEXT TO TRUFFLES, I ADORE CAVIAR, AND I USUALLY INCLUDE BOTH ON MY NEW YEAR'S BASH MENU. ■ FOR A SUPER PRESENTATION, I ARRANGE THE CAVIAR, CHAMPAGNE CREAM MIXTURE, AND TRADITIONAL GARNISHES IN PARFAIT GLASSES. IT LOOKS GOOD AND IT TASTES GOOD! WHAT MORE CAN YOU ASK FOR! MAKE THE PARFAITS A COUPLE OF HOURS IN ADVANCE AND KEEP CHILLED IN THE REFRIGERATOR BEFORE PASSING ON TRAYS.

In a small saucepan over medium-high heat, combine the salt, white pepper, Champagne, and 2 cups of the milk and bring just to a boil. Mix ½ cup of the hot milk mixture into the beaten egg yolks and whisk to blend. Mix this into the hot milk mixture remaining in the pan.

Dissolve the cornstarch in the remaining ½ cup milk, add to the pan, and cook, whisking until the mixture thickens slightly, 6 to 8 minutes. Pour into a glass bowl, place a sheet of plastic wrap over the surface to prevent a skin from forming, and let cool. Refrigerate for 4 hours.

To assemble, remove the Champagne cream from the refrigerator and whisk until smooth. Spoon 1 tablespoon of the chopped eggs into the bottom of a parfait or wine glass. Then layer 1 teaspoon of the chopped red onion, ½ teaspoon of the chopped parsley, 2 teaspoons of the caviar, 2 tablespoons of the Champagne cream, and 1 tablespoon of the salmon roe on top. Continue layering, using another 1 tablespoon chopped eggs, another 1 teaspoon red onion, ½ teaspoon parsley, and 2 tablespoons Champagne cream mixture, then another 1 tablespoon chopped eggs, 1 teaspoon chopped red onion, ½ teaspoon parsley. Top with 1 teaspoon of the caviar. Repeat the process to make 7 more parfaits. Cover and chill completely before serving.

½ teaspoon salt
¼ teaspoon freshly ground white pepper
½ cup Champagne
2½ cups milk
3 tablespoons cornstarch
4 large egg yolks, lightly beaten
1½ cups finely chopped hard-boiled eggs
½ cup finely chopped red onion
¼ cup finely chopped fresh parsley leaves
½ cup sevruga or osetra caviar
½ cup salmon roe

MAKES 8 SERVINGS

ANGEL HAIR PASTA WITH BLACK TRUFFLES

I JUST LOVE ANYTHING WITH TRUFFLES—I KNOW THEY'RE EXPENSIVE, BUT FOR A NEW YEAR'S PARTY, I BLOW IT OUT! JILL, MY DAUGHTER THE VEGETARIAN, SAYS THIS DISH IS ONE OF HER FAVORITES, SO THIS ONE IS FOR HER! ■ TO SHAVE A TRUFFLE, USE A TRUFFLE SLICER, A SMALL GADGET WITH AN ADJUSTABLE BLADE MOUNTED ON A STAIN-LESS-STEEL FRAME. THE BLADE IS HELD AT A 45-DEGREE ANGLE AND THE TRUFFLE IS PRESSED DOWN AND ACROSS IT, ALLOWING THE BLADE TO SHAVE OFF SMALL SLIVERS AND SLICES. OR YOU CAN USE A SHARP THIN-BLADED KNIFE TO MAKE THE SHAVINGS.

4 quarts water

3/4 teaspoon salt

3/4 pound angel hair pasta

1/2 cup plus 2 tablespoons truffle oil

1/4 pound Parmigiano-Reggiano cheese, grated

1/2 teaspoon freshly ground black pepper

1/4 cup snipped fresh chives or finely chopped green onions or scallions (green part only)

1 black truffle, shaved

In a large pot, bring the water and 1/4 teaspoon of the salt to a boil. Add the pasta and cook until *al dente*, about 4 minutes. Drain and place in a mixing bowl. Add 1/2 cup of the truffle oil, 3/4 cup of the cheese, the remaining 1/2 teaspoon salt, the black pepper, and chives and toss to mix.

To serve, garnish with the shaved truffle, drizzle with the remaining 2 tablespoons truffle oil, and sprinkle with the remaining cheese. Serve immediately.

MAKES ABOUT 12 SMALL SERVINGS

HOT MAYONNAISE-GLAZED SCALLOPS

I LOVE THE TEXTURE OF SEA SCALLOPS, SLIGHTLY CHEWY BUT SWEET. IF YOU CAN'T FIND SEA SCALLOPS, SUBSTITUTE THE SMALLER BAY SCALLOPS. WHICHEVER YOU USE, BE SURE THAT THEY ARE FRESH AND HAVE A SWEET SMELL AND A FRESH, MOIST SHEEN. ■ YOU COULD ALSO USE ABOUT ¾ POUND SHRIMP IF SCALLOPS ARE NOT AVAILABLE IN YOUR AREA.

Preheat the oven to 400°F.

In a food processor or blender, combine the egg, mustard, hot sauce, lemon juice, Worcestershire, salt, black pepper, and red pepper flakes. Process until smooth, about 30 seconds. With the motor running, pour in the oil in a slow, steady stream. The mixture will thicken. Refrigerate until ready to use.

Put the scallop shells on a baking sheet. Season both sides of the scallops with the salt and black pepper. Put two scallops in each shell and spoon about 2 tablespoons of the mayonnaise over them. Bake on the top rack of the oven until the mayonnaise is golden brown, about 10 minutes. Garnish with the green onions and serve hot.

FOR THE MAYONNAISE (MAKES ABOUT 1½ CUPS)

1 large egg (see Note on page 13)
1 teaspoon Dijon mustard
1 tablespoon Homemade Pepper Sauce (page 274)
2 tablespoons fresh lemon juice
1 teaspoon Worcestershire sauce
½ teaspoon salt
⅛ teaspoon freshly ground black pepper
¼ teaspoon red pepper flakes
1 cup olive oil

FOR THE SCALLOPS

12 large scallop shells (available at gourmet shops)
24 large sea scallops, each cut horizontally in half
½ teaspoon salt
½ teaspoon freshly ground black pepper
¼ cup chopped green onions or scallions (green part only)

MAKES 12 APPETIZER SERVINGS

LEMON ICEBOX PIE

DURING THE WINTER MONTHS, THERE'S FABULOUS CITRUS AVAIL-ABLE IN OUR LOCAL MARKETS FROM THE ORCHARDS IN PLAQUEM-INE AND ST. BERNARD PARISHES, LOCATED SOUTH OF NEW ORLEANS, TOWARD THE MOUTH OF THE MISSISSIPPI RIVER. ONE OF MY FAVORITE CITRUS FRUITS FROM THIS AREA IS WHAT IS KNOWN AS THE MEYER LEMON. IT IS SWEET AND MILD, AND NOT A TRUE LEMON, BUT RATHER A LEMON AND ORANGE CROSS. IT IS THIN-SKINNED AND VERY JUICY, AND IDEAL, ACCORDING TO MR. LOU, THE HEAD PAS-TRY CHEF AT EMERIL'S, FOR MAKING THESE LEMON ICEBOX PIES. ■ YOU'LL NEED EIGHT 4-INCH TARTLET PANS TO MAKE THIS.

Preheat the oven to 350°F.

Make the piecrust. In a medium-size mixing bowl, combine the graham cracker crumbs and melted butter, mixing to blend.

Put ¼ cup of the mixture into each of eight 4-inch individual fluted tartlet pans with removable bottoms. Using your fingers, press the crust into the bottom and up the sides of the pans. Put them on a baking sheet and bake for 15 minutes. Remove from the oven and let cool completely on a wire rack.

Make the filling. In a medium-size saucepan, combine the sugar and cornstarch and whisk until blended. In a small mixing bowl, combine the lemon juice and

FOR THE PIECRUST
2 cups graham cracker crumbs
¼ pound (1 stick) unsalted butter, melted and slightly cooled

FOR THE FILLING
1 cup sugar
½ cup cornstarch
1 cup fresh lemon juice
1 cup water
6 large egg yolks, lightly beaten

FOR THE MERINGUE
6 large egg whites
¼ cup sugar

water. Slowly whisk this into the sugar-and-cornstarch mixture. Over medium heat, bring to a gentle boil and whisk occasionally until the mixture begins to thicken, about 5 minutes.

Add ¼ cup of the hot mixture to the beaten egg yolks and whisk to blend. Add this mixture to the saucepan and whisk until thick enough to coat the back of a wooden spoon, about 5 minutes.

Pour about ⅓ cup of the mixture into each of the tart shells. Place them on a baking sheet and refrigerate until the filling sets, about 2 hours. Carefully remove the tarts from the pans and place on a baking sheet.

Make the meringue. Preheat the oven to 450°F.

Combine the egg whites and sugar in a large mixing bowl and beat on high speed with an electric mixer until stiff peaks form. Spread the top of each tart with an equal portion of the meringue. Bake on the top rack of the oven until the meringue is lightly brown, about 6 minutes. Let cool before serving.

MAKES 8 TARTS

LOUISIANA CALENDAR OF EVENTS

January

Sugar Bowl
New Orleans
(504) 525–8573
Battle of New Orleans
Anniversary
Chalmette
(504) 589–4430
Louisiana Fur and Wildlife
Festival
Cameron
(318) 775–5785
Oyster Scavenger Hunt
Lafitte
(504) 689–4757
Mid-Winter Fair &
Rodeo
Lafayette
(318) 482–6441
Chinese New Year's
Festival
Metairie
(504) 832–0702
Creole Heritage Day
Melrose
(800) 259–1714
Cajun Music Festival
Westwego
(504) 899–0615

February

Boudin Festival
Carencro
(318) 896–FEST

Vietnamese Tet
Celebration
Marrero
(504) 254–5660
Lundi Gras Street Party
Mamou
(318) 468–3272
Mardi Gras Parades
Lafayette
(800) 346–1958
Lake Charles
(800) 456–7952
Houma
(800) 688–2732
Shreveport
(800) 551–8682
Chic-à-la-Pie Parade
Kaplan
(318) 643–2400
Ark-La-Miss Rodeo
Monroe
(318) 329–2338

March

Bonne Fête
Baton Rouge
(800) LA–ROUGE
Black Heritage Festival
New Orleans
(504) 581–4629
Cajun Fun Fest
New Iberia
(318) 364–5116

Irish-Italian Festival
Lake Charles
(800) 456–7952
French Quarter St. Patrick's
Day Parade
New Orleans
(504) 525–5169
Irish Channel Parade
New Orleans
(504) 565–7080
French Quarter St. Joseph's
Day Parade
New Orleans
(504) 522–7294
St. Patrick's Parade
of Jefferson
Metairie
(504) 522–7294
Downtown Irish Club's
St. Patrick's Day Parade
New Orleans
(504) 947–1104
New Orleans Spring Fiesta
New Orleans
(504) 947–0103
Louisiana Redbud Festival
Vivian
(318) 375–5300
Oak Alley Spring Arts &
Crafts Festival
Vacherie
(800) 44–ALLEY
Black Heritage Festival
Lake Charles
(318) 475–5923

Tennessee Williams
  Literary Festival
New Orleans
(504) 581–1144
Oyster Festival—
Amite
(504) 748–5161

April

French Quarter Festival
New Orleans
(504) 522–5730
Bunk Johnson Festival
New Iberia
(888) 9–IBERIA
Catfish Festival
Winnsboro
(318) 435–3781
Strawberry Festival
Pontchatoula
(504) 386–6677
Cajun Day Celebration
Port Allen
(225) 774–1940
Étouffée Festival
Arnaudville
(318) 754–5912
Holiday in Dixie
Shreveport
(318) 865–5555
Cajun Joke-Telling Contest
Opelousas
(318) 942–3562
Crescent City Classic
New Orleans
(504) 861–8686
State Chili Cook-off
  Contest
Gonzales
(225) 644–5307

Festival International
Lafayette
(318) 232–8086
New Orleans Jazz &
  Heritage Festival
New Orleans
(504) 522–4786
Contraband Days
Lake Charles
(318) 436–5508
Crawfish Festival
Breaux Bridge
(318) 332–6655
Breaux Bridge Crustacean
  Festival
Breaux Bridge
(318) 332–6945

May

First Bloom Festival
Shreveport
(318) 938–5402
River City Fest
Logansport
(318) 872–1177
Festival in the Park
Bogalousa
(318) 735–5731
Cochon de Lait Festival
Mansura
(318) 964–2887
Contraband Festival
Lake Charles
(318) 436–5508
Zoo-To-Do
New Orleans
(504) 581–4629
Festival Ray★la★ne
Rayne
(318) 234–1666

Fête d'Amérique Française
New Orleans
(504) 581–9569
Cajun Heartland State Fair
Lafayette
(318) 265–2100
Jambalaya Festival
Gonzales
(225) 647–9566
Greek Festival
New Orleans
(504) 282–0259
Zydeco Extravaganza
Lafayette
(318) 234–9695

June

Mamou Cajun Music
  Festival
Mamou
(318) 468–3272/2300
Peach Festival
Ruston
(318) 255–2031
Church Point Buggy
  Festival
Church Point
(318) 684–2739
Bayou Liberty Pirogue
  Races
Slidell
(800) 634–9443
French Market Tomato
  Festival
New Orleans
(504) 522–2621
Louisiana Blueberry
  Festival
Mansfield
(318) 872–1310

New Orleans Wine and
Food Experience
New Orleans
(504) 529–9463
Ark-La-Miss Music Festival
Oak Grove
(318) 428–2161
Crab Festival
LaCombe
(504) 892–0520
Festival des Cadiens
Westwego
(504) 899–0615

July

Essence Music Festival
New Orleans
(504) 896–8300
Seafood Festival
Mandeville
(800) 634–9443
Watermelon Festival
Franklinton
(504) 839–7855
Bastille Weekend
Lafayette
(800) 992–2968
Bastille Day Celebration
Kaplan
(318) 643–8319
International Grand Isle
Tarpon Rodeo
Grand Isle
(504) 736–6400
Watermelon Festival
Farmerville
(318) 368–3947
Marshland Festival
Lake Charles
(800) 737–2873

August

South Lafourche Seafood
Festival
Galliano
(504) 537–5800
Lafitte Seafood Festival
Lafitte
(504) 689–4754
Reggae and Cultural
Festival
Carencro
(318) 896–FEST
"Le Cajun" Music Awards
Festival
Lafayette
(800) 346–1958
Louisiana Wildfowl
Festival
New Orleans
(504) 834–8878
Shrimp Festival and
Blessing of the Fleet
Delcambre
(318) 685–4462
Laura Plantation Week
Vacherie
(225) 265–7690
Duck Festival
Gueydon
(318) 898–6600
St. Helena Forest Festival
Greensburg (504)
222–4682

September

Louisiana Shrimp &
Petroleum Festival
Morgan City
(504) 385-0703

Rayne Frog Festival
Rayne
(318) 334-2332
Creole Zydeco Festival
St. Martinville
(318) 394-4635
Pecan Ridge Bluegrass
Festival
Jackson
(225) 629-5852
Creole Festival
French Settlement
(225) 698-9886
Bayou Blues & Zydeco
Fest
Lake Charles
(318) 475-5123
Festivals Acadiens
Lafayette
(800) 346-1958;
in Louisiana,
(318) 232-3808
Louisiana Sugarcane
Festival
New Iberia
(888) 9-IBERIA
Alligator Festival
Boutte
(504) 785-0530
Wooden Boat Festival
Madisonville
(504) 845-9200

October

Cattle Festival
Abbeville
(318) 893-2491
Cracklin' Festival
Bourg
(504) 594-7410

Cotton Festival
Ville Platte
(318) 363-7348
Gumbo Festival
Bridge City
(504) 436-4712
Natchitoches
Pilgrimage
Natchitoches
(800) 259-1714
Laurel Valley Village Fall
Festival
Thibodaux
(504) 446-7456
Cotton Festival
Bastrop
(318) 281-1406
Rice Festival
Crowley
(318) 783-3067
Pepper Festival
St. Martinville
(318) 394-5125
Yambilee Festival
Opelousas
(800) 210-5298
Andouille Festival
LaPlace
(504) 652-9659

November

Louisiana Swine Festival
Basile
(318) 432-6624
Pecan Festival
Colfax
(318) 627-5196

Celebration of the Giant
Omelette
Abbeville
(318) 893-6517
Southdown Fall Festival
Houma
(504) 851-0154
Gumbo Cook-off &
Festival
Ville Platte
(318) 363-1878
Cracklin' Festival
Port Barre
(318) 585-6673
Caldo Festividad
St. Bernard
(504) 682-5493
Christmas Festival of
Lights
Natchitoches
(800) 259-1714 or
(318) 352-8072

December

Christmas in the
Country
St. Francisville
(225) 635-6717
Barge Parade of Lights
Natchitoches
(800) 259-1714
Orange Fair & Festival
Buras
(504) 564-2951
Algiers Bonfire
New Orleans
(504) 565-6315

City Harbor Lights Parade
& Festival
Morgan City
(800) 256-2931
Christmas Festival of
Lights
Natchitoches
(800) 259-1714
Bonfire on the Levee
Oak Alley—Vacherie
(800) 44-ALLEY
Festival of the Bonfire
Gramercy/Lutcher
(225) 869-9752
Bonfire Fête
Laura Plantation, Vacherie
(225) 265-7690
Bonfire Christmas
Celebration
*Tezcuco Plantation
Burnside*
(504) 562-3929
Caroling in Jackson Square
New Orleans
(504) 522-5730
Christmas Eve Bonfires
on the Levee
Gramercy/Lutcher
(225) 869-9752
New Year's Eve
Jackson Square
New Orleans
(504) 566-5009

SOURCE GUIDE

Turkey frying and seafood boiling rig
METAL FUSION INC.
712 St. George Avenue
Jefferson, LA 70121
(504) 736-0201

Cajun Injector
P.O. Box 97
Clinton, LA 70722
(800) 221-8060
www.cajuninjector.com

Foie gras
HUDSON VALLEY
FOIE GRAS
80 Brooks Road
Ferndale, NY 12734
(914) 292-2500

King cake babies and Mardi Gras accessories
ACCENT ANNEX
1420 Sams Avenue
New Orleans, LA 70123
(800) 322-2368

Steen's 100% Pure Cane Syrup
C. S. STEEN SYRUP
  MILL, INC.
P.O. Box 339
Abbeville, LA 70510
(318) 893-1654 or (800)
  725-1654
www.steensyrup.com

Crawfish, shrimp, oysters, and whole fish
NEW ORLEANS FISH
  HOUSE
921 South Dupre Street
New Orleans, LA 70125
(800) 839-3474

Spices, crab and shrimp boil mixes, and Creole mustard
ZATARAIN'S
(504) 367-2950
www.zatarain.com

Andouille, boudin, and soft-shell crabs and other seafood
LIL' FISHERMAN
3301 Magazine Street
New Orleans, LA 70115
(504) 897-9907
and
7420 West Judge Perez
Arabi, LA 70032
(504) 271-9907

Cheeses
MAYTAG CHEESE
  COMPANY
(800) 247-2458

EMERIL'S RESTAURANTS AND STUFF

Emeril's Restaurant
800 Tchoupitoulas
New Orleans, LA 70130
(504) 528-9393

NOLA Restaurant
534 Rue St. Louis
New Orleans, LA 70130
(504) 522-6652

**Delmonico Restaurant
and Bar**
1300 St. Charles Avenue
New Orleans, LA 70130
(504) 525-4937

**Emeril's New Orleans
Fish House**
3799 Las Vegas Boulevard
    South
Las Vegas, NV 89019
(702) 891-7374

Delmonico Steakhouse
AT THE VENETIAN
    RESORT HOTEL
    CASINO
3355 Las Vegas Boulevard
    South
Las Vegas, NV 89109
(702) 414-3737

**Emeril's Restaurant
Orlando**
6000 Universal Boulevard
    at Universal Studios
    City Walk
Orlando, FL 32819
(407) 224-2424

And for a taste of Emeril
in your own kitchen,
you can order
- The Essence of Emeril
  Spice Pack
- *Emeril's New New
  Orleans Cooking* cook-
  book
- *Louisiana Real & Rustic*
  cookbook
- *Emeril's Creole Christmas*
  cookbook
- *Emeril's TV Dinners*
  cookbook

All other merchandise
    from:

Emeril's Homebase
638 Camp Street
New Orleans, LA 70130
(504) 524-4242
or visit us on our website
    at
http:\\www.emerils.com

index

butter sauce:
  lemon, poached trout with parsley potatoes and, 82–83
  pecan-pesto, goat cheese-stuffed soft-shell crabs with a, 158–159

Cabbage:
  braised, with corn beef hash, 110
  in crunchy slaw, 179
cakes:
  angel food, with marinated peaches, 181
  Black Forest, 76–77
  celebration, 310–312
  chocolate strawberry shortcake, 136–137
  funnel, 66
  king, 42–43
  raspberry crumb coffee, 268–269
  strawberry sabayon, 138–139
calamari tomato sauce, baked macaroni with, 118
candies:
  bonbons, 313
  three-chocolate bark with spiced pecans and dried cherries, 54–55
caramelized:
  onion bread pudding, seared duck with, 98–99
  salmon in new potatoes, 247
caramel sauce, 85
carrot ring, Suzanne's, 290–291
caviar:
  in crabmeat deviled eggs, 264
  oysters on the half-shell with *mignonette* sauce and, 93
  parfait, 320
celebration cake, 310–312
celery root mayonnaise, crabmeat with, 80–81
Champagne:
  in caviar parfait, 320
  in royal cup, 316

chanterelles, pan-seared escolar with crabmeat and, 94–95
cheddar cheese:
  in crawfish bread, 146–147
  in ham and cheese bites, 129
  in jambalaya grits, 149
  and pork sausage omelette, 282–283
  in scalloped potatoes, 200
  in spinach and cheese quiche, 266–267
  in warm pimiento cheese-stuffed tomatoes, 186
cheese:
  and ham bites, 129
  and spinach quiche, 266–267
  -stuffed tomatoes, warm pimiento, 186
  see also specific kinds of cheese
cherries:
  in Black Forest cake, 76–77
  dried, three-chocolate bark with spiced pecans and, 54–55
chess pie, chocolate, 48
chicken livers, in country pâté, my way, 210
chocolate:
  in bonbons, 313
  brownies, Lizzie's, 214–215
  cake, Black Forest, 76–77
  chess pie, 48
  coeur à la crème, 50–52
  grapes, Emeril's martini with, 102
  icing, 215
  and peanut butter praline ice cream sandwiches, 203–205
  strawberry shortcake, 136–137
  sweet potato bars, 260–261
  three-, bark with spiced pecans and dried cherries, 54–55
choux pastry, in gougère, 246
chunky garden gazpacho, 187
cilantro, in crunchy slaw, 179

clambake, 194
cobbler, Fifield's blackberry, 148
cocktails, *see* drinks
coconut:
  in bonbons, 313
  pie, sweet dough, 132–133
coeur à la crème, chocolate, 50–52
coffee cake, raspberry crumb, 268–269
cold cucumber soup, 156
coleslaw, crunchy, 179
cookies:
  pecan florentines, 161
  sugar, 52
corn(meal):
  bread, jalapeño, 286
  in clambake, 194
  dogs, andouille, 63
  and shrimp salad, 213
  tortilla chips, 185
corn and goat *queso,* 202
  shredded pork *flautas* with, 201–202
corn beef hash, braised cabbage with, 110
country pâté, my way, 210
crab(meat), 173–175
  with celery root mayonnaise, 80–81
  claws, marinated, 175
  deviled eggs, 264
  dip, hot jalapeño, 174
  goat cheese stuffed soft-shell, with a pecan-pesto butter sauce, 158–159
  pan-seared escolar with chanterelles and, 94–95
  in seafood gumbo, 253
  in stuffed artichokes, 153
cranberry pie, holiday, 292–293
crawfish, 163–169
  bread, 146–147
  dressing, trout stuffed with, 169
  in Mr. John's veal chops with smoked Gouda cheese macaroni, 72

Gouda cheese, smoked:
    macaroni, 74
    macaroni, Mr. John's veal
        chops with, 72–74
gougère, 246
Grand Marnier:
    in chocolate strawberry
        shortcake, 136–137
    in Fifield's blackberry
        cobbler, 148
    in orange crepes, 16–17
    in royal cup, 316
    in strawberry sabayon cake,
        138–139
grapes, chocolate, Emeril's
    martini with, 102
greens, wilted, with pecan-
    crusted rabbit and
    Creole dressing, 12–13
grilled Creole mustard-
    marinated quail with
    smothered field peas and
    andouille, 20–21
grits, jambalaya, 149
Gruyère cheese, in gougère, 246
gumbo, 249–253
    duck and andouille sausage, 252
    seafood, 253
    ya-ya, 250–251

Ham:
    and cheese bites, 129
    in jambalaya grits, 149
    in muffuletta salad, 212
    in shrimp Clemenceau, 218
haricots verts, in petits filets with
    blue cheese *glaçage,* 96
hash, corned beef, braised
    cabbage with, 110
hen, in gumbo ya-ya, 250–251
herb-and-salt-crusted red
    snapper, 34
Hilda's mahimahi with seasonal
    vegetables, 70–71
holiday cranberry pie, 292–293
hollandaise sauce, 15
hors d'oeuvres:
    caramelized salmon in new
        potatoes, 247

gougère, 246
    see also appetizers
hot dogs, in clambake, 194
hot mayonnaise-glazed scallops,
    322

Ice cream:
    mint julep, 160
    pie, bananas Foster, 36–37
    sandwiches, peanut butter and
        chocolate praline,
        205–207
    vanilla-praline, 204
icing, chocolate, 215
Irish soda bread, 108

Jalapeño:
    corn bread, 286
    crab dip, hot, 174
jambalaya:
    crawfish and sausage, 64
    grits, 149

King cake, 42–43
kirsch:
    in Black Forest cake, 76–77
    in chocolate strawberry
        shortcake, 136–137

Lamb:
    pistachio-crusted rack of,
        32–33
    roasted leg of, with a bouquet
        of spring vegetables,
        130–131
    stew, 111
lemon:
    butter sauce, poached trout
        with parsley potatoes
        and, 82–83
    icebox pie, 324–325
    in planter's punch, 211
lettuce, iceberg, in Emeril's
    wedgie salad, 256
Lizzie's chocolate brownies, 214
lobster toast, 220
Louisiana:
    garlic bread, 199
    oyster and sausage bake, 150

Macaroni:
    with calamari tomato sauce,
        baked, 118
    smoked Gouda cheese, 74
    smoked Gouda cheese, Mr.
        John's veal chops with,
        72–74
mahimahi, with seasonal
    vegetables, Hilda's,
    70–71
marinated crab claws, 175
martinis:
    with chocolate grapes,
        Emeril's, 102
    NOLA blue glacier, 62
mascarpone cheese, in
    strawberry sabayon cake,
    138–139
mashed potatoes, 159
    goat cheese, 33
mayonnaise, 129
    celery root, crabmeat with,
        80–81
    -glazed scallops, hot, 322
meatball poorboys, garlic,
    22–23
mignonette sauce, oysters on the
    half-shell with caviar
    and, 93
mint julep ice cream, 160
Monterey Jack cheese:
    in crawfish bread, 146–147
    in Frito pie, 65
    in hot jalapeño crab dip, 174
    in scalloped potatoes, 200
    in warm pimiento cheese-
        stuffed tomatoes, 186
mortadella, in muffuletta salad,
    212
Mr. John's veal chops with
    smoked Gouda cheese
    macaroni, 72–74
muffuletta salad, 212
muscat sabayon, 95
    in pan-seared escolar with
        crabmeat and
        chanterelles, 94–95
mushrooms:
    and beef risotto, 257

ribs, duo BBQ, 196–197
roasted, and french fry
poorboy, 152
roasted pig, 178
see also bacon; ham; sausage
potato(es):
andouille mash, oyster stew
with, 299
french fry, and roasted pork
poorboy, 152
goat cheese mashed, 33
mashed, 159
new, caramelized salmon in,
247
new, in clambake, 194
parsley, poached trout with
lemon butter sauce and,
82–83
roasted, 131
scalloped, 200
in shrimp Clemenceau, 218
soup, 109
truffle pizza, 300–301
praline(s):
ice cream sandwiches, peanut
butter and chocolate,
203–205
peanut butter and chocolate,
205
-vanilla ice cream, 204
provolone:
in garlic meatball poorboys,
22–23
in muffuletta salad, 212
pudding, caramelized onion
bread, seared duck with,
98–99
puff pastry:
in crawfish vol-au-vent, 168
dome, escargots in, 30–31
in exotic mushroom tarts,
11
in ham and cheese bites, 129
pumpkin soup, 287

Quail, grilled Creole mustard-
marinated, with
smothered field peas and
andouille, 20–21

quiche, spinach and cheese,
266–267

Rabbit, pecan-crusted, with
wilted greens and Creole
dressing, 12–13
raspberry crumb coffee cake,
268–269
red rooster, 298
red snapper, salt-and-herb-
crusted, 34
relish tray, 307
rice:
in crawfish and sausage
jambalaya, 64
in duck and andouille sausage
gumbo, 252
orange, roasted squab with,
308–309
risotto, beef and mushroom,
257
roasted:
leg of lamb with a bouquet of
spring vegetables, 130–131
pork and french fry poorboy,
152
potatoes, 131
squab with orange rice,
308–309
royal cup, 316
rum, in planter's punch, 211

Sabayon:
strawberry cake, 138–139
see also muscat sabayon
salads:
Emeril's wedgie, 256
muffuletta, 212
shrimp and corn, 213
salami, in muffuletta salad, 212
salmon, in new potatoes,
caramelized, 247
salmonella, warning about, 13
salsa, Creole tomato, 184–185
salt-and-herb-crusted red
snapper, 34
sandwiches:
garlic meatball poorboys,
22–23

roasted pork and french fry
poorboy, 152
sandwiches, ice cream, peanut
butter and chocolate
praline, 203–205
sauces:
calamari tomato, baked
macaroni with, 118
caramel, 85
hollandaise, 15
homemade pepper, 274–275
mignonette, oysters on the half-
shell with caviar and, 93
pecan-pesto butter, goat
cheese-stuffed soft-shell
crabs with a, 159–160
see also butter sauce; muscat
sabayon
sausage:
and crawfish jambalaya, 64
and oyster bake, Louisiana,
150
pork, and cheese omelette,
282–283
see also andouille
Sazerac cocktail, 10
scallop(s):
hot mayonnaise-glazed, 322
seviche, 28
toast, 220
scalloped potatoes, 200
seafood gumbo, 253
seared duck with caramelized
onion bread pudding,
98–99
seasoning, Creole, 13
seviche, scallop, 28
shell pasta, in muffuletta salad,
212
sherry, in celebration cake, 310
shortcake, chocolate strawberry,
136–137
shredded pork flautas with corn
and goat queso, 201–202
shrimp:
bisque, 304–305
Clemenceau, 218
and corn salad, 213
Creole, 14–15

Every Day's a Party ■ Oyster Festival ■ Sugar Bowl ■ Cigar Dinner ■
Anniversary ■ Ash Wednesday ■ Emeril's Tenth Anniversary ■ St. P
Fest ■ Mother's Day ■ Crawfish Festival ■ Crab Festival ■ Father's I
Shrimp Festival ■ Festivals Acadiens ■ Sugarcane Festival ■ Pirogu
Cook-off ■ Halloween ■ Alessandro's Christening ■ Pepper Festiva
Christmas Dinner ■ New Year's Eve ■ **Every Day's a Party** ■ Oyster Fe
■ Mardi Gras ■ Hilda and Mr. John's Anniversary ■ Ash Wednesday ■
Easter ■ Strawberry Festival ■ Jazz Fest ■ Mother's Day ■ Crawfish F
■ Fourth of July ■ Boat Party ■ Shrimp Festival ■ Festivals Acadiens
Party ■ New Iberia Gumbo Cook-off ■ Halloween ■ Alessandro's C
Christmas Tree Trimming ■ Christmas Dinner ■ New Year's Eve ■ Ever
Night ■ Valentine's Day ■ Mardi Gras ■ Hilda and Mr. John's Annivers
■ St. Joseph's Day ■ Easter ■ Strawberry Festival ■ Jazz Fest ■ Mo
Market Tomato Festival ■ Fourth of July ■ Boat Party ■ Shrimp Fest
Annie and Tom's Toasting Party ■ New Iberia Gumbo Cook-off ■ Hall
■ Thanksgiving ■ Christmas Tree Trimming ■ Christmas Dinner ■ New
Dinner ■ Twelfth Night ■ Valentine's Day ■ Mardi Gras ■ Hilda and M
■ St. Patrick's Day ■ St. Joseph's Day ■ Easter ■ Strawberry Festi
Father's Day ■ French Market Tomato Festival ■ Fourth of July ■ Bo
■ Pirogue Race Picnic ■ Annie and Tom's Toasting Party ■ New Ibe
Festival ■ Omelette Festival ■ Thanksgiving ■ Christmas Tree Trimm
Festival ■ Sugar Bowl ■ Cigar Dinner ■ Twelfth Night ■ Valentine's I
■ Emeril's Tenth Anniversary ■ St. Patrick's Day ■ St. Joseph's